The End of
Southern
Exceptionalism

The End of
Southern
Exceptionalism

*Class, Race, and
Partisan Change
in the
Postwar South*

BYRON E. SHAFER

RICHARD JOHNSTON

Harvard University Press
Cambridge, Massachusetts · London, England
2006

Library of Congress Cataloging-in-Publication Data

Shafer, Byron E.
The end of Southern exceptionalism : class, race, and partisan change
in the postwar South / Byron E. Shafer and Richard Johnston.
p. cm.
Includes bibliographical references and index.
ISBN 0-674-01934-2 (alk. paper)
1. Southern States—Politics and government—1951–
2. Political parties—Southern States.
3. Social classes—Southern States.
4. Southern States—Race relations.
I. Johnston, Richard, 1948–   II. Title.
F216.2.S46 2006
975'.043—dc22   2005050268

Contents

Preface   vii

1. The Nature of the Puzzle   1

2. Economic Development and a Politics of Class   22

3. Legal Desegregation and a Politics of Race   51

4. Class, Race, and Partisan Change   92

5. Social Forces and Partisan Politicians   134

6. Old South, New South, No South?   173

Notes   201
References   207
Index   215

❧ Preface

THIS BOOK CAN be traced to the chance interaction of two events that will long since have become invisible to all but its authors. The first was a seminar—and an extended seminar argument—at Oxford University, introduced and chaired by Byron Shafer. An Inaugural Lecture by Nelson Polsby of the University of California at Berkeley, then a visiting professor of American Government at Oxford, produced a fierce argument in this subsequent seminar. Polsby had asserted that economic development was more central than racial desegregation to the evolution of the postwar South in the U.S. Congress, and, with the obvious exception of the late Leslie Stone, Chief Commentator for the BBC World Service, all the local Americanists took strong exception: Nigel Bowles, Desmond King, David Goldey, and Alan Ware in particular.

Some weeks later, Byron recounted these events to Richard Johnston of the University of British Columbia at an informal working session aimed at finishing an edited collection on postwar politics within the G-7 nations (Shafer 1996), in which Dick contributed the Canadian and Byron the American chapters. By then, all that could safely be said by way of professional summary was: (a) that no one in the Southern argument appeared to have much systematically relevant evidence, but (b) that if economics was the root cause of the demise of the old South, then a new Republican Party would have arisen in one set of places, whereas if race was the root cause, it would obviously have arisen in another. Dick listened for a bit, then grew impatient. "Well, we can know that. I mean, it should be easy enough to formalize and test those possibilities."

The first product of this effort was a piece on the postwar House of Representatives, previewed at the 2000 meetings of the American Political Science Association, a piece that ultimately found a home in the *British Journal of Political Science* (Shafer and Johnston 2001). The results were as striking as they were unexpected. Seen through the lens of the postwar House, economics and social class clearly trumped desegregation and racial identity as engines for partisan change. Moreover, race actually worked in a way that was opposite to the dominant argument in the literature of Southern politics: Republicans did worse among whites in areas with large black populations than in those without this implicit "threat" to continued white dominance.

Despite the obvious power of these two great social forces, economic development and legal desegregation, two key political factors—the provision of Republican challengers and, especially, the presence (or absence) of Democratic incumbents—still crucially shaped electoral outcomes. This led us to see whether the House analysis could be extended to the other major elective institutions of American national government, namely the Senate and the presidency. Accordingly, the second product of this accidental enterprise was a paper on class, race, and candidate impacts more generally, previewed at the 2002 meetings of the American Political Science Association (Shafer and Johnston 2002).

The parade of substantive surprises continued. In particular, Congress—both the House and, in a weaker fashion, the Senate—behaved very differently in institutional terms than did the presidency. While class continued to trump race as an engine for partisan change, race now worked, for the presidency, in the way that the existing literature suggested: whites in blacker areas were *more* likely to vote Republican. As a result, where analysis of the impact of two social forces in the House had brought political intermediaries back into the picture, this difference in voting behavior between Congress and the presidency brought institutional structures back into the story as well.

It also brought the analysis back around to the voting behavior that had started this entire progression. Needless to say, the ultimate registrar of all these influences in both of our papers—the place where the degree of their influence was effectively determined—was the mass electorate. As always, this electorate brought its own mix of background characteristics, social contexts, and, last but not least, individual policy attitudes to bear on its response. And the impact of this mix looked considerably different than it had when we began with two influences on one institution.

Both papers were honored by the section on Political Organizations and Parties (POP) of the American Political Science Association as the best paper of their respective years. Yet by the time we had drafted the second APSA paper, it was clear that these data contained further puzzles which we ourselves did not understand, and that their proper unpacking required simultaneous consideration of economic development, legal desegregation, and strategic responses by intermediary elites, along with voting decisions by a (growing) mass electorate, all filtered through differing institutional structures. Which meant that we needed to write a book rather than yet another article.

The realization of this book depended, of course, on fifty years of political behavior by residents of the American South, as well as on the interactions of two authors, at home and jointly in Oxford, Vancouver, and then Madison over a number of years. Its realization also depended on a small but crucial supporting cast, whose contribution can be only inadequately acknowledged here.

Once Dick had created the initial dataset, its ongoing maintenance became the responsibility of Daniel Liam Singer, research assistant to Byron at Oxford while working on a D.Phil. of his own. Dan added substantially to the dataset, while executing most of the original analyses which convinced us that there was indeed a larger project here. He was the one who had to carry this total project as it ventured into unknown territory.

Stuart N. Soroka, then research assistant to Dick in Vancouver and now on the Political Science faculty at McGill University, became a Prize Research (postdoctoral) Fellow at Nuffield College, Oxford, which allowed him to continue his methodological and theoretical contributions to the project. Although Stuart was only intermittently involved in the total effort, his involvements came at precisely those times when we needed a third opinion on some major analytic sticking-points.

David C. W. Parker, subsequently research assistant to Byron in Madison, ultimately contributed the greatest amount of overall support. He was responsible for tweaking the dataset and considering the main analytic alternatives, while checking (and rechecking) our calculations all along the way. His patience, when an apparently robust finding had to be examined in yet another way, was constantly tested. His reliable ability to pass that test is why we could quite literally not have done it without him.

Stacey L. Pelika, as successor to Dave, acquired the closing supportive duties on the manuscript. No doubt she will long remember that she was in fact hired to support a quite different project. Yet she tackled the set of analytic difficulties that always seem to cluster at the end of any large project with energy and initiative. And at the very end, she bore without complaint the burden of making sure that all tabular material was in alignment.

A small cast of professional colleagues—Southerners both indigenous and transplanted—read the manuscript at various points and improved it immensely. Charles O. Jones (presently of Virginia) prevented us from making some remarkably simple errors of analysis. Harold F. Bass, Jr. (presently of Arkansas) spent time with us at every APSA meeting along the way, trying hard to ground us in the practical details of Southern politics. Chuck and Hal, along with Bryan D. Jones (formerly of Alabama) and Nicol C. Rae (currently of Florida), then read the entire manuscript in the final stage. Richard F. Fenno, Jr. (honorary resident of Georgia) managed to escape manuscript duty, but suggested the distinction between cosmopolitans and locals that plays such a major role in Chapter 5.

Finally, Michael A. Aronson, Senior Editor for the Social Sciences at Harvard University Press, took the manuscript under his wing from the very first moment when we were ready to discuss it with anyone outside this support team. His colleague, Mary Ellen Geer, then served as both manuscript editor and production manager. It is always a trick—and often a partial contradiction—to appreciate an entire supporting cast, to thank them for their help, but to absolve them from the product. Yet we do.

The End of
Southern
Exceptionalism

1

The Nature of the Puzzle

HIGH ON THE LIST of transformative changes in American politics during the postwar years is partisan transformation of the South. Given the historical background—a populous one-party region, unshakable in attachment and behavior for nearly a century beforehand—such a transformation would loom large merely on its own. Yet serious partisan change in the American South inevitably brought a cascade of further changes in its wake—first regional, then national.

Serious partisan change in the South, by definition, meant a change in partisan balance for the nation as a whole. Overall, this always seemed most likely to benefit the party previously disadvantaged in the region— the national Republicans. Yet the actual process by which partisan change came to the South, that is, the real identity of the underlying engine(s) for change, always had the potential for producing other, potentially countervailing shifts. Either way, partisan change in the South automatically meant a shift in the strategies by which the two major parties attempted to assemble nationwide majorities, in order to control the presidency but equally to control Congress. At one time Democrats began by assuming an overwhelming dominance in one-third of the nation, while Republicans began by writing it off. Both strategies died with the birth of serious Southern Republicanism.

As a result, both the social coalitions assembled by the two parties and the policy programs those parties offered were destined to change. Pieces of the old one-party South would inevitably join various pieces of the national Democratic and Republican Parties, doubtless creating further tensions as they did. Yet the result was almost sure to be more programmatic and ideological coherence in both parties, courtesy of the demise of a one-party region that had choked such differences in its huge home area. So that in the end, serious partisan change in the South meant that the major institutions of American national government would just *work differently*. Everything about the presidency, from its electoral politics to its policy attachments, was linked to—embedded in—a national party system. The same could be said of Congress: Senators and Representatives, individually and collectively, were critically linked to the main contours of an old (and new) party system, at home and in Washington.

These are grand claims, to which a broad array of observers would nevertheless quickly assent (Tindall 1972; Wolfinger and Arseneau 1978; Lamis 1984; Wattenberg 1991; Rohde 1996; Black and Black 2002; Green 2002). Moreover, the issue of where this comprehensive change came from is itself surprisingly consensual. It is here that we would disagree. The book that follows comes to a set of conclusions different from much of the literature of Southern politics, different both in its collection of individual propositions and in its composite picture. What emerges from an invasion of this literature with a handful of theoretical propositions plus the apparently relevant data is the following argument:

- that the engine of partisan change in the postwar South was, first and foremost, economic development and an associated politics of social class;
- that the impact of legal desegregation and an associated politics of racial identity had to be understood through its interaction with economic development, and otherwise as much for braking the pace of change as for accelerating it;
- that during the long transition away from the political patterns of the old South, the impact of class, race, and their interaction was powerfully conditioned by the structure of the institutional arenas for that impact, namely, the presidency, the Senate, and the House;
- that policy preferences in the general public for the realms most directly tied to class and race, that is, social welfare and aid to blacks, shifted in a partially autonomous fashion but came to play a larger and larger role in a new Southern politics;
- that the place of intermediary elites in this dynamic lay not in their individual idiosyncrasies but in the simple provision of Republican challengers and, even more crucially, in the distinction between locals and cosmopolitans among Democratic incumbents;

- and that when there finally was a new pattern to Southern ｐ ⊣
  one that was impressively uniform across states and across ii
  tions, it was the result of a confluence of economic developmen
  cial desegregation, and candidate responses which no one hac
  tended, but which no one could ultimately derail.

The Historical Backdrop

The smothering one-party character of Southern regional politics had long been a diagnostic feature of American politics generally, indeed of a sequence of national party systems in the years following the Civil War. In the highly competitive two-party world of the years immediately afterward, an important part of national politics involved policy aimed at reintegrating the South, and especially its black population, into national life. In this, the Southern Democracy was aggressively opposed to national— read "Northern Republican"—policy on Reconstruction, viewing it as an outside attempt to transform local life. Southern Democrats offered a critical and growing contribution to national Democratic totals in response.

In the dominant Republican system that followed, which lasted from the 1890s until the Great Depression, the Southern Democracy, with Reconstruction ended and blacks gradually removed from political life, became the inalienable core of the national Democratic opposition. In this, it was comfortable with the national party preference for a federal government that interfered neither economically nor culturally in local affairs. In return, election in and election out, the South could be relied upon to send an overwhelming phalanx of Democrats to Congress and to offer its electoral votes as a bloc to the Democratic presidential candidate.

With the coming of the Great Depression and then the New Deal, this dominant Republican system was replaced with a dominant Democratic one nationwide. In a sense, the Southern Democracy was now in the national majority, guaranteeing presidential and congressional majorities for national Democrats. In a different sense, however, it was often the key to the opposition, providing the critical counterweight to national—read "Northern Democratic"—policy preferences and initiatives. And for still other purposes, a "three-party system" was effectively in operation, featuring Northern Democrats, Northern Republicans, and Southern Democrats.

What did not change, after the partisan settlement of 1876 and during all these subsequent party systems, was the practical absence of a fourth group—Southern Republicans. That is, what did not change was an overwhelming Democratic dominance within the region, along with its conditional association to the national party. Three separate national party systems appeared in the years between the end of the Civil War and the end of the Second World War, and the policy role of the Southern Democracy shifted a bit within each. But that Democracy essentially altered very little in its partisan contours (Patterson 1965; Miller 1956).

Yet change everywhere was to be, at last, the story of the postwar South. There was vibrant economic development, moving the South from subsistence agriculture to a modern economy. There was a veritable civil rights revolution, dismantling the formal organization of Southern racial life. And there was, simultaneously, a nascent and then an increasingly vigorous Southern Republican Party. When it finally arrived, one of the most enduring patterns of American politics, a pattern visible by the 1850s and evident still in the 1960s, would be swept away.

A search for the real roots of partisan change in the postwar South is thus a prerequisite for understanding all the other changes that would follow inescapably once this enduring constraint on the shape of American politics had shattered. At the same time, a search for these roots is a precondition for understanding the direction of *contemporary* American politics. At a minimum, this implies careful separation of the partisan impact of the two great social forces shaping postwar Southern society, economic development and legal desegregation, along with careful consideration of their interaction. Yet if these propositions appear almost elementary as an analytic strategy, they bump up against an established literature of Southern politics—charming and richly contextualized, but also unsystematic and deeply inbred—which effectively assumes the opposite:

- This literature assumes that the analyst must proceed, not with hypotheses and variables, but with the accumulation of local knowledge. Measures derived from the rest of the country and generalizations extracted from these measures will be trumped by the "fabric" of life in the South.
- By our time, this literature also assumes that we know the answer which must result: *Southern politics was, is, and will be principally about race.* It is not that other factors do not acquire some mention; it is just that they serve more as elements of enrichment or complication, rather than as theoretical alternatives.

- In getting to such a conclusion, finally, the literature frequently just elides—combines and thereby confuses—the impact of two great social influences, those of class and race, implicitly dismissing what we take to be the core of the analytic puzzle.

Few other aspects of American politics (and no other geographic region) have generated as much focused work. We ourselves would never have proceeded without it. Yet that very focus brings its own problems, for it brings with it the presumption that this regional politics is sufficiently distinctive that it must be addressed largely in terms of itself, rather than importing into Southern political analysis the theoretical propositions, empirical data, and methodological techniques that would seem natural to an examination of most aspects of politics in most other realms. Instead, the uniquely Southern aspects of the South's history and institutions often serve as the starting point for analyses of Southern politics.

Moreover, the field shares some remarkably consensual propositions about the result. That is, those who differentiate themselves as students of Southern politics have reached a kind of closure about the nature and dynamics of politics in the American South. There are noteworthy exceptions, and we utilize them appreciatively in the book that follows. Yet this is a literature noted for the extent to which disciples elaborate, even just reiterate, the basic contours of an argument about the centrality of race. In a militantly ethnographic body of work, a myriad of other factors do make an appearance, but rarely such that they constitute propositions that would challenge a dominant-factor explanation; rarely such that they could even plausibly be judged for their comparative contribution to political change; rarely, indeed, such that they actually delineate the massive contribution of race itself as an influence on a *differentiated,* changing politics.

One further result of this situation is that the data which would most commonly be mobilized to test—to affirm or to refute—these grand propositions are curiously thin on the ground. Evidence does get marshaled, but in an unsystematic, even anecdotal, fashion. By contrast, the centerpiece of our own effort is the creation of a dataset, and it alone might provide the justification for another book on the evolution of postwar Southern politics, especially given the centrality of this story to national politics during all these years. In other words, ours is an enterprise aimed at bringing the standard procedures of an orthodox political science into a realm famed for its local knowledge and elaborated lore.

Alternative Engines for Political Change

Despite seventy years of partisan stasis, the main alternative explanations for potential change in the partisan South—the two main causal engines for change if it ever came—were not just generally recognized but increasingly invoked in the relevant professional literature as the postwar era opened. One explanation did receive disproportionate attention, and that fact would be important to the evolution, not of the political South, but of the literature purportedly describing it. Yet both alternative shapes of a Southern political future were consciously articulated, even if their articulators might doubt the practical prospects of their own projections.

Earlier, really from the days of William Jennings Bryan until the Second World War, *agrarian radicalism* had been the change engine of choice, and the Democratic Party had seemed the natural theater for its resulting conflicts. One-party politics in an overwhelmingly agrarian economy appeared to require intense rural divisions within the dominant party if it was ever to undergo a fundamental shift. Yet by the beginning of the postwar period, agrarian radicalism was clearly being displaced by two alternative sources of putative political change. One was legal desegregation and a politics of race; the other was economic development and a politics of class. And both appeared as likely to achieve their influence through the Republican as through the Democratic Party.

The foundation stone for both arguments in the immediate postwar years was to be *Southern Politics in State and Nation* by V. O. Key, Jr. Just as W. J. Cash's *The Mind of the South* had earlier become the definitive treatment of Southern culture, so Key's *Southern Politics* would become the defining text on Southern political life. Accordingly, as the postwar era began, it was Key who most effectively impelled the first great explanation for the distinctive character of Southern politics—and thus the first great social change that might ultimately crack it:

> In its grand outlines, the politics of the South revolves around the position of the Negro. It is at times interpreted as a politics of cotton, as a politics of free trade, as a politics of agrarian poverty, or as a politics of planter and plutocrat. Although such interpretations have a superficial validity, in the last analysis the major peculiarities of southern politics go back to the Negro. Whatever phase of the southern political process one seeks to understand, sooner or later the trail of inquiry leads to the Negro.

Yet it is far from the truth to paint a picture of southern politics
as being chiefly concerned with the maintenance of the supremacy
of white over black. That dominance is an outcome, but the ob-
server must look more closely to determine which whites and which
blacks give southern politics its individuality. The hard core of the
political South—and the backbone of southern political unity—is
made up of those counties and sections of the southern states in
which Negroes constitute a substantial proportion of the population. In these areas, a real problem of politics, broadly considered, is
the maintenance of control by a white minority. (Key 1949, 5)

On the other hand, Key himself advanced a second major line of argument about buttresses for the existing character of Southern politics, and
hence about the social change that might cause those buttresses to crumble. Because he wavered not only in the relative emphasis but also in the
rhetorical tone of his two larger arguments, disciples would not always
credit both. Yet Key did insist that two great crises, not one, had shaped
and then extended Southern political solidarity. These were, in his words,
"the war of the 'sixties and the Populist revolt of the 'nineties" (Key 1949,
6), and he remained insistent that the social and political impact of the latter not be lost in the more dramatic context of the former:

In the second great crisis whose influence persists—the Populist revolt—political cleavages often fell along the same lines as in the dis-
pute leading to the War. The details of the pattern differed, of
course, from state to state, as did the timing of the great upsurge of
agrarian radicalism. Yet everywhere the most consistent, the most
intense rural resistance to Populists and like radicals of the day came
from the black-belt whites. They had valiant allies in the merchants
and bankers of the towns and in the new industrialists. Against
these defenders of the status quo were arrayed the upcountrymen,
the small farmers of the highlands and other areas where there were
few Negroes and where there was no basis for a plantation economy.
And they were joined by many of the workers of the cities which
were beginning to grow, as well as by many poor white farmers of
other regions.
    The black-belt whites, the townsmen, and all the allied forces of
conservatism staved off radical agrarianism, although not without
leaving a residue of a belligerent attitude that for decades found ex-

pression in support for leaders who at least talked, if they did not always act, against the "interests." And in crucial campaigns even now, the counties of several states divide about as they did in the elections of the agrarian uprising. (Key 1949, 7–8)

Modern political scientists rarely speak in such a concrete, specific, and engaged voice. Yet one can easily convert both arguments into theoretical propositions. In the first, social life in the South was organized around *de jure* segregation. Anything that threatened segregation would thus be genuinely revolutionary. A social revolution could hardly avoid changing the political character of the American South. Put differently, it was segregation that underpinned partisan solidarity. A civil rights movement was the great potential threat to segregation. Partisan solidarity would almost surely crumble if legal desegregation and an accompanying politics of race came to the political forefront.

Converted into a theoretical proposition, the second argument too is easily abstracted. Economic life in the South was organized around agriculture. Anything that changed the agricultural nature of the economy would be inevitably and thoroughly disruptive to the larger society. An economic revolution could hardly avoid spilling over into, and changing, the political character of the American South. Put differently, it was *underdevelopment* that buttressed partisan solidarity. Economic growth and the accompanying politics of class were the great potential apposition to underdevelopment. Partisan solidarity would almost surely crumble in their wake.

Moreover, with this second argument, the prior political evolution of the rest of the country offered a practical embodiment of just such a change. Or at least, where an agricultural economy still suppressed class distinctions in the South, a politics of class had become a signature characteristic of the New Deal party system outside it (Sundquist 1973; Ladd with Hadley 1975). Presumably, modernization of the Southern economy should thus bring this non-Southern politics, at long last, to Dixie.

Many of Key's disciples, continuing to honor the master in an era where his historical analysis did not automatically apply, implicitly downplayed this second possibility (economic development) by explicitly featuring the first (racial desegregation). One further reason to revisit partisan change in the postwar South is to redress this balance. Yet Key himself did not help these disciples by raising the two main theoretical alternatives and then implicitly eliding them. Some of this was Key as neo-Beardian: if politics should "normally" be about economics, then if it was apparently about race, the two had to be intimately connected. Accordingly, we began this study by consciously formulating the opposite proposition:

- If legal desegregation and a politics of racial identity were the driving force behind the rise of a Southern Republican Party, then it would appear among whites in areas where blacks were most numerous. But if economic development and a politics of social class were the driving force, then a new Southern Republican Party would appear instead in areas with a new and rising white-collar population. Given that black areas were poor areas generally, it seemed likely that these hypotheses were opposite, not parallel, in their implications.

In the analysis to follow, this grand alternative hypothesis likewise will need to be adjusted, elaborated, and nuanced in numerous ways. But as an opening guide to research, it has the undeniable advantage of not assuming the outcome—and imposing that outcome upon the analysis. In our view, then, the master's insistence on the parallel nature of economic and racial divisions directed attention *away from* their analytic separation, and away from their practical interaction as well.

Nevertheless, it remains true that in Key's time, any effort to compare and contrast two alternative explanations—explanations of the *absence* of political change—would have been largely beside the point. A successful one-party resolution was indisputably in place, one that had obviously triumphed in the face of both latent challenges. As a result, Key's further critical task was just to offer up the means, by way of the active agents and their practical strategies, whereby this resolution was maintained. A large part of his seminal account can be seen as addressing precisely this task, going state by state to examine the individual politicians and the areas of their social support which, together, constituted the political order of the old South. In this view, it was the behavior of these "Bourbon Democrats" and their inheritors that seamlessly blended the two grand engines of incipient change, while simultaneously dismissing them both, to produce that lasting one-party resolution. In the hands of a master miniaturist, the resulting composite picture was not a pretty one:

The almost overwhelming temptation, especially in areas with many Negroes, is to take advantage of the short-run opportunity to main-

tain the status quo by using, or tolerating the use of, the race issue to
blot up the discontents of the lesser whites. By this means, the gov-
erning class can kill off or minimize pressures for improved governmental services from whites and find support for low public out-
lays for the benefit of the Negro. It is naïve, of course, to interpret
southern politics as a deliberate conspiracy among the better-off
whites to divide the mass of people by tolerating Negro-baiting.
Nevertheless, with a high degree of regularity those of the top economic groups—particularly the new industrialists—are to be found
in communion with the strident advocates of white supremacy. In
the political chaos and demoralization that ensue, alert men with a
sharp eye for immediate advantage take and count their gains. (Key
1949, 662–663)

Careful consideration of these same arguments in the light of data unavailable to Key is the central purpose of this book. His disciples, on the
other hand, did not just follow the master in eliding the impact of economic and racial change. They were much more attracted by his first line
of argument than by his second. The result should probably be unsurprising. The disciples were to continue to find legal desegregation rather than
economic development to be the main engine for the partisan change
which would become increasingly apparent to all, and hence race rather
than class to be the main means for creating a new resolution, in a new
Southern politics.

A forceful and compelling version of this summary view appears in a recent presidential address to the Southern Political Science Association. In
a piece that draws the argument together succinctly, from its title onward,
Earl Black sets it out as "The Newest Southern Politics." In our reading, it
is noteworthy that (a) all of the analytic distinctions are based on race, and
(b) race appears to be sufficient to denominate the behavior of the minority
racial group, but has nothing to say about the apparently decisive division
within the (white) majority:

The newest southern politics, as we have seen, involves three paths
to victory. After the 1994 southern House elections, a much smaller
group of white Democrats survived on the basis of biracial coalitions, an enhanced number of black Democrats established safe
seats based on black majorities, and—for the first time since Reconstruction—white Republicans controlled a majority of the southern

delegation. The rule of white majorities, the universal road to victory of the white Republicans, thus reappeared as the central tendency of the newest southern politics. (Black 1998, 607)

Social Change Arrives

Had he known where he was in history, V. O. Key himself might have been doubly happy with *Southern Politics in State and Nation*. On its own terms, the book was an immediate and then a lasting success. Two generations of scholarly offspring would sustain its themes and extend its analysis. Yet what Key was also doing, by writing in the late 1940s, was capturing a portentous historical moment. Looking backward, he was providing a richly textured description, built around the essential contours of a partisan world that, if you fuzzed the detail just a bit, might not have seemed all that different three or even four generations previously. Looking forward, however, these were contours that would shift within one further generation, and shatter within another.

Which is to say: all three grand aspects of change did arrive in the postwar years. The South was to undergo that revolution in civil rights and race relations. The South was to secure economic development on a scale unimagined by earlier theorists of social change. And the South was to acquire a major regional branch of the national Republican Party, to such a degree that it could contribute not only to Republican presidencies but also to Republican majorities in Congress, and even make a claim—and a major claim at that—on leadership posts within those majorities. The next fifty years were thus to produce a Southern political world that would have been unrecognizable through the lens of the previous one hundred (Fenno 1998; Bullock and Rozell 1998).

The postwar boom for the entire United States was to be historic, with a new economy, a new occupational structure, and new levels of personal affluence. Nevertheless, the South managed to narrow the gap with the rest of the nation on all such measures *at the same time* (Cobb 1993; Scranton 2001). Coming from farther back than the rest of the nation, it experienced a correspondingly greater economic shift, with the greater potential for partisan impact that came inevitably with greater change at a faster pace. Economic change on this scale could hardly fail to affect partisan politics in major ways. The intensity of this change—its compressed nature in historical perspective—only magnified the scope for impact.

The very basis of the Southern economy was to change profoundly. At the beginning of World War II, roughly 40 percent of the South was still employed in agriculture, a share twice that of the rest of the nation. By 1990, that figure was down to 1 percent, a smaller agricultural sector than the non-South. In its place, a modern occupational distribution inevitably emerged. The agricultural economy, and its agrarian society, were gone. An industrial, and then within short order a post-industrial, economy and society had appeared (Cobb 1984; Weinstein 1985).

As a result, there was a profound change in economic well-being, though this aggregate gain was hardly the whole story: a rising tide did not lift all boats, and that fact would be central to the postwar partisan evolution of the South. Nevertheless, in the aggregate, the South had managed a per capita income only half that of the rest of the nation at the beginning of World War II—at $3,002 in constant 1940 dollars, a mere 53 percent of the non-Southern figure. The 1950s, 1960s, and 1970s were all explosive by this measure, and the income gap was substantially closed by 1980, at $14,138 or 85 percent (*Statistical Abstract*, relevant years). The force of this change only gains emphasis from the fact that it was sustained despite having to incorporate an increasing stream of in-migrants from the North, bent on sharing this new prosperity (Weinstein 1985).

The economic South thus became a sharply different place within a historically short period of time. Once, within living memory of most of those who experienced the change, the Southern economy had been so backward as to be unable to sustain the familiar divisions of an industrial society—by class, by occupation, and by income—divisions that had come to characterize politics outside the South. Now, at a minimum, those incipient prerequisites of a different partisan politics had inescapably arrived (McKinney and Bourque 1971; Nadeau and Stanley 1993).

Bedrock change in the racial organization of Southern society was likewise about to occur, and if that story is familiar, this familiarity should not be allowed to dull its impact (Sitkoff 1981; Graham 1990). Race was a consideration in American politics long before *de jure* segregation arrived, and it would remain a consideration long after *de jure* segregation was gone. Nevertheless, legal segregation—formal, explicit, codified separation of Southerners classified, by whatever means, as black or white—was well established as a central organizing principle for Southern society in the immediate postwar years. The dismantling of this social system, if it came, would necessarily change the fundamental nature of that society.

Part and parcel of legal segregation were draconian limits on voter registration. Thus the dismantling of those limits was an early, obvious, and essential step in practical desegregation, one that produced an immediate shift in the relative standing of blacks and whites as active participants in the political system (Keech 1968; Lawson 1976; Stanley 1987). Registration by Southern blacks accelerated remarkably: 5 percent in 1940, 20 percent in 1952, 29 percent in 1960, but *65 percent* by 1969 (Bartley and Graham 1975). Voting by Southern blacks followed inexorably: they constituted 4 percent of the Southern electorate in the 1950s, 12 percent in the 1960s, 16 percent in the 1970s, and 22 percent—their proportionate share—by the 1980s (see Figure 3.1).

Accordingly, what was once a chasm between the races in the availability of the ballot was now a residual. The racial South too had become a very different place within a historically short—an even shorter—period of time. In the process, the world that racial segregationists had feared, railed against, and actively suppressed had effectively come to pass. In combination with economic change, racial change promised to transform Southern society. Partisan change, at least in hindsight, could hardly be far behind. Indeed, both the presidency and Congress would shortly testify to this change in the most unprecedented way possible, through the obvious and inescapable (re)arrival of a Southern Republican Party.

The Great Partisan Shift

The arrival of a new partisan political world would prove to be gradual in its appearance, multi-causal in its underpinnings, and, as a result, challenging to interpret. In that sense, too, it differed greatly from the world of Southern politics that it would displace. This older political world had possessed a clear and specific starting point, at least when measured through its signature pattern of partisan imbalance, along with an almost immediate realization. The resulting political order had then been very simply described.

This old world had begun most pointedly with the election of 1876, or rather, with the compromise of 1876 that resolved the election. In a deal that kept the presidency in Republican hands, national Republicans agreed to remove federal voting marshals from the South, thereby ending the period of Reconstruction. In short order, resurgent Southern Democrats effectively dismissed the nascent Southern Republican Party—for a further seventy-five years or so.

In the case of the presidency, the compromise of 1876 led instantly to the end of any Southern contribution to the electoral vote for Republican candidates (Figure 1.1). Within one election, the solidarity for which the South would afterward become famous was in existence presidentially. It was destined to be unruffled for upwards of seventy years, surviving the shift in the nation as a whole to a lasting period of Republican dominance after 1896 without so much as a Southern ripple. The Republican vote in the solid South did show an isolated uptick in 1928, the last presidential election before the Great Depression. In hindsight, this appears as nothing more than resistance to the quintessentially Northern character of presidential nominee Al Smith—immigrant-based, New York-accented, culturally "wet," and, perhaps worst of all, Catholic. Regardless, that blip was wiped away by the coming of the Great Depression and the New Deal.

Congress reflected the same underlying story. Southern Republican members of the House of Representatives from the Reconstruction period were quickly cut back to a handful of districts that had been Republican before the Civil War (Figure 1.1). These were almost entirely in the Appalachian Mountains of North Carolina, Tennessee, and Virginia, where the plantation economy and thus racial slavery had never had much relevance, so that the "lost cause" of Southern independence had never resonated much. A handful of idiosyncratic holdovers were squeezed away during the 1880s. A small apparent uptick in the 1890s was largely the result of a temporary Republican-Populist fusion in North Carolina. And the dire situa-

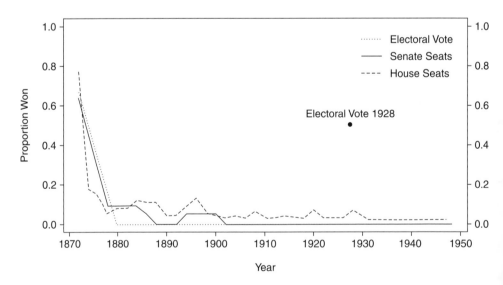

Figure 1.1   Lines of Republican Progress, 1872–1948.

tion thereafter was nevertheless trimmed further by the coming of the Great Depression and the New Deal in the 1930s.

This made it all the more remarkable that the Senate story could be even more desperate (Figure 1.1). Eight Republican Senators had already disappeared before the crucial election of 1876, as the Southern Democratic Party began its return to control of state legislatures. Five more Republicans disappeared that year, and one further election cycle eliminated four others. Louisiana and Mississippi gave up their lone holdouts in the early 1880s, and Virginia lost a pair of Republican Senators later that decade. Idiosyncratic political divisions restored one more Republican, that is, one Senator for one term, in North Carolina at the turn of the twentieth century. And then, from 1903 onward, there were no Republican Senators from the states of the Old Confederacy—literally none—until John Tower was elected as a Republican from Texas in a special election in 1961.

Contemporary analysts in the immediate postwar years could thus be forgiven their disbelief in the prospects of a Southern Republican Party (Heard 1952; even Converse 1966). There was the ongoing inertial weight of an obvious, existing, one-party dominance as backdrop. Despite the apparent demise of the white primary at the hands of the Supreme Court in the 1940s, there remained major institutional means to sustain this dominance: the literacy test and the poll tax most notably, on top of idiosyncratic administration of electoral rules at the local level. And there were class-based maneuvering and race-based intimidation if all else failed. Seventy-five years of partisan stasis testified to the strength of this combination.

Nevertheless, the first postwar generation stands out as the arrival date for a serious Southern Republicanism that would not, this time, prove to be merely a blip. The presidential harbinger arrived first, appearing in the early 1950s (Heard 1952; Seagull 1975; Lamis 1984). Its congressional counterpart arrived a bit later, but constituted a more stable and relentless embodiment when it came. Either way, it should have been clear by the 1960s that economic change was here to stay. By the 1970s, it would be clear that the same could be said of racial change. Habit buttressed by institutional manipulation would then prove insufficient to deter partisan change in the face of two such forces together.

While the same underlying social forces were contributing changed Republican prospects to all three institutions, it was the presidency, by way of a new presidential Republicanism, that registered them first (Figure 1.2).

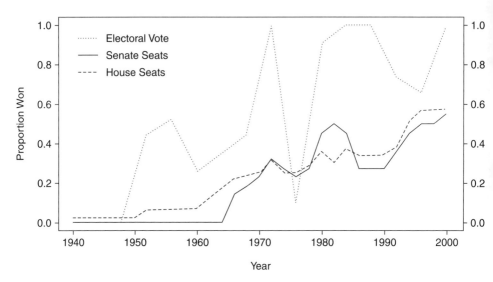

Figure 1.2   Lines of Republican Progress, 1940–2000.

The three elections of the 1940s still reflected the old world of Southern politics: there was no electoral vote from the South for any Republican candidate. The opening election of the 1950s was different. By 1952, a serious presidential Republicanism was on the dial, though at the time it seemed possible that this Eisenhower surge was just a personal tribute. Yet by 1972, only a generation later, there was a Republican majority for President in the South, the first Southern Republican majority since 1876.

On the other hand, by comparison to the situation in the House or the Senate, these gains remained potential rather than reliable. John Kennedy managed to knock the first surge back in 1960. Jimmy Carter took the line of further progress back nearly to zero as late as 1976. But by 1992, even a national nominee who was a certified Southern Democrat, Bill Clinton of Arkansas, could not resurrect a presidential majority in his home region. In other words, what was still hopeless at the time V. O. Key went to press was incipiently in existence by the next succeeding election; moved into majority territory only a generation later; and could not be dislodged by even a highly successful native son a generation after that.

In most ways, the House of Representatives told the same story, albeit in a superficially opposite fashion. A tiny rise for Republican seats in the House did join the surge of electoral votes for Eisenhower in the 1950s, though it accomplished little more than restoring the upper limits of the old Southern Republicanism before the Great Depression lowered them additionally (Figure 1.2). Contemporary observers could be forgiven for viewing this as normal fluctuation within an established order. In the early 1960s, however, the share of Republican seats in the House moved sharply upward, and, as we shall see in Chapter 2, this breakthrough represented more than just a further increase in aggregate numbers: it was to be underpinned by voting patterns that were fundamentally different.

Thereafter, what was noteworthy about the line of Republican progress in the Southern House, by comparison to that line for the presidency, was its relentlessness. From the late 1960s through the early 1990s, there was just a long, slow assertion of the Republican alternative. Along the way, this line did draw small additional increments from presidential advances in some years and suffer small additional decrements from presidential problems in others. Yet its overall trajectory was more noteworthy for the tiny character of these interruptions. Republican support largely expanded on the back of economic development while being restrained, to jump ahead of the story, by the civil rights revolution. In any case, in 1994, for the first time since 1876, the Southern Republican Party moved into majority territory in the House of Representatives as well—under the leadership of a Southern Republican, Congressman Newt Gingrich of Georgia.

The Senate story was distinguished from that of the House by a later start and a bit more electoral volatility. Otherwise, their paths of Republican progress were hardly worth distinguishing (Figure 1.2). Because there were no entire states constituted from Appalachian Republicanism, party prospects in the upper house of Congress started farther behind: there were no Republican Senators from the Old Confederacy in the 1940s, and still none in the 1950s. Yet once Republican progress began in the Senate, it too moved relentlessly, along almost the same trajectory as the House.

This Senate line gathered speed in the late 1960s and early 1970s. The lone subsequent point of notable difference with the House then came in 1980, when Ronald Reagan pulled an especially large crop of senatorial candidates into office with him, suggesting the possibility of an earlier arrival of majority status in the Senate. Reagan, however, gave back some of these Senators in 1986, so that it was ultimately to be 1994, as with the House, when Senate Republicans finally crossed into majority territory— never thereafter ceding that status, at least as this is being written.

These three lines of historical progress, taken together, have encouraged analysts to posit a "presidency-driven," even a "top-down," story of partisan change (Aistrup 1996). This view has the advantage of powerful simplification. Yet even when the focus is only the difference among institutions during this process of change, we think that a presidential story oversimplifies the picture. The presidency could run well ahead of Congress at key points, as it did in 1972. But it could also crash back behind it in short order, as it did just four years later. And it could suggest a modest Republican decline, for example from 1988 to 1996, when Congress was showing a strong Republican advance.

Worse yet, an analysis that privileges the presidency risks suggesting that political change was a product, not of fundamental shifts within the social base for partisan politics, but rather of an institutional—a constitutional—dynamic. We think it makes more sense to look on the presidency as reflecting the potential for both growth and retreat, and Congress as representing "the base" beyond which neither was likely to be consolidated in the long run. Most of the resulting change would indeed well up from below, though some of it would also be imposed from above. Moreover, even if much of it would register first by way of the presidency, it could not be treated as characterizing a "new Southern politics" until it had been institutionalized in Congress.

In other words, by showing a greater volatility of electoral outcomes, the presidency would indicate a profound change in underlying Republican potential but also the extent to which successful Democrats could claw it back. With a later start and slower growth, Congress would show much less volatility and, as a result, much more apparent inevitability in this same partisan shift. Accordingly, in the chapters that follow, we attempt to keep all three institutions in focus at all times. Our aim in so doing is to try to allow institutional structure to interact with social change in a manner that does not presuppose the outcome, a manner that permits institutional structure to become part of the overall explanation, not its defined essence.

Pursuing the Nexus of Partisan Change

A historical overview of electoral outcomes for the major institutions of national politics in the American South attests both to the long period of partisan stasis after Reconstruction and to the coming of partisan change after the Second World War. Yet a better way to grasp the remarkable shift in the *dynamic* of Southern politics is just to compare the place of the South in two dramatic Republican surges, at opposite ends of the postwar era. The national Republican Party managed to recapture control of Congress in the first fully postwar election, that of 1946, without the aid of a Republican candidate for President. The national Republican Party did

Table 1.1   The Changing Role of the Southern Republican Party: Regional
Contributions to National Upheavals

Year	Non-Southern Democrats	Southern Democrats	Southern Republicans	Non-Southern Republicans	All Other
A. The Congressional Upheaval of 1946					
1944	142	103	2	188	0
1946	84	103	2	245	1
1948	160	103	2	169	1
B. The Congressional Upheaval of 1994					
1992	182	77	48	127	1
1994	144	61	64	165	1
1996	155	54	71	153	2

not manage the same feat again, a congressional capture without presidential assistance, until 1994, forty-eight years later, when it did so resoundingly (Table 1.1).

Yet if those are formally equivalent events, the practical role of the South in their execution could hardly have been more different. The opening contest of the postwar era, in 1946, featured massive partisan volatility in the North, coupled with amazing partisan stasis in the states of the Old Confederacy. In this first fully postwar congressional election, the national Republican Party surged to majorities in both houses of Congress for the first time since 1928, only to give back both majorities at the re-election of Harry Truman, Democratic President, a mere two years later. In the process, Northern Republicans went from 188 House seats in 1944, to 245 seats (and a majority) in 1946, then back to 169 seats in 1948. Northern Democrats, conversely, went from 142 seats in 1944, to 84 seats in 1946, to 160 seats in 1948. Southern Democrats, however, stayed at 103, 103, and 103 in those years; and Southern Republicans went from 2 to 2 to 2.

The same story for 1994 can capture, concisely and powerfully, the now-changed dynamic of this partisan situation. By 1994, every aspect of the situation, and hence an entire national party system, was different—and the South was now the essence of the difference. In that tumultuous year, Northern Democrats went from 182 seats in 1992 to 144 seats in 1994 to 155 seats in 1996, while Northern Republicans went from 127 to 165 to 153: a Democratic majority to a Republican majority to an effective partisan wash. But Southern Democrats went from 77 seats in 1992 to 61 seats in 1994 to 54 seats in 1996, while Southern Republicans went from 48 to 64 to 71: powerful, monotonic, opposite movements. Indeed, this time, those movements were powerful enough to keep the Republicans in control of the House when Democrat Bill Clinton was solidly re-elected as President in 1996.

All of this led us to one guiding operational conclusion: that unpacking the effects of economic development and legal desegregation on partisan change in the postwar South required a complex dataset which could withstand major and multiple demands.

- At bottom, this unpacking required a dataset that would permit us to untangle the influence of two main causal agents, economic development and legal desegregation, and through them, class and race, on voting for public office.
- It required a dataset that could examine individual voting behavior, while simultaneously considering individual social backgrounds and individual policy preferences, most especially on issues of social welfare and aid to blacks.
- It required a dataset that could introduce contextual influences, especially the characteristics of electoral districts in which those individuals lived, characteristics which themselves reflected both economic and racial evolution.
- It required the ability to disentangle key aspects of elite maneuvering, by congressional challengers or incumbents as well as by presidential candidates based inside but also outside the American South, and to locate crucial differences among them.
- And of course, it required capturing the ultimate outcome, partisan wins and losses for national public office, institution by institution.

Three principal data collections were merged here to create such a dataset, and to permit such an analysis. An attempt to take these data seriously is critical to what follows.

1. The first of these was the cumulative file for the *American National Election Studies,* mostly tapped for individual-level data, including social background, voting behavior, and issue preferences.[1]
2. Second was the decennial census, mostly used for aggregate demographics of congressional districts. In earlier years, these were drawn from the *Congressional District Data Book;* in later years, they were drawn instead from the decennial volumes on congressional districting by Congressional Quarterly Press.[2]

3. Third was a more diverse set of specialized compilations for election outcomes, including *Candidate and Constituency Statistics of Elections in the United States, 1788–1990; Guide to U.S. Elections; America Votes; A Statistical History of the American Electorate;* and the *Almanac of American Politics*.[3]

Accordingly, it became possible to work with composite district demographics and specific personal backgrounds, elite candidate provision and mass public response, aggregate electoral outcomes and individual voting behavior. We think the result differs from much of the earlier work in several ways: in organizing the analysis, militantly and repeatedly, around *two* great changes in Southern social structure; in blending mass public attitudes, most especially on social welfare and civil rights, with objective social change; in highlighting the place of critical intermediaries—political parties and, most especially, partisan elites—as they addressed a changing society; in having concrete institutional outcomes as the focus, in terms of wins and losses for the House of Representatives, the Senate, and the presidency; and, last but not least, in using the best available data for addressing all of the above.

What results is a story of the transformation of Southern politics, familiar in its main elements but with, we hope, fresh contours and a different balance. With obvious portents in the 1950s and substantial beginnings in the 1960s, the coming of a serious and competitive Republican Party in the years following World War II ended—annihilated, really—the one-party character of a large American region. In so doing, it contributed one of the handful of genuine structural shifts that established the contours of modern American politics. The rise of a Southern Republican Party fundamentally changed the nature of politics in a major American region, of course. At the same time, it changed the character of American politics nationwide.

2

Economic Development
and a Politics of Class

ECONOMIC DEVELOPMENT WAS destined to come to the postwar South, and the politics of social class that might be expected to come with economic change did inexorably follow. Both would prove central to the rise of a Southern Republican Party. By the time they arrived, a politics of class would long since have become established—old news—in the non-South, where it had served for more than a generation as a diagnostic characteristic of the New Deal party system. Nevertheless, even if all that were not true, it makes sense to begin the story of postwar partisan change in the South by way of economic development and class politics for another, obvious reason.

Economic development and legal desegregation, and with them a politics both of class and of race, would remain intertwined during the postwar years in the American South. Yet if the racial reorganization of Southern society was to be the more dramatic and emotive of these two impacts, the economic reorganization of Southern society was effectively under way first. Or at least, and critically for our purposes, its impacts are present earlier in the data. A one-party South had, by definition, repressed the main cleavage, social class, which had defined the non-Southern—the New Deal—party system elsewhere, with a blue-collar Democracy facing a white-collar GOP. Its restoration, bringing the South back into the partisan union at long last, would finally make that party system fully national.

Beginning with the politics of class does, in turn, imply beginning with a focus on the white South. During the 1950s, there was some natural increase in the share of the Southern electorate contributed by black Southerners, the key trigger for a reorganization in the politics of race. Yet into the 1960s, this was still an inconsequential number of black voters: a region that was 20+ percent black had a black electorate in the 1950s, after it had begun to grow, of about 4 percent. That fact alone almost mandates an opening focus on the white South and its divisions, first incipient and then very real, on lines of economic interest. Nevertheless, it is worth remembering that even in this most-black section of the United States, the Southern electorate was and would remain overwhelmingly white, so that any major divisions among white Southerners would perforce be a crucial part of the postwar Southern story.

Curiously, much existing analysis of this fundamental structural shift, from economic development to class politics to resurgent Southern Republicanism, has remained rooted in descriptions of the Southern political world *pre-change*. It is as if an analysis appropriate to the 1920s, even the 1890s, has merely been brought forward with the dials adjusted. A major secondary purpose of this chapter, accordingly, is to help shift the overall frame of reference for the analysis of Southern politics, away from one more appropriate to the old order. A major secondary benefit of beginning with class politics is that it does precisely that.

The reconstitution and then invigoration of a basic class cleavage in the American South is thus the essential opening part of the story. And the critical body of data for such an analysis, of economic growth, class division, and Republican prospects, is the series of opinion surveys that was to become the National Election Studies (NES). Serendipitously, their creation was to coincide with the rise of Southern Republicanism. That series received a kind of unofficial "pre-test" in 1948, with a small sample and very limited questions.[1] But the real start of what was to become the central tool for the study of voting behavior in the United States came in 1952. Accordingly, this analysis needs to begin there as well.

Fortunately, the pattern of politics that V. O. Key set out for the old South can still be discerned easily with 1950s data in the case of Congress, and can be teased out of that data in the case of the presidency. On the other hand, while it would have been ideal to have some composite measure of social class when addressing the impact of economic change on the white electorate, the NES presents obvious problems in this regard. Shifting occupational categories, coupled with shifting means for their assessment, along with different ways of treating spouses and/or breadwinners, make direct analyses in terms of "social class" as a comprehensive concept highly problematic, especially in the earlier years which are critical to this particular story.

Nevertheless, the NES does categorize by *family income* across the whole period from 1952 to 2000. While these are still income bands rather than precise figures, they do allow an easy division into terciles for the nation as a whole: bottom, middle, and top thirds by income. Moreover, such a division has a special advantage for an examination of the South. If income terciles are calculated for the nation as a whole, then the South can begin poor (with a disproportionate bottom third) and grow richer (with a top third growing disproportionately), as in fact it did.

Social Class and Southern Republicanism: The House

For two main reasons, it makes additional sense to begin searching for the institutional impacts of economic change on partisan outcomes by way of the U.S. House of Representatives (Rohde 1991; Polsby 1997; Fenno 2000). From one side, as we have seen in Chapter 1, House votes and aggregate House outcomes were much less volatile than presidential votes and Electoral College outcomes. The main story-line is thus easier to recognize through the House. From the other side, the presidential candidacy of Dwight Eisenhower was such an important individualized phenomenon in the 1950s that, without some further analytic background, his candidacy risks opening the story through a potentially idiosyncratic focus. It is not immediately obvious how the analyst should separate the man from the moment.

Yet Eisenhower is ultimately a specific instance of a more generic problem. For the presidency as an institutional lens is always open to precisely the sort of analysis we hope to avoid, one focused on individuals and idiosyncrasies—a different kind of "local knowledge"—rather than on social forces, institutional structures, and regularized behavior by the mass public. Moreover, because the presidency provides a single contest every four years, major idiosyncratic elements will intermittently present a second set of continuing problems, involving the proper basis for aggregation. We address these initially in Tables 2.3 and 2.5 below. By contrast, the House offers more than a hundred contests every two years, so that its analytic charm is the opposite. The wiping away of specific individuals encourages a focus on larger trends shaping aggregated cohorts.

All three nationally elective institutions of American government—the presidency, Senate, and House—need ultimately to enter the analysis, since all three were available to register social change and its partisan impact, and especially since both their common stories and their institutional differences are important. Yet the advantage of beginning with House elections is not just that there are sufficient House districts to allow an analysis that is not specific to personalities. It is also that, whereas the presidency often led in the registration of electoral trends, the House was the body that most obviously consolidated them into stable and ongoing patterns of politics. For interpretive purposes, then, the common insistence on the primacy of the presidency, a priori, can be actively distortive.

In any case, Table 2.1 starts the analysis of the change underlying this postwar trajectory by looking at House elections by decade from the 1950s onward.[2] At the beginning of this period, Southern Republican congressmen were confined to a handful of Appalachian districts, which were among the poorest in the entire nation. For our purposes, their confinement meant that any class relationship was automatically attenuated. Nevertheless, in

Table 2.1   Social Class and the Coming of Southern Republicanism: The House

Decade	Income Terciles				Range (High-Low)
	Low	Mid	High	Total	
A. Republican Percentage among All Whites					
1950s	18	15	15	16	-3
(N)	*(200)*	*(140)*	*(220)*	*(560)*	
1960s	25	28	35	29	+10
(N)	*(223)*	*(208)*	*(225)*	*(656)*	
1970s	24	33	38	32	+14
(N)	*(271)*	*(317)*	*(296)*	*(884)*	
1980s	26	37	48	38	+22
(N)	*(232)*	*(305)*	*(313)*	*(850)*	
1990s	41	60	70	60	+29
(N)	*(254)*	*(329)*	*(423)*	*(1006)*	
B. Republican Percentage among All Whites in Contested Districts					
1950s	40	32	25	31	−15
(N)	*(80)*	*(59)*	*(100)*	*(239)*	
1960s	31	37	44	37	+13
(N)	*(137)*	*(113)*	*(122)*	*(372)*	
1970s	34	44	50	43	+16
(N)	*(184)*	*(217)*	*(201)*	*(602)*	
1980s	34	49	53	47	+19
(N)	*(131)*	*(202)*	*(230)*	*(563)*	
1990s	40	58	64	56	+24
(N)	*(225)*	*(270)*	*(338)*	*(833)*	

the old world of Southern politics, the relationship that did appear was inverse to the pattern outside the South. Which is to say: the poor were modestly more likely to vote Republican (Table 2.1A).

This situation changed, and the engine for a shift toward Southern Republicanism stood abruptly revealed, in the 1960s. Indeed, from one decade to the next, the overall relationship actually reversed. A politics of economic interest had evidently arrived. The wealthiest tercile was now most likely to vote Republican, the poorest tercile least likely—in a turn that was never in any way threatened thereafter. And while the move from the 1950s to the 1960s was the strongest overall shift, all subsequent decadal changes were to move further in the same direction.

Table 2.1A does contain what will prove to be the overall story of partisan change among Southern whites during all the postwar years. Yet its aggregation still very much masks the extent of the change, even in just this one institution, because it still includes many who *could not* vote Republican for the House of Representatives because they had no Republican candidate. Accordingly, the analysis should really be restricted to white Southerners who possessed both a Democratic and a Republican congressional alternative. When this restriction is imposed, the same patterns recur, writ larger still.

The column marked "Total" still shows relentless Republican progress across all these years, decade by decade (Table 2.1B). In the 1950s, even when the analysis is limited only to those districts that did indeed have Republican candidates, the party could attract less than a third of the total vote. By the 1990s, the Republican Party had reached majority status, at least among white voters, and it had done so on a far broader base of competition. Rather than drawing a third of the vote within the minority of seats that it could manage to contest, it drew a majority in a world where remarkably few seats lay beyond its aspirations.

More to the point of explaining this growth, however, is the class shift that accompanied and underpinned it. The 1950s, as captured by these individual-level data in tabular form, stand out as the decade of the old South, a piece of the same world that V. O. Key had captured with ecological data graphed onto maps. As such, the Republican vote that did exist still featured a clear class inversion: the wealthy were least likely to vote Republican, the poor most likely to do so.

The 1960s then reversed these old class patterns and laid the groundwork for Republican gains, forging a new link between partisan choice and social class, a link that had characterized the North at least since the New

Deal. From the 1960s and ever onward, at least as this is being written, the wealthy became most likely to vote Republican, in the South and not just in the North. In our terms, the top tercile became most likely to vote Republican, the bottom tercile least likely to do so.

But in fact, there was more. At the beginning of this switch, it was the top income tercile that really contributed the great change, detaching itself from the Democrats and moving to support the Republicans. This proved to be a fearsome shift: the top tercile went on to reach majority status for a Republican House by the 1970s. The middle tercile followed at a distance, getting to that same point only in the 1990s, when it brought the party as a whole to (white) majority status. By then, the top tercile was approaching the two-thirds mark in Republican support.

At the same time, the bottom tercile, creeping upward with overall Republican successes, had only just achieved the level of support it possessed even in the 1950s. Low-income Southerners participated in the new class politics of the 1960s by actually moving *away* from a newly energized Republican Party. In a new class politics, that party apparently lacked attraction for the low-income South, at least when examined by way of the House of Representatives, our benchmark for a stable and recurring partisan vote. In fact, low-income (white) Southerners were no more Republican in the 1990s than they had been in the 1950s.

A politics newly built around social class should also have been a politics newly built around social welfare as a policy concern, as it turned out to be. This was not just because societal divisions and issue cleavages cohere naturally and logically: no social basis, no policy difference. Nor was it just because when politics in the North had shifted from an essentially geographic to an essentially economic division, social welfare issues had been part and parcel of that change. Nor was it only because the essence of the dominant policy agenda of the immediate postwar era, the New Deal agenda of Presidents Franklin Roosevelt and Harry Truman, was economics and social welfare. Rather, all three preconditions were present. On the other hand, they had been present in the North for a generation without infusing Southern politics to nearly the same degree (Ladd with Hadley 1975; Geer 1992).

Fortunately, the National Election Studies asked one or more social welfare questions from the very first survey in 1948 onward. Even more fortunately, the longest-running single focus in the entire series is built around a welfare item first asked in 1952, so that its progeny can be used for a simple check on the policy implications of this Southern class shift. Tapping gov-

ernmental interventions on behalf of employment opportunities and economic well-being, this became the effective "marker item" whose surface
content addressed welfare policy:

> *Some people feel that the government in Washington should see to it that*
> *every person has a job and a good standard of living. Others think that*
> *the government should just let each person get ahead on their own.*

In 1952, what was to become "a job and a good standard of living" was
instead the many-headed mandate "unemployment, education, housing,
and so on"; for 1956 and 1960, it was just "a job"; for 1964, just "a good
standard of living"; and at that point, it became "a job and a good standard
of living" in every year thereafter. For the 1950s, there was only a two-part
answer: agree/disagree. For the 1960s, there was a four-part answer, from
strongly agreeing with the first premise through strongly agreeing with the
second. And for the 1970s onward, there was a seven-point range of agree-
ment. At a minimum, then, it is possible to have a consistent liberal versus
conservative dichotomy for the entire postwar period, with "0" the liberal
point and "1" the conservative point. Table 2.2 reflects this dichotomy.

Arrayed this way, the pattern of issue preferences and their relationship
to partisan politics parallels the pattern of class memberships and their
partisan relationship, with an opening twist. In the 1950s, preferences on
welfare policy were not so much inverted as simply unrelated to a Republi-

Table 2.2   Welfare Attitudes and the Coming of Southern Republicanism:
The House

Republican Percentage among All Whites in Contested Districts

| | Welfare Attitudes | | Range |
	Liberal	Conservative	(High–Low)
1950s	31	31	0
(N)	(137)	(64)	
1960s	24	38	+14
(N)	(59)	(125)	
1970s	36	48	+12
(N)	(112)	(224)	
1980s	27	58	+31
(N)	(99)	(213)	
1990s	32	68	+36
(N)	(171)	(462)	

can or Democratic vote. This is, of course, the time when lower-income individuals were more likely to be voting Republican in the South. Yet the national parties had largely aligned themselves the other way around, and welfare policy was central to this alignment: national Democrats supported the welfare programs of the New Deal, while national Republicans opposed them. Moreover, just to confuse matters further in the South, national Republicans from poorer constituencies could be quite moderate on welfare issues, while *Southern* Democrats could stand almost anywhere in this policy realm.

The result among white Southerners was a lack of any policy alignment. This is presumably another reflection of the old South, where most individuals had acquired their partisan attachments in a direct line to the Civil War and Reconstruction, events with no obvious relevance to modern welfare preferences. Yet the moment a change in class attachments to the two political parties arrived, in the 1960s, it brought with it a change, and a lasting one, in policy attachments. Conservatives on social welfare were now more likely to pull the Republican lever, liberals on social welfare to vote Democratic. And this relationship only got stronger as the postwar era aged.

Moreover, the main secondary effect from a class inversion—the distinctive paths of low-income versus high-income Southerners within the overall picture—was likewise recapitulated with welfare preferences. With social class, the top tercile led the move to a new congressional Republicanism. This was the stratum of society that made the original break, while the bottom tercile remained impervious to Republican attractions. In an echo of the same phenomenon, Republican progress over time occurred almost entirely among those with conservative preferences on social welfare, while the congressional Republican Party scored hardly any gains at all among those with liberal preferences (Table 2.2). Remarkably, they still stood in the 1990s where they had stood in the 1950s, despite massive partisan change around them.[3]

Social Class and Southern Republicanism: The Presidency

In the immediate postwar years, however, all this change was still to come, and congressional politicking in the old South looked as sleepy as ever. The same could not be said of presidential politicking. If Congress was to begin (at least superficially) as an indicator of stasis in Southern politics, an implicit argument that the old order adapted and endured, the presidency was to elicit an immediate stream of predictions that something major had changed, was changing, or would inevitably change. Most of these predictions were not otherwise consistent with each other. Moreover, the volatility of postwar presidential outcomes, now in the American South as well, meant that each seemed temporarily to disconfirm its predecessor.

Nevertheless, the same underlying structural factors that were transforming the South, and that were to change congressional politics so dramatically, were in fact transforming presidential politics as well. Such an outcome was not an absolute necessity. In theory, presidential politicking might have been so different from congressional politicking, through either differing policy substance or differing electoral strategy, that grand factors shaping the one would still largely bypass the other. In practice, they did not, and with structural shifts as large as these—with economic development and racial desegregation on this scale—it is hard in retrospect to see how they really could have.

For seventy-five years, Republican candidates for President had been awaiting a serious and recurrent Republican vote from the American South. With the House, the harvesting of any such vote, the partisan product of social change, was partially dependent on the recruiting of candidates to capitalize upon it: no congressional challenger, no Republican vote. With the presidency, this secondary problem did not exist—there had been Republican presidential nominees across the South since the end of the Civil War. It was just that there had been no rising Republican vote to harvest.

In 1952, that vote arrived. Moreover, it arrived in its modern form—the new South and not the old—with a new class connection, that is, with the class connection that it would have offered in the North for a generation before (Eulau 1962). Dwight Eisenhower not only drew a vastly expanded Southern vote for President, by comparison with Thomas Dewey in 1948 or Wendell Willkie in 1944; he also opened the era in which Republican candidates attracted that vote most heavily within the top income tercile, least heavily within the bottom (Table 2.3A).

John Kennedy was to wrest the presidency back for the Democrats eight years later. What he did not do was to restore the old class order. The sharpness of this class cut in the Republican vote for President then jumped up again in the 1960s. At one end of the income spectrum, the Republican vote among low-income Southerners actually managed to fall, to its lowest level of the postwar era. But at the other end of the spectrum, the Republican vote among high-income Southerners continued upward, so that the gap between high- and low-income terciles essentially doubled. In

Table 2.3   Social Class and the Coming of Southern Republicanism:
The Presidency

Decade	Income Terciles			Total	Range (High-Low)
	Low	Mid	High		
A. Republican Percentage among All Whites					
1950s	43	47	53	48	+10
(N)	(200)	(134)	(201)	(535)	
1960s	37	38	56	43	+19
(N)	(143)	(103)	(106)	(352)	
1970s	56	64	72	64	+16
(N)	(223)	(256)	(238)	(717)	
1980s	51	63	77	65	+26
(N)	(125)	(194)	(167)	(486)	
1990s	38	54	57	51	+19
(N)	(228)	(289)	(323)	(840)	
B. Republican Percentage of the White Two-Party Vote					
1950s	43	47	53	48	+10
(N)	(200)	(134)	(201)	(535)	
1960s	44	47	62	51	+18
(N)	(121)	(83)	(95)	(299)	
1970s	56	66	73	65	+17
(N)	(222)	(251)	(235)	(708)	
1980s	51	63	77	65	+23
(N)	(125)	(194)	(167)	(486)	
1990s	41	58	65	56	+24
(N)	(211)	(271)	(285)	(767)	

the process, the modern pattern—had anyone known—was effectively established.

It is possible to make this change look additionally like the story for the House of Representatives, thereby emphasizing its common roots, by focusing on the Republican share of the two-party vote, since a major independent candidacy by George Wallace in the 1960s, along with a lesser independent effort from Ross Perot in the 1990s, does color all the numbers in Table 2.3A. Again, a class reversal in the old Southern pattern of the vote was already present in the 1950s (Table 2.3B). Again, it jumped up sharply in the 1960s. But seen this way, the line of Republican progress did not vacillate thereafter. Seen this way, in other words, the class escalator remained relentless for the presidency too.

All of this helps to remove any individual peculiarity—any potential Eisenhower idiosyncrasy—from the coming of a Republican vote for President in 1952. In principle, it would have been possible for Eisenhower, the great American hero of his time, to expand the Southern Republican vote across the board, and for an expanded vote to acquire a class differentiation *after* he had left the political scene. This clearly was not the story. Instead, sharply rising Republican prospects in the South were tied to the arrival of a partisan attachment to income differences. In the process, Eisenhower served as the vehicle to register a pattern of class voting opposite to what had existed before, not as a transition to that outcome, much less as a brake upon it.

The candidate himself would probably have been horrified at this contribution—no class warrior, he. Nevertheless, he was to serve as the crystallizing vehicle for a new and different attachment between social class and Republican voting for President in the South. Moreover, this attachment did not go on thereafter to drag all income levels up in roughly proportional fashion, as economic growth progressed and the postwar period aged. As with the House, the top income tercile led the charge to a new Republicanism. And as with the House, despite unprecedented general Republican growth, the bottom tercile, the poorest third of the white South, remained disproportionately immune to Republican attractions.

The presence of a serious Republican vote for President in the first postwar election for which we have individual-level data does deny to the presidential tables one element of drama that the congressional tables possessed. With the Republican vote for Congress, one can see the Republican vote arrive *and* see that it represents a class reversal when it does (Table 2.1). That is, we possess the necessary "before" and "after" elections, before and after that reversal of the voting relationship to social class. With the Republican vote for President, one can see this arrival but not the change in class connection that came with it, at least not directly. Strictly speaking, there is no "before."

This missing data point is really a small matter, given the background situation. There was, after all, a remarkable absence of economic growth in the South before the 1940s. A poor agricultural economy had been only further devastated by the Great Depression. There was likewise a remarkable absence of a Republican presidential vote, in a line of electoral votes still running effectively at zero (Figure 1.2). When this Republican vote did appear, on the other hand, it arrived in the company of a clear income differentiation (Table 2.3). And this contextual before-and-after logic could be directly confirmed with individual-level data in Congress (Table 2.1).

There is, however, one further means of looking for this temporal comparison in the case of the presidency, and if it is hardly ideal in terms of its measurement, it does coincide powerfully with the old South argument of V. O. Key and the new South patterns revealed in the House. What this also affirms, once more, is that the Republican surge around the Eisenhower candidacy, for all the attractions of its hero-candidate, was essentially a vehicle for tapping Southern economic development, with its new politics of economic interest.

The way to do this additional investigation is to classify congressional districts according to whether they actually possessed a Republican candidate for Congress in 1952, before Eisenhower was nominated and then went on to expand the presidential vote. Districts that possessed Republican House candidates before Eisenhower thus become "old Republican"; all others are classified as "new." Even then, the National Election Study did not code survey respondents in 1952 according to their congressional district. But the NES did code respondents that way in 1956 and thereafter, so that it is possible to look for structural resonances from the old South, and for contemporary differences between the old and the new.

Looked at this way, these differences—the geological strata of Southern politics—stand out strongly (Table 2.4). For the 1950s, in fact, four things stand out:

- First, despite the superficially seismic impact of Dwight Eisenhower, old Republican areas were still considerably more sympathetic to the Republican candidate for President. That did not change.
- Second, old Republican areas simultaneously demonstrated the class inversion characteristic of the old South: the poor were most likely to vote Republican, the wealthy least likely to do so. By contrast, new Republican areas had this class tilt reversed—"righted."
- As a result, the difference in the class-based range of Republican support in old versus new Republican areas was huge: −12 percent in old areas to +19 percent in new ones, a massive reverse alignment.
- And just to emphasize the nature of the change, this difference was at its most extreme among low-income whites: Eisenhower was hugely attractive to them in old Republican areas, garnering 60 percent of their votes, but notably unattractive in newer areas, at just 31 percent.

Table 2.4   The Timing of a Class Reversal: The Presidency

Republican Percentage among All Whites

	Income Terciles			Range		
	Low	Mid	High	(High-Low)	Total	[*N*]
A. The 1950s						
Old Republican Areas	60	58	48	−12	56	[124]
New Republican Areas	31	44	50	+19	42	[250]
B. The 1960s						
Old Republican Areas	44	32	57	+13	46	[112]
New Republican Areas	35	41	55	+20	42	[240]
C. The 1970s						
Old Republican Areas	58	67	71	+13	65	[268]
New Republican Areas	55	63	73	+18	64	[449]

The 1960s then began an evolution, showing the gradual but insistent dominance of the new order, infusing but not yet obliterating the old (Table 2.4B). The gap in Republican presidential prospects between old and new Republican areas remained alive, with a real but rapidly declining advantage to old Republican areas. Yet by the 1960s, both areas showed the impact of the new (not the old) class-based voting patterns. These were strongly present (and strongly positive) in the new Republican areas, more shakily present—apparently still in transition—in the old.

By the 1970s, the old South had disappeared (Table 2.4C). Old and new Republican areas were making an essentially equal contribution to the national Republican vote. Moreover, both now gave Republican presidential candidates a healthy majority. Old and new Republican areas could no longer be distinguished by the relationship between presidential voting and social class either; both now offered roughly the same percentage of support from lower-, middle-, and upper-income voters. This also meant that old and new Republican areas could no longer be distinguished by the behavior of their low-income denizens.

Policy implications, at least in the social welfare realm, followed logically from these class impacts (Table 2.5A). Unlike the situation in voting for the House, the modern class pattern was already present in overall voting for the presidency by the 1950s, with the rich more Republican and the poor more Democratic. Not surprisingly, the modern pattern of welfare preferences was likewise present, with conservatives voting Republican and

Table 2.5   Welfare Attitudes and the Coming of Southern Republicanism:
The Presidency

| | Welfare Attitudes | | Range |
	Liberal	Conservative	(High-Low)
A. Republican Percentage among All Whites by Decade			
1950s	43	53	+10
(N)	(207)	(93)	
1960s	37	56	+19
(N)	(84)	(198)	
1970s	56	72	+16
(N)	(145)	(368)	
1980s	51	77	+26
(N)	(103)	(273)	
1990s	38	57	+19
(N)	(161)	(427)	
B. Republican Percentage among All Whites by Grouped Presidencies			
Eisenhower-Kennedy	43	53	+10
(N)	(207)	(93)	
Johnson-Nixon	46	66	+20
(N)	(136)	(345)	
Carter-Reagan	44	69	+25
(N)	(151)	(355)	
Bush-Clinton	27	63	+36
(N)	(189)	(470)	

liberals voting Democratic. This relationship was then confirmed and en-
larged in the 1960s. Again unsurprisingly, the relationship between welfare
preferences and the vote, having taken root a decade before the same relationship surfaced for the House, remained substantially stronger for the
presidency (compare with Table 2.2).

It would be possible to disaggregate the 1950s of Table 2.5A into old
and new Republican areas, in the same manner as shown in Table 2.4. But
in the case of welfare attitudes, there would be little point. Both new and
established Republican areas showed the modern relationship to welfare
attitudes by the 1950s, with liberals being Democratic and conservatives
Republican. Established areas were still more Republican overall, as they
would have to be. But within both older and newer areas, welfare ideology

conduced toward Republican support in the modern fashion (table not shown).

One should not, however, miss the element of distinctiveness in this. With social class, older areas had shown an inverse relationship to the modern pattern; only the newer areas came with the modern relationship fully formed. With welfare ideology, on the other hand, the modern relationship arrived fully formed everywhere. In other words, in the old world of Southern politics, class attachments (dating to the Civil War) were inverse, but ideological attachments had come to reflect the policy positions of the national parties. In the newly emergent Southern world, by contrast, both class attachments and ideological positions were consistent with the modern world when they arrived, for they simply had no "old world" from which they needed to become disentangled.

Table 2.5A, however, is one of those tables where the process of aggregating presidencies by decade rather than in equal groupings, putting two elections in some decades and three in others, suggests that subsequent developments were less linear—more wobbly—than was probably the case. Accordingly, Table 2.5B takes the same relationship between welfare preferences and the vote and presents it in three-election aggregates. The positive relationship between welfare conservatism or liberalism and voting Republican or Democratic is unchanged for the earliest period, the Eisenhower-Kennedy elections. That relationship is still confirmed and enhanced in the next period, the Johnson-Nixon elections. But it then moves up in an essentially straightforward fashion through the next two periods as well, that is, through the Carter-Reagan and then the Bush-Clinton elections too.

Social Class and Southern Republicanism: The Senate

The other branch of Congress, the Senate, requires several short digressions on institutional structure and its impact on data-handling before we can proceed to analysis of the link between economic development and partisan change. Part of this is statistical in an elementary way. With the presidency, while there was a presidential contest only every four years, that contest did feature a Republican candidate in every voting district. With the Senate, especially in the early years, it did not. For the House, although the provision of Republican candidates was also a major challenge, there were over a hundred contests every two years, over five hundred every decade. But for the Senate, that is, for the eleven states of the Old Confederacy with their twenty-two Senators serving six-year terms, there were on average *seven* contests every other year, and thus only about thirty-five per decade.

As a result, some of the statistical manipulations that are possible for the House and the presidency are just impossible with the Senate, and many others present a "choppier" picture. The situation is made worse by the fact that the NES is a national—not necessarily a regional—random sample, so that a year with few Senate elections on the calendar, and fewer contested elections within them, can also find them seriously under-sampled. This problem is at its worst for the 1950s and early 1960s, when NES samples tended to be more tightly clustered in geographic terms. The best we can do is to raise these cautions when the particular analysis appears to make them especially pertinent.

Otherwise, when the focus is institutional arrangements with the potential to shape a relationship between social change and partisan shifts, there are some respects in which the Senate looks more like the presidency than the House. For example, the Senate and the presidency have effectively the *same* electoral districts, so that both allocate the spoils of victory, either a full term in office or a full complement of electoral votes, to the plurality winner statewide. In most regards, however, the Senate is institutionally closer to the House than to the presidency, starting with the fundamental facts that both are collective (rather than individual) and legislative (rather than executive) institutions.

House and Senate districts did differ in potentially important ways. To begin with, the individual Southern states comprised as few as 6 and as many as 22 congressional districts in the 1950s, as few as 4 and as many as 30 by the 1990s. This meant that House districts were inevitably more homogeneous than any single state could be. Seen the other way around, however, the more important consequence is that Senate districts, being a blend of their House components, varied less among themselves—among the states—than did these component parts. There was just inherently less variation among the 11 states of the Old Confederacy than among the 106 congressional districts of the 1950s or the 123 of the 1990s.

As a result, when partisan change began, the social changes that were contributing to it had the potential to register earlier in some minority of House seats, where they were always more concentrated. In the crucial example, there were congressional districts with white-collar majorities well before there were any Senate districts (that is, states) that could make this claim. Thereafter, this differential variance between House and Senate districts meant that relationships between changing social characteristics and changing partisan behavior were likely to be stronger across House as opposed to Senate districts. In the crucial example here, there would always be a minority of House districts that were disproportionately white, along with a minority of House districts that were disproportionately black—disproportionate in both cases to any Senate seat—so that when racial context mattered, it ought to have mattered more in the House.

Yet despite clear differences in their electoral districting, the Senate and the House often behaved in highly parallel ways, and this fact will sometimes prove to be a route around the statistical problems that the small number of Senate seats can introduce. Two House-Senate comparisons underline this parallelism. The first involves voting behavior and can be presented year by year. If we compare the mean Republican vote in contested districts across the postwar years, the two bodies are effectively indistinguishable (Figure 2.1A). Because there can be as few as two or three contested Senate elections from the South in any given year, we cannot reasonably compare outcomes—wins and losses—by year, but we can aggregate these by decade (Figure 2.1B). Once more, the resulting differences are inconsequential.

Moreover, it may be surprising to discover how closely the Senate hewed to both the House and the presidency stories. That is, it is possible to see the same class reversal arrive with the Senate as it did with the House and the presidency, and it is even possible to isolate the apparent timing of the change. At first glance, aggregated by decade, both the 1950s and the 1960s show only unsystematic flux in the relationship between income terciles and a Republican vote for the U.S. Senate, so that the overall effect of a class reversal cannot be elicited until after 1970 (table not shown). By then, the story had become the same.

In fact, however, this appears to be one of those cases where imposition of a temporal cut appropriate to the House and the presidency is modestly misleading with the Senate data. For even with a serious shortage of open seats and a chronic dearth of Republican candidates, it is possible, by examining Senate results year by year, to let the data themselves aggregate the early years a bit differently. If the point is to isolate the sharpest available shift from the old world (with its class inversion) to the new, then alternative ways of dividing the 1960s should be permitted. If they are, then Table 2.6 is the result.

A. Voting Behavior by Year: Contested House and Senate Compared

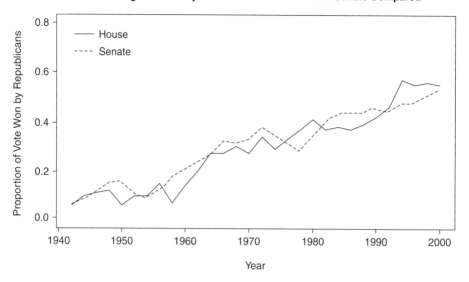

B. Electoral Outcomes by Decade: Contested House and Senate Compared

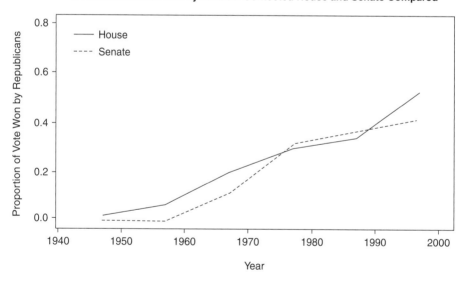

Figure 2.1   The Congressional Story Revisited.

Seen this way, for the period from the beginning of the National Election Studies through 1966, there was no evident patterning to the relationship between income terciles and Republican voting for the U.S. Senate in the American South. There was then a sharp jump toward the modern pattern from 1968 onward. That pattern was sustained in the 1980s. And

Table 2.6   The Timing of a Class Reversal: The Senate

Republican Percentage among All Whites in Contested States

Decade	Income Terciles				Range (High-Low)	Decadal Change
	Low	Mid	High			
1952–1966	26	20	27	25	+1	—
(N)	(139)	(95)	(122)	(356)		
1968–1980	42	44	53	47	+11	+10
(N)	(227)	(259)	(257)	(743)		
1982–1990	35	38	46	40	+11	0
(N)	(162)	(208)	(222)	(592)		
1992–2000	43	56	64	56	+21	+10
(N)	(165)	(226)	(288)	(679)		

it jumped again in the 1990s, as Republicans moved to majority status. Cut this way, the Senate looks powerfully like the House, and the apparent time lag in its responsiveness shrinks substantially. The Republican breakthrough occurred perhaps four years earlier in the House than in the Senate, but that was all.

A direct link to policy conflicts from this class shift, however, did lag the most for the Senate. Direct links to public preferences on social welfare were already there with the presidency in the 1950s, and they were destined to grow only stronger (Table 2.5). These same links arrived for the House in the 1960s, the point at which the old class inversion righted itself in this institution too, and they grew thereafter for the House as well (Table 2.2). Yet they did not really arrive for the Senate until the 1980s, at least a decade after the old class inversion had disappeared (Table 2.7). If the class inversion characterizing postwar politics arrived a bit later with the Senate, then, its social welfare link arrived later still.

On the other hand, what came to characterize both the House and the presidency with regard to the place of public preferences on welfare policy could not be delayed indefinitely, and indeed it was not. The world of the old South for the Senate, like that same world when examined through the House, featured nearly no relationship between welfare attitudes and Republican voting. By the 1980s, that relationship was instead strongly present. By the 1990s, it was surging, becoming every bit as strong as the link to welfare attitudes for the other two nationally elective institutions, almost as if to make up for the delay. In other words, some mix of institutional and

Table 2.7   **Welfare Attitudes and the Coming of Southern Republicanism: The Senate**

| | Republican Percentage among All Whites in Contested States | | |
| | Welfare Attitudes | | Range |
Decade	Liberal	Conservative	(High-Low)
1950s	22	25	+3
(N)	*(109)*	*(56)*	
1960s	37	41	+4
(N)	*(41)*	*(110)*	
1970s	50	53	+3
(N)	*(104)*	*(301)*	
1980s	26	49	+23
(N)	*(119)*	*(299)*	
1990s	30	68	+38
(N)	*(141)*	*(359)*	

candidate characteristics kept the Senate from looking like the new South for a little longer, though not by much.

Economic Development as Partisan Engine

Economic development came to the American South in the years following World War II, in a manner that it had not experienced since well before the Civil War. And economic development proved to be directly associated with partisan change, most especially by way of the prospects, at long last, for a Southern Republican Party. The specific events of postwar politics still shaped these prospects in measurable ways: war and peace, boom and recession, achievement and scandal. So did the identities and abilities of individual candidates—for the presidency, for the Senate, and for the House. Yet what is more impressive, in the face of all these implicit sources of variation, is not just the relentlessness by which economic development remade Southern politics, but the essential *homogeneity* of its impact.

When the focus was the share of actual wins and losses for public office, as it was in Figure 1.2, then the picture of relentless Republican progress did show some differential volatility, institution by institution. But when the focus is instead the relationship between social class and partisan choice, as it has been throughout this chapter, then volatility was only ini-

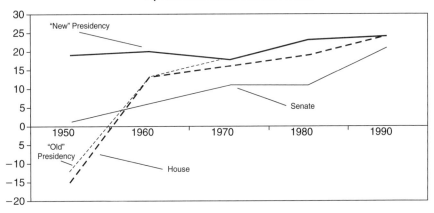

Percentage Difference in the Republican Vote between the
Top and the Bottom Income Terciles

Figure 2.2   Class Effects by Institution.

tial for all three institutions. Within an impressively short time, each came into line with the class patterns of the new and not the old South. Thereafter, what was striking was the extent to which the three separate institutions did *not* differ. Figure 2.2 plots the percentage difference in the Republican vote between the top and bottom income terciles by decade for the three governmental institutions, with the presidency divided into old and new areas for the early years.

At one extreme, the areas for a new Republican vote, those areas that had never previously provided a serious vote for Republican presidential candidates, arrived with the modern class relationship fully formed. This is the line for the "New" Presidency in Figure 2.2. Thereafter, these areas differed very little from decade to decade in the range of their success among upper-income as opposed to lower-income sectors of society. The aggregate total for the Republican candidate could still vary enormously, from 42 percent in the 1950s to 65 percent in the 1980s. But the class relationship within that aggregate varied almost not at all. It should also be noted that this was not the presidency "dragging up" the Republican vote. If institutional dynamics were the story, they should have appeared earlier and continued later. Rather, social forces were "welling up" from the bottom and being reflected in newly Republican areas.

It took a further decade for the older areas of Republican support, those that had always offered a serious vote to the Republican presidential candidate, to come into line with these new areas. Seen the other way around, however, it took *only* another decade: this is the line for the "Old" Presidency in Figure 2.2. The class relationships of the old South, where the lower-income sector was more likely to vote Republican rather than Democratic, naturally provided some resistance to the class relationships emerging in the new South. People had presumably been voting opposite to these new patterns—inversely—for generations. Yet it took only another decade before the difference between old and new Republican areas was close to elimination, not by splitting the difference but by settling on the new Republican pattern.

As the postwar era began, the House of Representatives actually looked most like the old presidency in terms of its voting relationships (Figure 2.2). This is the world sketched so richly by V. O. Key in *Southern Politics in State and Nation,* and it began with the strongest negative relationship between class and Republican support among the three nationally elective governmental institutions. Yet within a single decade, this pattern had reversed. Now, upper-income Southerners were voting Republican, lower-income Southerners Democratic, as they had in the North for a generation and a half, and as they would in the South forever after. By the 1960s, the House relationship was well on its way to convergence with the presidency. By the 1970s, it was effectively indistinguishable.

The Senate, finally, fell in between. At the start of the postwar era, voting relationships to social class were neither as inverted as they were for the House nor as contemporary as they were for newly Republican areas of the presidency (Figure 2.2). This initial ambiguity, coupled with the much smaller number of Senate contests, the presence of many long-lived incumbents, and some personal idiosyncrasies, appeared to delay the aligning impact of economic development on partisan politics. Yet by the 1970s, the Senate too had begun its move toward class convergence with the presidency and the House. By the 1990s, it had experienced a second sharp correction, essentially converging on the presidency/House pattern.

A tabular way to see the same thing is just to recast the postwar presidential vote in a fashion precisely parallel to the postwar vote for the House of Representatives (Table 2.8). In the real world of practical politics, it makes no sense to do this: the two parties had presidential candidates everywhere, after all, and the degree to which they attracted votes is the appropriate measure of presidential Republican strength (Table 2.3). Moreover, if our concern is with the transition from an old Republican vote to a new, then the proper calculation is the Republican vote in areas with an es-

Table 2.8   Social Class and the Coming of Southern Republicanism:
The Presidency in Contested House Districts

Republican Percentage among All Whites

Decade	Income Terciles			Presidential Range	House Range
	Low	Mid	High		
1950s	55	52	46	-9	-13
(N)	(71)	(60)	(93)	(224)	(201)
1960s	34	39	57	+23	+25
(N)	(106)	(75)	(74)	(255)	(234)
1970s	53	58	69	+16	+20
(N)	(141)	(156)	(169)	(466)	(418)
1980s	52	68	80	+28	+14
(N)	(62)	(127)	(117)	(306)	(285)
1990s	36	53	56	+20	+25
(N)	(204)	(234)	(275)	(713)	(609)

tablished Republican Party by the time of Dwight Eisenhower, versus the Republican vote in areas that were not previously characterized by an organized Republican presence (Table 2.4).

Yet there is no problem mechanically in looking at the effect of social class on Republican voting for the presidency in only those congressional districts that also possessed both Republican and Democratic House candidates, and comparing it with the effect of social class on Republican voting for the House in presidential years only, thereby creating a precisely parallel calculation. When this is done, the story the two institutions tell is remarkably parallel:

- Now, both the presidency and the House showed the old Southern class inversion for the 1950s.
- Now, that inversion was righted dramatically in the 1960s, with almost precisely the same amount of change.
- For both—compare Table 2.8 with Table 2.1—it was the upper-income tercile that shifted its loyalties to start this change.
- For both—same comparison—the lower-income tercile effectively sat in the 1990s where it had in the 1950s.
- By the 1970s, the presidency and the House, calculated in this way, had converged on the same point.
- By the 1990s, they had moved on, to a point of Republican progress that was nevertheless essentially the same.

Table 2.9   Welfare Attitudes of Partisan Voters: The Presidency, the House, and the Senate

Mean Welfare Scores for Party Voters by Decade

	The Presidency			Contested House			Contested Senate		
Decade	Dems	Reps	Margin	Dems	Reps	Margin	Dems	Reps	Margin
1950s	.27	.36	+.09	.33	.36	+.03	.33	.32	−.01
1960s	.60	.81	+.21	.67	.78	+.11	.72	.75	+.03
1970s	.64	.76	+.12	.71	.78	+.07	.73	.72	+.02
1980s	.50	.84	+.34	.64	.86	+.22	.64	.83	+.19
1990s	.54	.87	+.33	.56	.84	+.28	.54	.85	+.31

In any event, a new Southern politics had clearly emerged by the 1960s. Implicitly present by the 1950s, it was to acquire its fully modern form by the 1970s. And it would move relentlessly in the same direction thereafter. What was this politics about, the new politics that came with a changed economic universe and its new social alignments? The obvious answer is "social welfare," and it is obvious in two senses. First, a politics of social class was likely to be most centrally about social insurance and material (re)distribution. And second, the politics of the New Deal order—the Northern, class-based politics of the time—was profoundly about just that.

It came as no surprise, then, when the main events of a great class reversal were reflected in economic ideology. To see this, Table 2.9 takes the contents of Tables 2.2, 2.5, and 2.7, showing the relationship of welfare attitudes to the coming of Southern Republicanism, and calculates them "the other way around": the mean economic liberalism/conservatism of those who voted Republican or Democratic for each of these three national offices in all of the five postwar decades, where higher numbers are more conservative. What results is another variant of a familiar picture:

- There was little or no difference in the welfare preferences of Democratic and Republican voters for the House or the Senate in the old world of the 1950s. Partisan attachments had not been formed through welfare attitudes, and they did not reflect them. There were, however, clear and strong beginnings of a difference—to go with an evident class reversal—in the case of the presidency.
- Partisan voting for President moved forward to an even stronger link with public preferences on welfare policy in the 1960s, and partisan voting for the House now assumed the same alignment. Only

the Senate continued its lack of alignment with welfare policy conflict—not reverse alignment, just non-alignment.

- Both the presidency and the House actually fell back a bit in the
1970s, before moving forward strongly in the 1980s. At this point
the Senate moved, belatedly but strongly, to join them. Welfare policy differences between partisan voters were still greatest with the
presidency, least with the Senate, but even for the latter, the relationship no longer looked problematic.

- And that led to the strong policy differences of the modern era, in
which Democratic voters were sharply more liberal and Republican
voters sharply more conservative on welfare issues across all three
national institutions. Not only had all three relationships strengthened over time, they were also at their most congruent across the
three great institutions by the 1990s.

Class Politics and the New South

Huge social forces reconfigured postwar society in the American South.
Partisan shifts followed more or less ineluctably. Economic development,
in particular, began its take-off as the Second World War ended. In truth,
wartime industry had already helped in this transition, and the overall
boom in the postwar economy then took over. This postwar American
boom would be remarkable nearly everywhere, but the South actually caught
up with the rest of the nation during its occurrence. Out-migration in
search of a better life was a continuing motif of the old South, though the
loss of the economically ambitious could only exacerbate the problems they
left behind. Remarkably, in-migration in search of a better life would be a
counter-motif in the new South—the famous Michigan-to-Texas, rust-
belt-to-sun-belt stories of the 1980s being only a dramatic vignette (Gober
1993).

In turn, the coming of economic development, and with it a new class
structure, led to a crucial class reversal in partisan politics. Once—and presumably for generations before we have individual-level data to confirm
the relationship—class attachments to the political parties were inverse.
Inverse, that is, with regard to the situation in the North and to the overall New Deal order. The better-off in the South leaned Democratic, the
worse-off Republican. This was not so much a class alignment directly as it
was an indirect reflection of the social base of partisan identifications at the
time of the Civil War, but it nevertheless contributed an inverse class relationship.

Regardless, in the immediate postwar years, that relationship began to change. At long last, it came into alignment with the situation in the North, and the Republicans, not the Democrats, thereby became the party of the better-off. This also meant, portentously, that the Republicans were now aligned with the growth segments of Southern society (Figure 2.3). As its economic prospects grew, so did their political prospects: economic development proved a relentless partisan escalator for a new Southern Republican Party. One of the two great engines for partisan change in the American South was finally on the scene, pumping away. Figure 2.3 just retells that story in one more way.

Following on from this class reversal—part and parcel of it, but with a partially autonomous relationship to the partisan outcome—was a shift in policy conflict for the postwar South. As in the North, so in the South: a political order built upon social class was also a political order themed around social welfare. Class politics could, in principle, support any policy conflicts that were capable of being aligned with class differences. But in the late New Deal era, these were first and foremost conflicts over social welfare, and while these might be joined by other concerns as the postwar era aged, they would actually never recede. Indeed, they would only advance.

The simplest way to bring all of this together in a single exhibit, thus providing a final summary device, is by means of elementary cross-tabulations between welfare preferences and income terciles (Table 2.10).

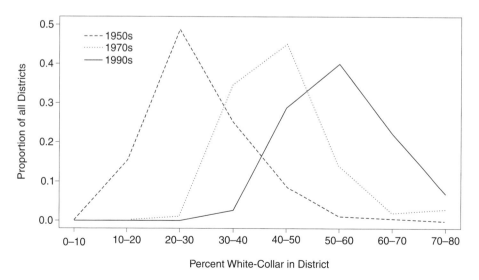

Figure 2.3   The Class Escalator: White-Collar Shares by Congressional District.

Table 2.10   Social Class, Welfare Preference, and Partisan Change, 1952–2000

Republican Percentage among All Whites

	A. Presidency Income			B. Senate Income			C. House Income		
Welfare Attitude	Low	High		Low	High		Low	High	
	1950s			1950s			1950s		
Lib	38 (90)	44 (54)	+6	23 (64)	30 (30)	+7	39 (57)	30 (44)	−9
Con	72 (18)	48 (48)	−24	50 (26)	31 (54)	−19	38 (13)	30 (37)	−8
	+34	+4		+27	+1		−1	0	
	1960s–1980s			1960s–1980s			1960s–1980s		
Lib	37 (131)	56 (59)	+19	33 (85)	38 (53)	+5	29 (98)	33 (57)	+4
Con	59 (185)	75 (329)	+26	45 (137)	53 (274)	+8	36 (151)	54 (309)	+18
	+22	+19		+12	+15		+7	+21	
	1990s			1990s			1990s		
Lib	25 (55)	25 (44)	0	23 (40)	30 (44)	+7	29 (52)	34 (50)	+5
Con	49 (78)	69 (169)	+20	55 (62)	73 (149)	+18	55 (91)	74 (190)	+19
	+24	+34		+32	+43		+26	+40	

Welfare preferences are presented as a liberal-conservative dichotomy, since that allows a consistent scale over fifty years. Social class is captured by comparing top and bottom income terciles. The postwar years are divided into the old order of the 1950s, the transitional period of the 1960s through the 1980s, and the new world of the 1990s.[4] And the presidency, the Senate, and the House are analyzed separately, to capture any institutional differences along the way.

Cell entries are then just the percentage voting Republican.[5] Even in this simplified format, the evidence from the 1950s is fragile, with small sample sizes and item formats that saw respondents opting more for the "Don't Know" category than they would in subsequent years. We think that the bivariate format of earlier tables in this chapter is a better representation of relationships at this period in many regards. Nevertheless, the picture that emerges here of the opening years of the postwar era is easily recognizable from what has gone before.

The House remained the world of the old South. There was no policy relationship to the vote, and the class relationship, which clearly did exist, was inverse. That is to say: liberals or conservatives on social welfare did not differ in their partisan choices, but the *poor* were more likely to vote Republican and the rich Democratic. By contrast, social change was already beginning to reach into voting for the presidency, so that it offered a more complex picture of the impact of social class and welfare preferences. Welfare ideology had arrived as an influence, with conservatives more likely to vote Republican for President than liberals, though this was especially true among low-income voters. And the wealthy had become more likely overall to vote Republican, the poor to vote Democratic, though this effect was concentrated among welfare liberals and did not apply to welfare conservatives.

On the other hand, there were so few low-income conservatives on social welfare that they should probably be disregarded. If they are, the story of the presidency in this period is that both class and race had become aligned, in what would come to be recognized as the modern pattern. The wealthy were more Republican than the poor, and welfare conservatives more Republican than welfare liberals, within each tercile. This was in striking contrast to the House, where the poor were more Republican than the wealthy, and where welfare preferences remained irrelevant within both groups. The Senate then approximated the presidency more than the House, again showing the beginnings of modern impacts from both social class and welfare preference, though in a weaker fashion than with the presidency.

The transitional decades, from the 1960s through the 1980s, bring more robust data and tell a very different story:

- For all three institutions, social class had become aligned with partisan choice. The upper tercile was going Republican, the lower tercile Democratic, and policy preferences were no longer a confusing factor in this relationship. This effect was strongest for the presidency and weakest for the Senate, though the greatest *change* came in the House, where an actual negative relationship had been reversed.
- For all three institutions, policy preference too was now aligned with

partisan choice. Conservatives were voting Republican, liberals Democratic, and social class was no longer a confusing factor in this relationship. Again, the effect was strongest for the presidency. And again, it was the House that had made the largest overall shift, though low-income voters still lagged; it was upper-income voters who had most fully come into alignment with the other two institutions.

• That said, the main point was a powerful symmetry emerging among all three institutions. High-income conservatives were uniformly most Republican. Low-income liberals were uniformly least Republican. And there was little to choose between high-income liberals or low-income conservatives in terms of their Republican proclivities.

The modern era, the 1990s, is then easily recognizable as a further evolution of this transition period. The overall class effect remained, and remained unconfused by the impact of policy preferences. The overall attitudinal effect remained as well, though by the 1990s, it was clearly the stronger of the two: differences between liberals and conservatives were larger than differences between the poor and the rich for every institution. As a result, the overall symmetry was additionally neat. Now, upper-income conservatives were the most Republican; lower-income conservatives came next; upper-income liberals followed them; and lower-income liberals were the least Republican. On the one hand, welfare liberals, rich or poor, were pretty uniformly resistant to Republican attractions. On the other, this was not much of a firewall against Republican gains: the vast majority of white Southerners were welfare conservatives.

In the end, then, what emerges most strikingly is the consistent pattern of a new Southern politics, one built upon—indeed, generated by—economic growth, social class, and an underlying class reversion. The basic class change, away from the pattern of the old South but still visible in the 1950s, was a hugely powerful phenomenon. Yet the impact of policy preferences on social welfare also became a powerful relationship as the new South consolidated, culminating in a remarkably powerful effect of its own by the 1990s. Thus in the end, there was a composite political world strikingly different from the one that had gone before, and had lasted for so long.

3

Legal Desegregation
and a Politics of Race

ECONOMIC DEVELOPMENT WAS under way in the years immediately after the Second World War in the American South, and the resulting alteration of an economic base and its class structure was having an impact on partisan politics by the early 1950s, as we have seen. Yet economic development as social change was also gradual, indirect, and implicit. The same could not be said of the second great social change affecting partisan politics in the postwar years. The "civil rights revolution" and the resulting alteration of the racial organization of Southern life arrived in response to dramatic, and highly visible, social conflict. After generations in abeyance, these stimuli arrived in a concentrated rush. And they arrived with the stated expectation of changing Southern politics.

Symbolically, the civil rights revolution was to be one of the signature events of the postwar era. Operationally, its direct impacts were secured by means of explicit legislative action and self-conscious administrative intervention. The Civil Rights Act of 1964 and the Voting Rights Act of 1965, in particular, directly attacked both the racial structuring of Southern society and the racial basis of Southern politics (Graham 1990). Yet these very facts, the very drama and concentration of the arrival of legal desegregation, drew the attention of scholars in a way that economic development did not, encouraging students of postwar Southern politics to extend the lead argument of V. O. Key, Jr., that "sooner or later the trail of inquiry leads to the Negro" (Key 1949, 5).

As we shall see, their attention was fully justified. In the aftermath of these reforms, there were practical impacts with the potential for reshaping partisan politics nearly everywhere one looked. Yet that very fact also en-

couraged scholars to apply the basic argument in a manner that was lacking nuance at the least, and occasionally was just incorrect. Accordingly,
we begin this chapter by introducing the black South back into the analysis, much as the civil rights revolution reintroduced black Southerners
to Southern politics. That is the main explicit purpose of the chapter, and
it pursues this purpose through the newly enfranchised black electorate,
through the restructured composite electorate created by this enfranchisement, and through an older white electorate that would surely respond,
one way or another, to racial change.

Yet there is a major secondary purpose to this chapter as well. For in the
process of pursuing the changing impacts of a politics of race, it is possible—indeed, it is necessary—to add sophistication to the manner in which
they are usually addressed. It is necessary, first, to add precision to the
changing impacts of a politics of race, for it was not some simple, single phenomenon. Yet it is also necessary to diversify those impacts, in
terms of the social contexts in which they occurred and the policy attitudes
with which they were associated. And it is necessary, finally, to embed the
impact of a changing racial politics in political institutions that actually
expressed this politics very differently. When this is done, three results
stand out:

- First, the partisan attachment of these new Southern black voters
  was to be central to everything that followed. In their case, an overwhelming attachment to the national—the Northern—Democratic
  Party, and not to the Southern Democrats nor to the national Republicans, dwarfed all other influences on their political behavior.
- Second, their arrival was to restructure the Southern electorate as a
  whole, in class and not just racial terms. Black Southerners themselves effected much of this change, adding a huge leaven of low-
  income voters to the electorate. But the institutional mechanisms
  that guaranteed their participation also brought a shift in the class
  structure of the *white* electorate, pulling it in the same direction
  and—this time—affirming suspicions long harbored in the literature of Southern politics.
- Finally, the arrival of Southern blacks into the real (rather than just
  the hypothetical) electorate was to offer grounds for a newly energized politics of race among white Southerners too, should they
  choose to pursue it. When they did, this white racial politics drew
  the attention of scholars in a manner that often eclipsed the first

two impacts of racial desegregation, and in a much more undifferentiated fashion than institutional distinctions would actually require.

Analytically, this latter politics—on the part of white Southerners in a racial context that had been transformed—was the most complex, and therefore the most revealing, part of the story. In a sense, its most remarkable aspect was the *lack* of apparent change in the pattern of congressional voting, though this was also a tribute to the ability of congressional politicians to finesse a huge societal shift. Before racial reform, whites in blacker areas voted more Democratic, whites in whiter areas more Republican. After reform, the same was true.

Yet at the same time, presidential voting assumed precisely the opposite pattern, a pattern long hypothesized, either anticipated or feared, by students of Southern politics. Presidential candidates could not sustain old voting patterns across the same social divide. Before reform, whites in blacker areas had voted more Democratic, whites in whiter areas more Republican for President—just like Congress. After reform, however, whites in blacker areas voted more *Republican*, whites in whiter areas more Democratic.

Finally, and just as remarkably, the relationship between white preferences on race policy and white voting also shifted strongly. Before the civil rights revolution, racial liberals voted Republican while racial conservatives voted Democratic. After the civil rights revolution, this pattern reversed. Moreover, it reversed in all three institutions—conservatives voting Republican, liberals Democratic—so that racial attitudes had a consistent impact across the House, the Senate, and the presidency, while racial contexts primed Congress and the presidency, simultaneously, in opposite directions.

Racial Desegregation and the Coming of a Northern Democracy

Forty years later, it is easy to forget that a very substantial minority of Southern blacks had long been adherents of the Republican Party, the party that had freed the slaves and spearheaded the first great attempt to make them voting citizens. Likewise, it is easy to forget that the success of both the Civil Rights Act and the Voting Rights Act remained critically dependent on the support of Republican Senators. If it was Northern Democrats who spearheaded the legislative side of the civil rights revolution, it was Southern Democrats who led the fight against it. As a result, it was Northern Republicans—the national Republican Party—that provided the votes to make this legislation pass. A higher percentage of Republican than Democratic Senators voted for both the Civil Rights Act and the Voting Rights Act. Had Republicans been only as supportive of civil rights as Democrats, neither bill would have survived.

Nevertheless, it was Northern Democrats who principally initiated and sustained these legislative efforts. Thus when Southern blacks entered the electorate in a rush in the 1960s and 1970s, they entered as "national Democrats," despite the obstructive presence of white regional Democrats. While the total contribution by Southern blacks to the NES sample of Southern *voters* in the 1950s was inevitably small, the National Election Studies could still elicit evidence of the underlying partisan story. In these data, over 40 percent of the presidential vote by black Southerners still belonged to national Republican nominees in the 1950s (Table 3.1A). That share fell catastrophically in the 1960s—to 3 percent!—and it never really recovered. Black Southerners would thereafter echo the pattern of support for Republican presidential candidates nationwide, albeit at a great distance, ticking up a bit in the 1970s and 1980s in conjunction with the fortunes of those candidates. But this would always remain the faintest and most distant of echoes.

The historical vote by black Southerners for the Republican candidate, generated during Reconstruction and sustained in part by Democratic foreclosure, was thus gone presidentially. A side-look at the House and the Senate tells essentially the same story (Table 3.1B). The survey *N*

Table 3.1   The Demise of Black Republicanism

	% Republican	(N)
A. Presidential Vote by Black Southerners by Decade		
1950s	42	(33)
1960s	3	(74)
1970s	10	(174)
1980s	9	(130)
1990s	3	(219)
B. Presidential, Senate, and House Voting after Legal Desegregation		
Presidency	7	(523)
Senate	13	(493)
House	11	(670)

for the earlier period is additionally feeble in the case of this congressional electorate, but aggregating the three decades after the civil rights revolution shows a Republican vote of 7 percent for the presidency, 13 percent for the Senate, and 11 percent for the House—though in truth, this should probably be stated the other way around: as a *Democratic* vote of 93 percent for the Presidency, 87 percent for the Senate, and 89 percent for the House.

A social group with that sort of overwhelming partisan imbalance left nearly no room for any other influences on its vote. Black Southerners in the new South were to be even more monolithically Democratic than white Southerners had been in the old. For them, racial identification overwhelmed any other social basis for partisan distinction. As a result, the obvious missing element, so very consequential among white Southerners, was social class. The coming of a class reversal had been crucial to the rise of Republican voting among Southern whites. Yet there was nearly no room for a parallel effect among their black fellow citizens, and there was effectively none.

Black voters became Democratic voters, pure and simple. Class distinctions, such as they were, had nothing to add (Table 3.2A). The presidency showed a remarkably high and essentially uniform line of support for Democratic candidates. The Senate showed a "perverse" relationship, with the slightest trend toward the Democrats and *away* from Republicans in the top tercile. And the House showed a slightly larger trend in the opposite direction, if losing 80 percent of the small vote in the top income tercile of this social group can be considered a "Republican trend." Yet that was essentially all there was to say, for a demographic influence that was powerfully reshaping the white electorate at the same time.

Not surprisingly, given the lack of a class effect, there was no serious variation in partisan support among Southern blacks according to general preferences on social welfare. This is again in sharp contrast to the clear and strong relationship among Southern whites. Yet if nine out of ten Southern blacks voted Democratic for President after passage of the Civil Rights and Voting Rights Acts, welfare attitudes could add only the slightest increment or decrement to this relationship. There was the hint of a link for the presidency; the Senate was essentially a wash; and the House showed a slightly larger relationship (Table 3.2B). Overall, however, the point remained that, with little room for much further influence on the black vote, there was little further influence.

A different possibility for some internal differentiation within a new and

Table 3.2   The Rise of a Monolithic Voting Bloc

A. Social Class and Partisan Voting

Democratic Percentage among Black Southerners

1970s-1990s	Income Terciles		
	Low	Mid	High
Presidency	92	92	93
(N)	(290)	(128)	(61)
Senate	87	87	92
(N)	(240)	(122)	(59)
House	90	90	80
(N)	(249)	(117)	(58)

B. Welfare Attitudes and Partisan Voting

Democratic Percentage among Black Southerners

1970s-1990s	Welfare Attitudes	
	Liberal	Conservative
Presidency	93	90
(N)	(260)	(93)
Senate	88	89
(N)	(237)	(80)
House	91	84
(N)	(313)	(113)

exploding Southern black electorate involved the social *contexts* that these individuals inhabited. With many other social groups (Tingsten 1937; Butler and Stokes 1969), members of the group who lived in areas where that group was disproportionately concentrated did show different behaviors, including political behaviors, from members who lived in areas where the group was comparatively less numerous. In other words, members in areas where the group was numerous were more likely to display the modal behavior of the group, while members in other areas were more likely to deviate from it.

In the 1950 census, blacks constituted more than one in four Southerners. They still constituted more than one in five in 2000, despite substantial white in-migration and black out-migration. These figures made the South as a region racially distinctive, but they naturally subsumed a much greater range of racial contexts, from electoral districts where blacks were a tiny percentage to those where they verged on being the majority.

For many subsequent analyses, especially in Chapters 4 and 5, we shall use this full range, the actual racial composition of congressional districts. For an initial look at the impact of racial context, however, it is easiest just to take the later 20 percent figure—more than one in five—as a cutpoint. In practical terms, once black Southerners constituted more than 20 percent of the potential electorate, they would more or less automatically require some adjustment from the white Democrats whom they were supporting: some acknowledgement, some integration, or failing that, some confrontation. Along the way, the 20 percent cut emphasizes the momentousness of legal desegregation for all of southern politics in the 1960s, when the southern average was still well above that figure. And this division has the crucial collateral advantage of guaranteeing a substantial white population in more-black districts until very late in the analysis.

In any case, it is easy to divide Southern voting districts into those that were more and less black than this benchmark figure.[1] Such a division allows the possibility in practical and not just theoretical terms that new Southern black voters who found themselves in less-black (more-white) districts might exhibit some different voting behavior from those in more-black (less-white) districts as a direct result. Once again, however, the simple fact of Democratic predominance among all black Southerners—the overwhelming tendency of Southern blacks to come into the electorate as, in effect, Northern Democrats *and to stay that way*—eliminated most of this possibility in practice.

When black voters for the three main nationally elective institutions of American government are pooled across the three full decades after legal desegregation, presidential voters are overwhelmingly Democratic, regardless of blacker or whiter social context (Table 3.3A). The two houses of Congress do hint at a contextual effect: blacks in blacker districts were about 5 percent more likely to vote Democratic (and hence 5 percent less likely to vote Republican) than blacks in whiter districts for the House, about 6 percent more likely for the Senate. As we shall see, this congressional effect, small in its own right, was to be dwarfed in magnitude and consequence by the counterpart effect among whites. Racial context would indeed be important to the Southern story, but for whites, not for blacks.

The final possibility in such an analysis is that it would not have been racially relevant contexts but racially relevant *attitudes* that should have been expected to shape voting behavior among black Southerners. That is, those who believed that governmental aid targeted specifically to black Ameri-

Table 3.3   The Rise of a Monolithic Voting Bloc, Continued

A. Racial Context and Partisan Voting

Democratic Percentage among Black Southerners

1970s-1990s	<20% Black	>20% Black
Presidency	94	94
(N)	(152)	(371)
Senate	83	88
(N)	(113)	(347)
House	87	93
(N)	(126)	(353)

B. Racial Attitudes and Partisan Voting

Democratic Percentage among Black Southerners

1970s-1990s	Race Policy	
	Liberal	Conservative
Presidency	92	92
(N)	(222)	(109)
Senate	89	84
(N)	(216)	(103)
House	88	89
(N)	(290)	(143)

cans was a good thing might at least be more likely to vote Democratic than those who thought that racially targeted aid was not a good thing. Fortunately, although there are no civil rights items that span the entire NES in the way that the social welfare item on "a job and a good standard of living" does (see Chapter 2), there is an item on aid to black Americans that spans the aggregated period from 1972 onward, and it seems a reasonable proxy for this attitude:

> *Some people feel that the government in Washington should make every possible effort to improve the social and economic position of blacks and other minority groups. Others feel that the government should not make any special effort to help minorities because they should help themselves.*

Yet once again, on a policy division so apparently relevant to the arrival of black Southerners in practical politics, there was little relationship to the partisan choices they made thereafter (Table 3.3B). The presidency and the House showed effectively no difference; the Senate showed a tiny difference in the "proper" direction, with conservative blacks being a shade less Democratic. Regarding this latter relationship, however, it is worth recalling the overall value of the effect: if black Southerners were 20 percent of the regional population, if black conservatives were 33 percent of black Southerners, and if Republicans did 5 percent better among black conservatives in Senate elections, then that was a further aggregate contribution to the Southern Republican vote for the Senate of one-third of one percent—0.33 percent.

Legal Desegregation and the New Southern Electorate

Voting by black Southerners surged during the 1960s, under the dual protection of national law and federal marshals. As a result, the nature of the social base for Southern politics—the Southern electorate—was recast almost at a stroke (Lawson 1976; Stanley 1987). The postwar baseline for black participation in the politics of the old South, still visible in NES data for the 1950s, already represented some modest incremental gains (Bartley and Graham 1975; Bass and DeVries 1976). That baseline nevertheless experienced immediate and explosive growth in the 1960s, courtesy of a changed legal framework plus practical guarantees for its application. As we have seen, this new black electorate was all the more noteworthy for the fact that it was not further divided by other social considerations, by racial contexts, by racial attitudes, by welfare attitudes, or, most remarkably given the white Southern story of the postwar years, by social class.

On the other hand, it is important not to allow this racial homogeneity to mask a major contribution that this new black electorate was making, both directly and indirectly, to the *class* basis of Southern politics. For if the new black electorate was still disproportionately located in the lowest income tercile, then it almost had to be pulling the total electorate strongly in that direction. This is its direct effect, and, as we shall see below, it was certain and strong. Yet it is important to remember that it had long been argued that the electoral rules for the old Southern politics functioned as a barrier to participation by poor whites as well. So the potential for an indirect effect on the class composition of the Southern electorate by way of white voters was automatically present too in the aftermath of electoral reform.

Black Southerners may not themselves have been responsive to considerations of social class as distinct from racial identity. But they certainly held a class *position* in Southern society, and that position helped to underpin and augment considerations of economic voting in Southern politics. As a result, the composite class contribution of reforms aimed at ending black disfranchisement in the 1960s was substantial. Table 3.4 presents the aggregate of Southern voters for the presidency by decade, divided into top, middle, and bottom terciles by income. In the Southern electorate of the 1950s, an overwhelmingly poor electorate had nevertheless secured only a small edge for lower-income Southerners in voting totals. Upper-income Southerners, despite their relative paucity, were actually close behind (Table 3.4A).

Voting reforms in the 1960s then fueled a substantial class shift, sharply elevating the lower-income share of the total vote while sharply reducing the upper-income share. Poor Southerners became almost a majority of the total electorate. Moreover, this racially impelled class shift coincided with the arrival of the class reversal in Southern voting patterns that began with the presidency in the 1950s and reached both houses of Congress in the 1960s. Reforms justified on racial grounds obviously had a powerful class impact.

After the 1960s, these reformed electoral rules would go on to meet an economically booming Southern society, and the effects of that boom—plus, presumably, some differential voter turnout within it—would go on to alter these impacts in additional ways. While the lower-income tercile

Table 3.4   Racial Desegregation and the Class Composition of the Southern Presidential Electorate

Decade	Low	Mid	High	*(N)*
A. Share of Electorate by Income Terciles for the Full Southern Electorate				
1950s	39	25	36	(568)
1960s	45	29	27	(421)
1970s	38	33	29	(885)
1980s	32	38	30	(606)
1990s	32	34	34	(1033)
B. Share of Electorate by Income Terciles for the White Southern Electorate				
1950s	37	25	38	(535)
1960s	41	29	30	(352)
1970s	31	36	33	(717)
1980s	26	40	34	(486)
1990s	27	34	39	(840)

Note: Bolded decades are the ones before and after electoral reform.

continued to be the modal part of the Southern electorate in the 1970s, its share was already declining; it was the middle tercile that was continuing to grow (Table 3.4A). This growth continued through the 1980s, when the middle-income tercile became the modal part of the electorate. The upper-income tercile did not benefit in similar ways until the 1990s, when it finally reached parity with the middle tercile, a parity still below the electoral share that it had enjoyed in the 1950s, forty years before.

The numbers in Table 3.4, being based on the presidential vote, mask some modest further variation within the total electorate. While those who voted for President were obviously available to vote for Congress—always the House, usually the Senate—there was actually some ballot fall-off with these down-ticket offices in presidential years. As a result, figures calculated for the House or the Senate over this entire fifty-year period averaged a percentage point lower for the bottom tercile, a percentage point lower for the middle tercile, and two percentage points higher for the top tercile. In the same way, off-year elections could be expected to have a lower turnout on average than on-year (presidential-year) counterparts. As a result, House and Senate elections in presidential years for this same fifty-year period averaged four percentage points higher for the bottom tercile than in off-year elections, two percentage points lower for the middle tercile, and two percentage points lower for the top tercile (tables not shown).

Within all these numbers, the change from the 1950s to the 1960s, courtesy of electoral reforms rooted in the civil rights revolution, still stands out dramatically. At a stroke, the class composition of the Southern electorate was changed. Yet the old rules that were swept away, rules justified as keeping black Southerners out of the voting population and the ones targeted by the Voting Rights Act—the literacy test and the poll tax, along with their differential and discriminatory application—had long been argued to have a secondary class effect, serving as an additional barrier to the participation of poor whites. Accordingly, when the old rules were swept away, even the Southern white electorate ought to have undergone some change in its class composition.

As indeed it did (Table 3.4B). In this poorest region of the nation, upper-income whites had nevertheless managed to be the modal income group within the white Southern electorate of the 1950s. By the 1960s, the decade of legal reform in voting arrangements throughout the South, not only had they lost that position, but the modal group was actually lower-income whites. By the 1970s, the combination of electoral reform and economic growth meant that middle-income whites would become the modal category, and this situation would prevail through the 1980s as well. It was only in the 1990s, forty years later, that some combination of economic growth and active turnout brought upper-income whites back to the share of the white electorate that they had attained forty years before, in the 1950s.

A different but complementary way to tell this story is to focus, not on the modal class sector of the electorate, but on the sector that was growing most rapidly across time as a result of electoral reform, economic development, or, presumably, both. Viewed in this way, Table 3.4B is essentially a story of *middle-income ascendance*. While the dramatic change in the 1960s, when measured by modal categories, was from upper-income to lower-income voters, middle-income whites were already increasing their electoral share at a faster rate. They would continue to do so in the 1970s, and again in the 1980s. Only in the 1990s would they surrender this growth standard to upper-income whites.

Seen from one side of the partisan aisle, then, as long as the Democratic Party remained the preference of middle-income whites, the class shift in the 1960s electorate might have permitted Democratic partisan dominance to continue. Seen from the other side of the aisle, only when the Republican Party achieved majority preference with the white middle class could its triumph be complete. Seen either way, however, this was the great secondary effect of voting reform—rooted in the white community, expressed through social class.

What a focus on real gains and losses (rather than modal positions) also underlines is the *timing* of the way that electoral reform interacted with economic development in the postwar South. If it were possible to conceive of the civil rights revolution as happening a generation earlier—in the 1930s, say, as part of the New Deal, rather than in the 1960s—then electoral reform would have fallen on a very different Southern economy, with a very different class structure. Presumably, the numerical transfer from upper-income to lower-income whites would have been even more striking. But in fact, by the time electoral reform arrived, economic development was already well under way, so that Southern society—or at least, white Southern society—was evolving into a middle-income, not a lower-income, world.

Told by way of modal income sectors, then, this was a story of upper-class advantage, lower-class mobilization, and upper-class resurgence. Told by way of the growing income sector, it was a story of middle-class ascendance, from the 1960s through the 1980s. Told either way, however, it was undeniably a class story. Moreover, it was undeniably a white and not just a black class story, courtesy of legal desegregation and the political mobilization that came with it. Yet this second effect implied an increased Democratic edge, by way of a substantial extension of the class reversal of the white electorate, *only as long as the expansion of the black electorate did not alter the partisan implications of this white class story.*

Legal Desegregation and a White Politics of Race

The direct impact of black enfranchisement on partisan balance in the South was overwhelming. Its direct and indirect impacts on electoral composition were likewise impressive. Together, their potential influence on the rise of a Southern Republican Party ranged from conditionally damaging to absolutely disastrous. Yet that was not nearly all the grounds for a racial impact from the arrival of legal desegregation. In particular, none of this necessarily denied the prospects for a mass politics of racial voting among white Southerners. And indeed, a large literature has since pointed to precisely this possibility as a crucial ground—often privileged over economic development—for the rise of Southern Republicanism (Lamis 1999; Black and Black 2002).

In this scenario, while black enfranchisement would be directly advantageous to the regional Democratic Party, it could be indirectly advantageous to the regional Republican Party as well. The keystone of this latter literature has been the notion of "racial threat," the possibility that a new and disproportionately black electorate would cause white voters to move toward the Republican Party as a way to maintain their political influence on racial grounds (Giles 1977 and 1993; but see Voss 1996 and Abramowitz 1994). We shall return to this possibility explicitly. But before that, it is worth asking simply about the impact of *racial context* on white voting. We have seen only a mixed and modest impact from racial context on black voting. Yet once again, this did not require, by any practical extension, that there would likewise be no racial effect among whites.

Again, it is easy to examine the behavior of white voters according to the racial composition of their electoral districts. The easiest initial way to do this is to go back to the same cut-point used to distinguish racial contexts among black Southerners—districts that were more or less than 20 percent black—and look, now, at white Southern voters within those districts. Methodologically, a white reaction to the racial restructuring of politics that was insufficient to register by this measure was, at the very least, not very widespread. Practically, as before, when black Southerners constituted more than 20 percent of the total electorate, especially when they had previously constituted less than 5 percent, their presence could not very well be ignored by their white neighbors.

Accordingly, Table 3.5A shows the vote among whites for the House of Representatives for those districts that possessed both a Republican and a Democratic candidate, dividing them into those that were more-black or less-black than our benchmark figure. In the 1950s, when blacks were essentially missing from the House electorate in much of the South, the resulting relationship was hardly a response to black participation. Yet it did accord with the old Southern politics as described by Key. In other words, whites in more-black areas were considerably less likely to vote Republican than were whites in less-black areas, even for those districts where the Re-

Table 3.5   Racial Contexts and White Voters: The House

A. Racial Contexts and Partisan Voting

Republican Percentage among All Whites in Contested Districts

Decade	<20% Black	>20% Black	Range
1950s	33	27	−6
(N)	(106)	(110)	
1960s	44	27	−17
(N)	(190)	(188)	
1970s	48	36	−8
(N)	(398)	(258)	
1980s	60	29	−31
(N)	(361)	(260)	
1990s	55	61	+6
(N)	(725)	(201)	

B. Racial Contexts and Partisan Voting, Controlling for Social Class

Republican Percentage among All Whites in Contested Districts

	Income Terciles					
	Low		Mid		High	
Decades	<20% Black	>20% Black	<20% Black	>20% Black	<20% Black	>20% Black
1960s-1980s	40	29	56	29	58	38
(N)	(267)	(181)	(295)	(218)	(310)	(239)
1990s	39	44	56	65	64	67
(N)	(171)	(54)	(207)	(63)	(274)	(64)

publicans did possess a congressional challenger. This was a reflection of where Southern Democrats had been ensconced and where Southern Republicans had been able to mount a challenge for much of the previous century.

The central point, however, is that when the electoral world turned upside down in the 1960s, with the rapid influx of a large black component to the Southern electorate, this relationship did not change (Table 3.5A). If anything, it became stronger. Now, with blacks surging as a greater and greater share of the Democratic electorate, whites in more-black areas *remained* more likely to stay with the Democrats, and therefore less likely to shift to the Republicans. Initial Republican gains in the aggregate were entirely within the less-black congressional districts, a tendency which Table 3.5A still understates. For more-black areas were also less likely to get Republican challengers (see Chapter 5), so that many of the worst areas for an incipient new Republican Party are ruled out of the analysis here.

The same effect of racial context was repeated in the 1970s. And it was repeated in the 1980s, becoming stronger yet again. Republicans now had *majorities* among white voters in the more-white congressional districts. By comparison, they had progressed very little in the more-black districts. Instead of driving whites into the Republican Party, substantial black enfranchisement appeared to contain that party within areas where few blacks lived. Put differently, thirty years of evolution in Southern congressional voting still made it very difficult to find something called "racial threat" in the numbers. It was easy enough to see an impact of racial context, but that impact ran in the opposite direction.

Only in the 1990s did this impact finally disappear. Indeed, it actually reversed, with whites in blacker House districts becoming more likely to vote Republican than their counterparts in whiter areas. In other words, the particular impact of racial context which supporters of legal desegregation had feared for the 1960s, and which scholars of Southern politics had attempted to use in explaining the rise of a Southern Republican Party in the 1970s and 1980s, arrived only thirty years later for the House of Representatives, after black Southerners had become an integral part of Southern electoral politics. If racial context had a role to play in Republican prospects for the House, it was as a capstone for those prospects, not as an underpinning, much less as an initial impetus.

Nevertheless, it is also important to note that the end of this previous Democratic edge among whites in more-black districts arrived at the point when its demise mattered least. In the 1950s, 54 percent of white voters had lived in such districts; in the 1960s, 51 percent; in the 1970s, still 49 percent. This percentage dipped in the 1980s, to 35 percent, though the Democratic edge among these whites actually rose in return, largely compensating for the loss of numbers. In other words, the difference in white voting by racial context actually declined in conjunction with the disappearance of whites in more-black districts, as the share of white voters in these districts fell to (only) 22 percent in the 1990s.[2] The previous edge to the *Democrats* from racial context thus finally disappeared just as its numerical consequence plummeted.

On the other hand, Table 3.5A is not by itself sufficient to sustain this overall reading of the effect of racial context. Precisely because social class came to have such a strong pro-Republican effect on the white electorate, it is possible that voting results by racial context are merely a surrogate for class. In other words, because blacker areas were also poorer areas generally, it is possible that poorer whites too lived there disproportionately, and that what looks like electoral division based on racial context is instead electoral division based on economic development, masked. Some simple notion of "racial threat" is obviously not sufficient to summarize this effect even then, since the hypothesized impact simply does not appear. But social class might still be the key to understanding an apparent pro-Democratic bias among whites in blacker districts.

Therefore, Table 3.5B controls for income terciles—low, middle, and high—in comparing the Republican share of the vote by racial context. Little changes. For the period after the 1950s and until the 1990s, all paired comparisons—more-black versus less-black lower income, more-black versus less-black middle income, and more-black versus less-black higher income—show the same pattern as the overall relationship. Whites in more-black areas were comparatively more likely to vote Democratic. Whites in less-black areas were comparatively more likely to vote Republican. Until that effect was erased for the South as a whole, it was not erased in any income tercile. Likewise, when it finally did disappear—reverse—in the 1990s, it reversed in every income stratum.

The postwar Senate tells essentially the same story in a slightly attenuated version, though it does raise an immediate question about the proper unit for measuring racial context. In one sense, the *state* is the proper basis for comparison: states are, after all, the "districts" for Senate elections. Yet here, there are both theoretical and practical problems in relying on this measure. Theoretically, states as the basis of comparison are just too large to capture the effect of a "racial context," if one were there to be captured.

It is not clear, for example, why white voters in West Texas, with a nearly complete absence of blacks, should feel "threatened" by the widespread presence of black voters in East Texas, 800 miles away.

Moreover, methodologically, states as units of measurement sharply compress the range of more-black and less-black districts. That is, states cluster far more closely around the Southern racial mean than do congressional districts, with the result that they offer limited variance on the variable alleged to be shaping the behavior of white voters. Accordingly, whenever the analysis requires electoral districts for the examination of contextual effects, we shall use the congressional district as the unit of analysis.[3] This has the additional advantage of examining contextual influences on the partisan vote for House, Senate, and President by way of the *same* base unit, making results directly comparable. To that end, Table 3.6 shows the total vote for Republican senatorial candidates by decade, calculated on the basis of the congressional district in which the voter lived.

Seen this way, the Senate too shows the racial pattern of the old South in the 1950s, with whites in whiter areas more likely to go Republican, whites in blacker areas to go Democratic. In the 1960s, the Senate too (still like the House) did *not* reverse this pattern as new black Democrats flooded into the Southern electorate. For the 1960s, 1970s, and 1980s, however, the scope of the difference between more-black and less-black areas remained considerably smaller in the Senate than in the House. Either senatorial elections did not prime racial context in the same way that House elections did, or statewide aggregation, no matter how measured, did not produce the same effect. Finally, in the 1990s, the Senate too

Table 3.6   **Racial Contexts and White Voters: The Senate**

Republican Percentage among All Whites			
Decade	<20% Black	>20% Black	Range
1950s	27	13	−14
(N)	(71)	(112)	
1960s	40	32	−8
(N)	(182)	(126)	
1970s	52	47	−5
(N)	(347)	(285)	
1980s	40	39	−1
(N)	(419)	(233)	
1990s	56	60	+4
(N)	(594)	(163)	

moved mildly in the other direction, with whites in more-black areas shifting to slightly more Republican, though this represents far less change than the counterpart movement in the House.

Accordingly, even by this most elementary test, neither house of Congress provides support for the hypothesis of racial threat. There *was* an impact from racial context on white voters—from the presence or absence of a disproportionate number of black Southerners—but when it did appear, it was inverse to the established hypothesis. More-black areas remained kinder to Democratic candidates for national office, even among whites. It was less-black areas where Republican candidates scored their greater successes.

On the other hand, the presidency tells a sharply different story, so that if there is an empirical grounding to those works attributing a heavy emphasis in the rise of a Southern Republican Party to racial context, it arrives with the presidency. Civil rights as a voting issue had actually arrived on the national agenda in 1948, when President Harry Truman received a strong civil rights plank at the Democratic National Convention from restive Northern Democrats, in the process splitting his party and producing a Southern Democratic—the Dixiecrat—revolt. In response, both parties shied away from the issue in the 1952 presidential contest, and again in 1956.

By 1960, events had begun to outpace their strategic preferences, and both presidential candidates, John Kennedy and Richard Nixon, worked instead to find a position—some sort of straddle—that made them progressive on civil rights nationally while "unthreatening" on the issue in the South. By 1964, there was no straddle left in the Johnson-Goldwater contest: the two candidates drew the lines on governmental intervention in civil rights about as cleanly as they would ever be drawn. By 1968, in part as a direct result of that contest, the Civil Rights Act and the Voting Rights Act were national law, and a national administration was helping to reconstruct the racial basis of Southern life.

What began seriously under John Kennedy, then, was the institutionalization of the civil rights issue in presidential politics. What began seriously under Lyndon Johnson was nothing less than the alteration of the racial organization of Southern social life. Not surprisingly, within that framework, the 1950s looked like the old South with regard to racial contexts and presidential voting (Table 3.7). Republican presidential candidates ran better among white voters in the less-black areas of the South, Democratic candidates among white voters in the more-black areas. By the

Table 3.7   **Racial Contexts and White Voters: The Presidency**

	Republican Percentage among All Whites		
Decade	<20% Black	>20% Black	Range
1950s	50	45	−5
(N)	(167)	(199)	
1960s	38	46	+8
(N)	(180)	(173)	
1970s	61	69	+8
(N)	(396)	(369)	
1980s	62	66	+4
(N)	(325)	(208)	
1990s	51	53	+2
(N)	(743)	(192)	

1960s, however, the old order of racial segregation was being dismantled. It would have been very surprising if this upheaval had secured no reflection in partisan politics.

There was to be no such surprise. White Southern voters, during this most intense period of social change, did indeed switch to voting more Republican for President in those areas where racial change would inevitably be greatest (Table 3.7). That is, during the 1960s, the relationship between presidential partisanship and racial context actually reversed. Now, whites in more-black areas were likely to be comparatively more Republican for President, while whites in less-black areas were likely to remain comparatively more Democratic. That same relationship continued through the 1970s. It continued, in reduced fashion, in the 1980s. And it was still present as a shadow in the 1990s, where the residual difference was of additionally reduced consequence because the imbalance between the distribution of white voters had become so extreme: there were very few whites left in the more-black districts.

What resulted overall, then, was a much more mottled and curious pattern of voting influences for racial context than most summary hypotheses, new or old, would have countenanced:

- The old "racial threat" hypothesis had little apparent utility in understanding congressional politics. Worse, it worked essentially in the opposite direction. As a result, it had little utility as a summary concept for the partisan impact of legal desegregation.
- On the other hand, in the immediate aftermath of the civil rights

revolution, voting for President assumed precisely the contours hypothesized—feared or desired—by those who had imagined the impact of racial desegregation on the breakup of the political order of the old South.

• Finally, when voting patterns for Congress and the presidency were put back together, what was most clear about the utility of an overarching distinction based on racial context was the power of two great governmental institutions to structure its impact in different (indeed, opposite!) ways.

Yet before accepting this composite picture as the partisan impact of legal desegregation, it is necessary to revisit the argument concerning racial threat in one important regard. For it might reasonably be argued in response to all of the above that a true "racial threat" would have to be defined much more extremely than we have defined it here (as "greater than 20 percent black") in order to have a significant, measurable, behavioral impact. Indeed, V. O. Key had begun the story of the rise of the old order in Southern politics with the assertion that it was those areas of the South with an actual black majority that had been central to the institutionalized foundation of that order (Key 1949, 5). Perhaps we need to do the same?

On the other hand, by the time *Southern Politics* appeared, such districts were already too rare to serve as the underpinnings for any new political order. For the 1950s, there was, to be exact, only one congressional district in the American South with an implicit black majority. Accordingly, Key himself had already shifted the argument, asserting that black majorities had been central to the foundation of an order, but that it was those areas that were *more than 30 percent black* that constituted the institutional bedrock—the electoral incentive—for a politics of racial segregation.[4] This is the standard that Earl and Merle Black used subsequently to make the same sort of argument for postwar politics (Black and Black 2002), so perhaps this standard (rather than 20 percent) should be used here as the crucial cut-point when addressing racial threat rather than just racial context.

Nevertheless, when this is done, precious little changes. Comparing the pattern of politics for the three great institutions of elective national government in the three decades when racial context primed a Republican vote differently as between the presidency and Congress—with racial context redefined at the 30 percent level—just does not change the underlying story (Table 3.8A versus 3.8B). Seen this way, the House still anchors an institutional continuum for the impact of this difference, in which larger

Table 3.8   Racial Contexts and White Voters: The House, the Senate, and the
Presidency Revisited

A. Partisan Voting with a Racial Context at 20%

Percent Republican for All Whites

1960s-1980s	<20% Black	>20% Black	Range
House	52	31	−21
(N)	(949)	(706)	
Senate	44	41	−3
(N)	(948)	(644)	
Presidency	57	63	+6
(N)	(901)	(750)	

B. Partisan Voting with a Racial Context at 30%

Percent Republican for All Whites

1960s-1980s	<30% Black	>30% Black	Range
House	49	27	−22
(N)	(1197)	(458)	
Senate	45	37	−8
(N)	(1190)	(402)	
Presidency	58	63	+5
(N)	(1181)	(470)	

black populations *reduce* the prospects of Republican voting among whites
very substantially. Once more, the Senate follows the House pattern, but in
an attenuated fashion. And once more—still strikingly—the presidency re-
verses the story, such that larger black populations actually increase the
prospects of Republican voting among whites.

Needless to say, major institutional differences mediating the impact of
racial context are, in the process, sustained. In other words, the differential
impact of racial context on a Republican vote for the House, the Senate,
and the presidency is not some simple product of understating the real divisions between less-black and more-black electoral districts. A cut-point
of 20 percent black, based on racial divisions in the 1990s, does not differ
from a cut-point of 30 percent black, the cut favored in the historical literature. It would be possible, mechanically, to impose an even more demanding cut-point, at 40 percent. But by then, any division within white voting
patterns between more-black and less-black areas would be inconsequential. With a cut-point of 40 percent, less than 9 percent of the white South
would have lived in more-black districts.

Racial Attitudes and Republican Prospects

Racial context obviously worked in opposite ways as an influence on white voters, for Congress versus the presidency, and it continued to work in this opposite fashion for a full three decades. This makes it only more intriguing to know how racial *attitudes* operated in this new Southern politics. Yet here, unlike the relationships involving social class and economic liberalism or conservatism, relationships involving racial context and racial liberalism or conservatism do not contain an inherent set of hypotheses to serve as initial—test—answers to the question. That is, we cannot merely begin with attitudinal extrapolations from the underlying social structure.

Social class had offered a "natural," that is, an interest-based, hypothesis about the relationship between welfare attitudes and partisan support, at least once the party system featured one party (the Democrats) centered on governmental provision in social welfare, with the other party (the Republicans) centered on resisting it. Those most in need of welfare provision, presumably the less well-off, ought to have leaned Democratic; those least in need of welfare provision, presumably the better-off, should have leaned Republican. By extension, even within social classes, those favoring welfare provision ought to have leaned toward the Democrats, with those who opposed such provision leaning toward the Republicans.

What made the voting patterns of the old South distinctive was that neither relationship had actually appeared. Instead, even after the coming of the New Deal had institutionalized these relationships in the North, the link between social class and partisan choice had been inverted in the South, with the poor leaning Republican, while the link between welfare preferences and partisan choice had just been nonexistent. Once a class reversion occurred, however, the related policy linkage followed hard upon it. Both relationships had thus fallen into practical alignment in the hypothetically appropriate direction: the bottom tercile Democratic and the top tercile Republican, with liberals Democratic and conservatives Republican within each tercile.

The problem with racial policy, with governmental action specifically on behalf of black Americans, but also the potential added value, was that the underlying sociological influences offered no clear opening hypotheses. Should racial conservatism among white Southerners have been expected to be associated with more-black areas, presumably those areas where governmental aid to blacks represented more of a social upheaval, not to mention more of a fiscal drain? Should racial conservatism among white Southerners have been expected to be associated with less-black areas, presumably those areas where whites were less likely to know black Southerners as "real people," as daily acquaintances rather than artificial stereotypes? Or was there no necessary connection? (See Glaser 1994; more generically, Forbes 1997.)

Introducing racial attitudes into the story of legal desegregation and a politics of race will prove more difficult overall than introducing welfare attitudes into the story of economic development and a politics of class, because there is less substantive consistency in the opinion items asked by the NES in the realm of race policy for the full postwar period. Yet initially, with the question of the relationship of racial conservatism to racial context, and especially for the critical period of change in the American South, there is no problem at all. The NES does offer a consistent item on aid to blacks during the entire 1960s, and respondents to it can, as ever, be easily classified by more-black and less-black racial contexts:

> *Should the government in Washington see to it that black people get fair treatment in jobs, or should the government in Washington leave these matters to the states and localities?*

Accordingly, our first question is easily answered. During the 1960s, the critical time when the relationship between racial context and partisan choice changed for the presidency but not for Congress, racial attitudes—ideological liberalism or conservatism on race policy—were unrelated to racial context. The mean racial conservatism for white Southerners in less-black districts was almost precisely equivalent to the mean racial conservatism for white Southerners in more-black districts: 0.70 for the former (on an *N* of 233), 0.69 for the latter (on an *N* of 249). White Southerners in less-black areas were not more racially conservative; nor were they more racially conservative in more-black areas. White Southerners were just equally conservative in less-black and more-black areas.

Therefore, the next question becomes how racial attitudes were related to the vote. Given the institutional differences in the impact of racial context, there must actually be two parts to this question. First, how *did* racial liberalism or conservatism relate to a Democratic or Republican vote? And second, was this the same relationship across all three institutions—the House, the Senate, and the presidency? Nothing in the lack of a relationship between racial attitudes and racial context prevented whites from expressing their racial views through the ballot box, just as nothing in the lack of this prior relationship prevented them from expressing these views differentially, as between Congress and the presidency.

In addressing these questions, the matter of item consistency across the decades does make the analysis less neat than it was able to be with economic conservatism. In the matter of aid to blacks, the same item that we used to investigate the impact of policy preferences on race among black Southerners can be used among whites for the 1970s, the 1980s, and the 1990s:

> *Some people feel that the government in Washington should make every possible effort to improve the social and economic position of blacks and other minority groups. Others feel that the government should not make any special effort to help minorities because they should help themselves.*

Unfortunately, the 1950s and the 1960s each require a different base item, with specific rather than generic aid referents. Because the literature on Southern politics suggests that something major did happen in this area during the transition from the old to the new Southern politics, it seems worth trying to integrate these items into the analysis nevertheless.

One apparently artifactual effect of changing not just item content but item format was to shift the marginals for these items between the 1950s and the 1960s. During the 1950s, the key item varied a bit, sometimes mentioning housing and sometimes not, but its form was at least essentially stable:

> *If Negroes are not getting fair treatment in jobs and housing, the government should see to it that they do.*

As above, this changed in the 1960s to:

> *Should the government in Washington see to it that black people get fair treatment in jobs, or should the government in Washington leave these matters to the states and localities?*

In the 1950s, without any priming for the alternative, responses were more liberal in the aggregate than they would be in the 1960s, when the alternative answer was explicitly prompted. We do know, however, that the shift in the marginals for these two items across these two decades was not a diagnostically Southern phenomenon; it almost exactly paralleled that same shift in the North. In any case, if we confine ourselves to looking at the *re-lationship* between racial liberals and racial conservatives in their partisan choice, we should still be able to make some use of data from the 1950s and 1960s, before the decade of the 1970s gives us a fully consistent item there-after.[5]

Because two very different base items had to be used to add opinions on racial policy to the overall story of political change in the postwar South, Table 3.9 does have to be read in two pieces. Fortunately, each piece still has a major part of this story to tell. In the first of these, the 1950s and 1960s pull together substantively similar items in order to reach back into history, and their message is very clear. In elections for the U.S. Congress, both the House and the Senate, the 1950s were still the old South (Table 3.9A and B). Whites who were more liberal on racial policy were more likely to vote Republican; whites who were more conservative on racial policy were more likely to vote Democratic.

The role of racial ideology was thus effectively inverted. In the racial up-heavals of the 1960s, on the other hand, as Northern Democrats drove a legislative revolution in civil rights and as Southern blacks entered the electorate as in effect Northern Democrats, these patterns of policy associ-ation reversed. Now, whites who were more liberal on racial matters were more likely to vote *Democratic,* while whites who were more conservative on this measure were likely to vote Republican. Racial ideology had come to be aligned in the modern manner. The House, having started slightly farther behind, underwent a slightly larger change than the Senate, but that was all.

The 1970s, 1980s, and 1990s in Table 3.9 then use the second base item on racial policy from the NES, the one on generic aid to blacks. While the results from this item cannot be directly compared to those for the 1950s and 1960s, it does offer an unchanged content for the next thirty years. Moreover, the story it tells with regard to Congress is clear enough (Table 3.9A and B). By the 1970s there was an evident relationship between pol-icy preferences and partisan choice, with racial conservatives more Repub-lican, racial liberals more Democratic. This is the situation created by the upheavals of the 1960s, and it obviously remained in place, even though the precise numbers cannot be compared.

Those numbers *can* be directly compared from the 1970s to the 1980s, however, when the relationship grew. Indeed, it grew very considerably in the case of the House, making this one of the few instances where dif-ferences between the House and the Senate actually trace to the fact that

Table 3.9   Racial Attitudes and Partisan Voting

Republican Percentage among All Whites in Contested Districts

Decade	Aid to Blacks		Range
	Liberal	Conservative	
A. The House			
1950s	34	21	−13
(N)	(118)	(72)	
1960s	28	38	+10
(N)	(50)	(154)	
1970s	40	48	+8
(N)	(115)	(330)	
1980s	35	53	+18
(N)	(89)	(329)	
1990s	27	60	+33
(N)	(128)	(546)	
B. The Senate			
1950s	21	14	−7
(N)	(104)	(69)	
1960s	33	41	+8
(N)	(46)	(114)	
1970s	37	54	+17
(N)	(99)	(319)	
1980s	28	46	+18
(N)	(129)	(294)	
1990s	38	67	+29
(N)	(94)	(379)	
C. The Presidency			
1950s	45	50	+5
(N)	(229)	(216)	
1960s	41	47	+6
(N)	(91)	(220)	
1970s	55	72	+17
(N)	(121)	(380)	
1980s	45	74	+29
(N)	(99)	(255)	
1990s	20	62	+42
(N)	(110)	(467)	

it was the *Senate* that reached a stronger alignment earlier. That is, by the 1970s racial attitudes were strongly tied to Senate voting, at a level achieved by the House only in the 1980s. In any case, the numbers can be compared directly again for the 1980s to the 1990s, and the relationship grew stronger still, opening up a veritable policy chasm.

The gap in Republican voting for both the House and the Senate, between racial liberals and racial conservatives, thus increased regularly from the 1970s through the 1990s. At the same time, the gap between the House and the Senate effectively closed. In other words, there was very little institutional difference left in the role of racial ideology as underpinning for a Republican vote. What had arrived instead was a huge *partisan* difference over aid to blacks, with Democratic voters supportive and Republican voters opposed.

Moreover, this time, the presidency was different in only one regard (Table 3.9C). With the presidency, the 1950s and 1960s already showed a clear if modest relationship between public preferences on racial policy and partisan choice among presidential candidates, a relationship exemplifying the new, not the old, South. Apparently, in sharply expanding the Southern presidential vote for the Republican candidate, Dwight Eisenhower had attracted many Southern Democrats who were racial conservatives. In doing so, he had already reversed the old relationship to civil rights attitudes—liberals Republican, conservatives Democratic—that the House and Senate would reverse only a decade later.

Yet thereafter, the presidential, House, and Senate stories were to be in complete alignment, growing only more tightly bound as time passed. Moreover, it is once again possible to excavate for an older stratum of Republican voting within the Eisenhower upsurge of the 1950s, thereby affirming that the same change characterized the presidency as characterized the Congress. When the presidential vote of the 1950s is divided into the vote from established Republican versus newly mobilized areas, this change stands out boldly.

Established Republican areas, those possessing congressional candidates by the time of Eisenhower, were still much more likely to vote Republican overall; this is the "Total" column in Table 3.10. Yet in these older Republican areas, it was racial *liberals* who were more likely to vote Republican, while in newly Republican areas, it was racial conservatives who were more likely to do so. And the difference was very large. At one extreme, 60 percent of racial liberals were voting Republican in established areas; at the other, only 37 percent of racial liberals were voting Republican in the

Table 3.10   Racial Attitudes and Partisan Voting: The Presidency Revisited

Republican Percentage among All Whites

Decade of 1950s	Aid to Blacks		Total	Range
	Liberal	Conservative		
Old Republican Areas	60	50	56	−10
(N)	(65)	(36)		
New Republican Areas	37	46	41	+9
(N)	(123)	(78)		

newly emerging areas. Once more, this was a picture drawn from presidential voting of the old world of Southern politics versus the new. It was also a picture of an impressive difference that was about to disappear. Only a decade later, both established Republican and newly mobilized areas would have converged, with racial conservatives voting Republican for President in both areas. In other words, by the 1960s, it was racial conservatives who would be leaning Republican in every decade—for every office—thereafter.

Yet this parallel behavior needs to be set directly beside the other great development in the politics of race. Or rather, it gains additional, independent significance from the way that these attitudinal relationships, consistent across institutions, were superimposed upon opposite relationships to racial context. That is to say: from the 1960s onward, racial conservatism was likely to foster Republican voting and racial liberalism Democratic voting for both Congress and the presidency. Yet from the 1960s through the 1980s, whites in blacker areas were more likely to vote Republican for President, whites in whiter areas to vote Democratic, while at the same time, whites in blacker areas were more likely to vote *Democratic* for Congress, whites in whiter areas to vote Republican. Only in the 1990s would this apparent disjunction ultimately disappear.

On the other hand, an argument could be made that public preferences on race policy are the wrong measure of racial attitudes. In this line of argument, what was important was just racial feeling per se. It was this, at the very least, which should most logically have been associated with perceptions of racial "threat." The direct threat (if any) was not that government would change public policies; the threat was that black enfranchisement would change—even overwhelm—white influence. So perhaps a different measure would produce a different outcome? Perhaps it would even remove the apparent disjunction between the impact of racial contexts versus racial attitudes?

Fortunately, there is a simple way to tap these possibilities, though it does not have the full historical span that we would like. Beginning in the 1960s, the National Election Studies began to ask about attitudes toward blacks by way of a "feeling thermometer." With this device, the respondent is asked to rank the positive or negative character of his/her feelings toward a variety of stimuli—often social groups, sometimes particular politicians as well—on a scale ranging from 0 (very negative) to 100 (very positive). The text introducing this item varied a bit over time, but the 1960s version is typical:

> *There are many groups in America that try to get the government or the American people to see things more their way. We would like to get your feelings toward some of these groups. I have here a card on which there is something that looks like a thermometer. We call it a "feeling thermometer" because it measures your feelings towards groups. Here's how it works. If you don't know too much about a group or don't feel particularly warm or cold toward them, then you place them in the middle, at the 50 degree mark. If you have a warm feeling toward a group or feel favorably toward it, you would give it a score somewhere between 50 degrees and 100 degrees, depending on how warm your feeling is toward the group. On the other hand, if you don't feel very favorably toward some of these groups—if there are some you don't care for too much—then you would place them somewhere between 0 degrees and 50 degrees.*

Because there is no feeling thermometer regarding blacks for the 1950s, it is not possible to look for change in the relationship between white feelings toward black Southerners and their own partisan behavior at the point when this change was occurring explicitly for the House or Senate and just below the surface, in old but not new areas of Republican strength, for the presidency. On the other hand, the item—effectively the same item—does run from the 1960s through the 1990s, providing at least a consistent measure over all those years. What it manages to suggest, for all three institutions this time, is that it was policy preferences directly, not the racial feelings beneath them, that were more central to attitudinal relationships.

In the case of the House of Representatives, any relationship that existed between racial feelings and partisan choice was modest (Table 3.11A). Those who felt negatively toward blacks—who put themselves on the "cold" side of the feeling thermometer—were slightly more likely to vote Republican in every decade, with their greatest differentiation in the 1970s. The same could be said of the Senate (Table 3.11B): always modest,

Table 3.11   Racial *Feeling* rather than Race *Policy* as a Measure of
Racial Attitudes?

| | Republican Percentage among All Whites in Contested Districts | | |
| | Feeling toward Blacks | | |
Decade	Positive	Negative	Range
A. The House			
1960s	35	40	+5
(N)	(219)	(167)	
1970s	42	52	+10
(N)	(470)	(276)	
1980s	44	50	+6
(N)	(373)	(229)	
1990s	49	52	+3
(N)	(638)	(363)	
B. The Senate			
1960s	36	40	+4
(N)	(180)	(129)	
1970s	43	52	+9
(N)	(282)	(177)	
1980s	41	39	-2
(N)	(399)	(238)	
1990s	54	60	+6
(N)	(470)	(255)	
C. The Presidency			
1960s	42	45	+3
(N)	(214)	(143)	
1970s	59	71	+12
(N)	(437)	(291)	
1980s	61	69	+8
(N)	(296)	(221)	
1990s	50	54	+4
(N)	(561)	(335)	

strongest in the 1970s, but never worth much. And this time, the same could be said for the presidency as well (Table 3.11C). Those who felt more negative toward blacks were more likely to vote Republican, those more positive to vote Democratic, with the 1970s again as the high point, but with this relationship always second to racial policy as an influence.

To put it differently, the relationship to public policy, namely concrete aid to black Southerners, always dominated the relationship to racial feeling. A comparison between Tables 3.10 and 3.11 shows a considerably stronger relationship between the Republican vote and policy preferences rather than racial feelings at every point. This is clear-cut in the 1960s, when both effects were at their weakest. It remains clear-cut in the 1970s, when racial feelings had their strongest effect. And it is thereafter overwhelming. From the 1960s through the 1990s, it was policy preference, not group feelings, which aligned strongly—more and more strongly—with the Republican vote.

Legal Desegregation as Partisan Engine

Major economic change began to come to the postwar South by the 1950s, and with it an impact on partisan politics, though this political fallout would be celebrated only much later. Major racial change followed hard upon it, and if racial change arrived a bit later than economic development, at least in terms of its impact on partisan politics, it registered much more explicitly when it did arrive. The institutional catalyst for this change—a deliberate institutional catalyst this time, not an aggregate market effect—was legal desegregation. Some of its impacts were direct and immediate. Others were indirect, the result of adaptations by other elements of the Southern political order.

The most direct and immediate result of legal desegregation was that the share of the total electorate contributed by black Southerners shot up. The directly statistical impact of legal desegregation was thus hugely consequential: the potential Southern black electorate became a practical voting electorate within a remarkably compressed period of time. The long-run practical impact of this shift, on the other hand, was the product of three other aspects of the same great change: the partisan balance within this newest major sector of the Southern electorate; the degree of change that this contributed to the partisan balance for the South as a whole; and—part and parcel of both these aspects—how the *non-black* South reacted to them.

Figure 3.1 pulls together the black contribution to the Southern vote for the House, Senate, and President by decade. What it suggests is that, although efforts to desegregate the politics of the American South would involve additional years of federal intervention and many more years of federal monitoring, those efforts bore partisan political fruit almost immediately. Black voters flooded into the Southern electorate in a rush during the second half of the 1960s. They flooded in, overwhelmingly, as Democrats, and Northern Democrats to boot. At the same time, Republican voting by black Southerners actually collapsed. And the latter was not inevitably a consequence of the former. The Southern partisan landscape was effectively transformed—nearly, in hindsight, at a stroke.

In the first of these bedrock partisan facts, whatever the proclivities of the black electorate in the old South had been, the new black voters who surged into that electorate after 1965 chose overwhelmingly to arrive as Democrats. Before this time, there remained a substantial minority of black support for the Republican Party, though it was clearly in decline from the days when national Republicans had actively championed the Southern black man's cause. Nevertheless, seen as a share of partisan electorates in the decade before the civil rights revolution, the black contribution was still approximately *equal* as between Democratic and Republican candidates. After 1965, such support was effectively trivialized, and the scale of this disaster for an emergent Republican Party is hard to exaggerate: a black contribution to Southern Republicanism managed to fall despite the fact that the total black vote was variously tripling or quadrupling.

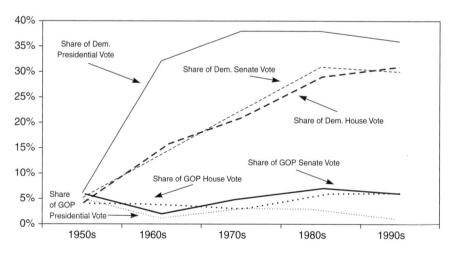

Figure 3.1   Black Contributions to the Democratic and Republican Vote.

Conversely, the black share of the vote for Democratic candidates, presidential and congressional, jumped up—and never thereafter faltered. At first glance, the black contribution to the vote for Democratic presidential candidates appeared to rise more quickly and remain reliably greater than its share for congressional candidates. Yet some of this apparently greater contribution by black voters to Democratic presidential candidates actually reflected disproportionate defeats nationwide—situations where the most loyal groups would inevitably bulk larger. Moreover, while most of these presidential elections were not close, many individual House and Senate races were, so that a growing Democratic contribution from black Southerners could matter much more to congressional than to presidential outcomes.

A second major impact of black enfranchisement followed from the way that this new, monolithic, and Democratic voting bloc changed the *class* composition of the Southern electorate. It should have been no surprise that black Southerners, among the very poorest demographic groups in the entire nation, pulled the Southern electorate strongly in their (lower-income) direction when they entered in substantial numbers. Yet in fact, the Southern *white* electorate itself reflected a reduced version of the same phenomenon.

It had long been argued that restrictive Southern voting arrangements, justified as privileging white voters, simultaneously privileged upper-income rather than lower-income individuals among them (Kousser 1974). The electoral reforms of the 1960s suggested that this was still true. In this poorest region of the nation, upper-income voters had actually managed to be the modal group in the Southern electorate among whites through the 1950s. At a stroke, the electoral reforms of the 1960s, implemented on black racial grounds but conferring change on white class grounds as well, awarded this status to lower-income whites instead. Thereafter, a combination of economic growth and differential turnout, as registered through more neutral administration of electoral rules, would determine the class composition of electorates.

This is not the same as saying that the combination would also determine partisan winners and losers. For the real partisan impact of this white class shift was also dependent in important ways on a third major aspect of legal desegregation and the associated politics of race: namely, the response of white voters to the arrival of a much blacker and more Democratic electorate. In Chapter 4 we will address the interaction of class and race in a more comprehensive and systematic—a multivariate—manner. In the meantime, it is obvious that two elements of this white response were crucial: the extent to which it was conditioned by racial context, and the extent to which it was conditioned by racial attitudes.

It is worth beginning with the fact that the impact of racial context was now a practical rather than just a theoretical question. More-black and less-black areas of the South now had greater or lesser black *voting populations*. Perhaps surprisingly, this fact registered very differently by institution. For Congress, especially the House, the impact of racial context ran opposite to fears of an implicit "racial threat": whites in blacker areas remained more likely to stay Democratic. For the presidency, however, the impact was reversed and those fears were realized: whites in blacker areas became more likely to go Republican. In other words, the impact of this second great social change in the American South was crucially mediated by the structure of elective political institutions. The same change had opposite partisan impacts on Congress versus the presidency.

Clearly, something was connecting social change to partisan outcomes in powerful—and powerfully different—ways. In Chapter 4 we will also examine this mediating process in more detail. What required less additional interpretation was the relationship between racial policy conflicts and ongoing partisan change. Liberalism or conservatism on a policy of governmental aid to black Americans shifted in its impact from the 1950s to the 1960s, and then grew steadily through the 1970s, the 1980s, and the 1990s. Positive or negative racial feelings, in the absence of any policy specifics, showed a weak echo of the same effect. And this time, both effects ran in the same direction for all three governmental institutions: racial liberals leaned Democratic, while racial conservatives leaned Republican.

A different way to summarize the same overall result is just to look at aggregate policy preferences on governmental aid to blacks, the stronger of these two attitudinal measures. To that end, Table 3.12 calculates the contents of Table 3.9 "the other way around," showing the mean racial liberalism/conservatism among those who voted Republican or Democratic for the presidency, the Senate, and the House in all five postwar decades. Again, higher scores are more conservative, lower scores more liberal. What stands out are the same institutionally general developments that were evident in the case of economic attitudes in Chapter 2 (Table 2.9), plus a difference between the presidency and Congress that was likewise in evidence there:

- First is the obvious patterning in policy relationships in the old South. For the 1950s, the House and the Senate showed this histor-

Table 3.12 **Racial Attitudes of Partisan Voters: The Presidency, the House, and the Senate**

Mean Score on Aid to Blacks among White Voters

Decade	The Presidency			Contested House			Contested Senate		
	Dems.	Reps.	Margin	Dems.	Reps.	Margin	Dems.	Reps.	Margin
1950s	.46	.52	+.06	.50	.32	-.18	.45	.29	-.16
1960s	.67	.74	+.07	.69	.76	+.07	.69	.76	+.07
1970s	.66	.81	+.15	.76	.78	+.02	.72	.82	+.10
1980s	.55	.81	+.26	.70	.84	+.14	.65	.79	+.14
1990s	.63	.93	+.30	.65	.89	+.24	.68	.88	+.20

ical world most clearly: Democrats were more conservative, Republicans more liberal on race. The 1950s surge in the presidency had already muddied this effect, but it can be resurrected by dividing the presidential vote into new versus old Republican areas. Established presidential areas too featured Democrats as conservative, Republicans liberal.

- A major reversal arrived in the 1960s. Congress, both the House and the Senate, now joined the presidency in the same overall direction: it was Democrats who were more liberal on race, Republicans who were more conservative. Moreover, this relationship had not just assumed the parallel, modern fashion for all three institutions, one that would last for the next four decades. The House and the Senate actually needed to produce a larger change in order to come into this alignment, and in the 1960s, they did so.

- The 1960s and 1970s cannot be compared precisely, because their attitudinal scores are based on different issue questions. But thereafter, both this second measure and the second story remained the same for all three institutions. Thus the change that appeared in the 1960s was recapitulated in the 1970s. That distinction expanded in the 1980s, and again in the 1990s. By that time, voting differences on racial policy had reached an impressive partisan differentiation.

- Fourth and last, but parallel to the situation with policy attitudes on social welfare, voting for President was more closely tied to racial attitudes for the 1970s, the 1980s, and the 1990s than was voting for Congress, for either the House or the Senate. In earlier years, the presidency "got there first." In later years, the gap between Republican and Democratic voters remained consistently larger for the presidency.

Race Politics and the New South

Economic development and a new politics of class had reversed old relationships among white Southerners. The Republican Party managed to put itself on the growth side of that equation. And economic growth dragged the party upwards in every decade after the 1950s. This was the great and continuing "Republican accelerator" for the postwar era in the American South. Legal desegregation and a new politics of race likewise reversed old relationships, or at least radically augmented a reversal already under way. With considerable irony, it was the Democratic Party that managed to put itself on the growth side of this equation. This was the great, though far more conditional, "Democratic brake" on Republican progress.

Such a description underlines the way that these two great social forces, economic development and legal desegregation, worked in noticeably different fashions. A key class reversal *was* essential to the impact of economic development; without it, the story of class politics would have been very different. Yet once that reversal had occurred, further economic change became an irresistible further contribution to Republican progress. It was not a simple linear story even then: the underlying class distinctions actually expanded as time passed. But economic change was relentless, and the associated class politics went hand in hand with partisan change.

By contrast, the big racial changes were essentially legal rather than demographic. The South did become modestly less black (more white) as the postwar era aged. But what really mattered was the way that the largely unchanging demographics of race applied—were applied—to partisan politics. The first big "application" came in the 1960s, with the civil rights revolution. At that point, established but hypothetical racial contexts became practical and direct influences on politicking. Then, thirty years later, an essentially stable racial demography was reapportioned in a strikingly different way. This second change will be addressed in Chapter 4. For now, the important point is that the resulting partisan shifts did not come from a change in overall racial balance, but from legal aspects of the application of an existing balance to partisan politics.

This difference in the demography of two great social changes gains further emphasis from their differing institutional impacts. Economic development and a new politics of class, while they arrived at modestly different times and resonated somewhat differently as between the House, the Senate, and the presidency, really contributed one general and overarching pattern. By contrast, legal desegregation and a revised politics of race, while arriving simultaneously in formal terms, saw three separate forms of institutional impact. An old world of institutional uniformity in the 1950s became a new world of striking difference between the presidency and Congress in the period between 1960 and 1990, before this difference collapsed into a new uniformity in the 1990s.

Summarizing two powerful sociological influences in this fashion does make the difference in their associated policy attitudes seem less surprising. Associated attitudes toward welfare policy followed logically from social class, in a double sense. The better-off were more conservative and the worse-off more liberal, where conservatives could be expected to vote Republican and liberals Democratic, once the South had joined the national party system. Moreover, within any given income stratum, the same relationship could be expected to apply—economic conservatives voting additionally Republican, economic liberals additionally Democratic. This too would have been true in the North since the 1930s. Now, it was true in the South as well.

In the case of racial identity, the counterpart situation was not as simply described. To begin with, black Southerners, those with the strongest racial identity, voted so overwhelmingly Democratic that nothing else mattered. By contrast, for thirty years, white Southerners were additionally differentiated both by racial context *and* by racial ideology. For racial context, whites in blacker districts were more likely to vote Democratic for Congress, Republican for President, and whites in whiter districts of course the reverse. For racial ideology, whites who were racially conservative were more likely to vote Republican for Congress or the presidency, while whites who were racially liberal were more likely to vote Democratic. Racial ideology and racial context were and remained unrelated in their impact. Yet the voting relationship to racial context ultimately declined, converging effectively to zero in the 1990s, while the relationship to racial ideology continued, growing only stronger.

Table 3.13 offers a different way to summarize these same developments, by looking at the *joint* impact of racial contexts and policy attitudes within the white Southern electorate. As with the final summary figure in Chapter 2, racial attitudes are retained as a simple liberal/conservative dichotomy in order to have comparability across the entire postwar period. Racial context is once again divided at plus or minus 20 percent black. The decades of transition, the 1960s through the 1980s, are contrasted with the old order of the 1950s and the new world of the 1990s. And the presidency, the Senate, and the House are presented separately, to capture any

Table 3.13   Racial Context, Aid to Blacks, and Partisan Change, 1952–2000

Republican Percentage among All Whites

A. Presidency — Racial Context

Racial Attitude	Low	High	
1950s			
Lib	51 (96)	38 (86)	−13
Con	47 (43)	48 (64)	+1
	−4	+10	
1960s–1980s			
Lib	47 (183)	48 (128)	+1
Con	63 (437)	69 (410)	+6
	+16	+21	
1990s			
Lib	23 (93)	* (17)	+1
Con	62 (358)	62 (109)	
	+42		

B. Senate — Racial Context

Racial Attitude	Low	High	
1950s			
Lib	32 (44)	13 (45)	−19
Con	12 (17)	11 (38)	−2
	−20	−2	
1960s–1980s			
Lib	33 (182)	30 (92)	−3
Con	51 (398)	46 (327)	−5
	+18	+16	
1990s			
Lib	40 (81)	* (13)	−7
Con	68 (310)	59 (69)	
	+28		

C. House — Racial Context

Racial Attitude	Low	High	
1950s			
Lib	43 (61)	27 (48)	−16
Con	11 (27)	26 (35)	+15
	−32	−1	
1960s–1980s			
Lib	45 (154)	22 (100)	−23
Con	56 (445)	38 (361)	−18
	+11	+16	
1990s			
Lib	28 (96)	* (23)	+8
Con	65 (376)	72 (116)	
	+30		

Note: Entries with an asterisk contain less than 5 percent of the total sample, and are suppressed. Summary numbers are calculated in a slightly different fashion as a result; see text.

institutional differences along the way. Cell entries are the percentage voting Republican.[6]

Once again, evidence from the 1950s is fragile. Yet one central circumstance did dominate this evidence, and thereby anchored voting patterns for all three institutions. This key point, the real story linking all three representations, was the disproportionately Republican support of whites in whiter areas who were also racial liberals. They were the bedrock of a Republican vote. It was their voting behavior that explained why whites in less-black (more-white) areas were disproportionately Republican. It was their voting behavior that had underpinned an older tendency for whites who were racial liberals to vote disproportionately Republican, although this was the part of the story that was already changing during the 1950s. Apart from their behavior, neither racial contexts nor racial attitudes made any consistent contribution to the Republican vote.

These individuals were the main explanation for why Republican candidates appeared to do better in less-black areas in the South as a whole. This was because, by and large, they resided in what had been areas of Republican strength since the formation of the national Republican Party before the Civil War. In the years immediately after World War II, they still did. Yet with the presidency, there were also hints of change. In drawing a Republican vote across the entire South, Dwight Eisenhower had inevitably increased that vote in more-black areas, the stronghold of the old Southern Democracy. As a result, the old racial disjunction was being reduced.

In the same way, these individuals were the explanation for why Republican candidates had long tended to do better among racial liberals than among racial conservatives. The Republican Party of the Civil War had been the party of abolition and then reconstruction. Remarkably, a hundred years later, it still was, at least as reflected in the attitudinal distribution of the vote. This time, however, the presidency did more than hint at change. With the presidency, whites in more-black areas were already more likely to vote Republican for President overall if they were racial *conservatives* rather than racial liberals, a tendency that would be generalized in the 1960s and would continue ever after.

The next three decades were to convert the incipient demographic and attitudinal deviations in this picture into major partisan developments, harbingers of a new Southern politics. As a result, during this long transitional era, policy preferences and racial contexts would tell a very different story from that of the 1950s. Moreover, the impact of these two developments would itself have important further differences. The first aspect of this change, the influence of policy preferences, would be generalized across institutions. But the second aspect, the influence of racial contexts, would be powerfully *differentiated* as between the presidency, the Senate, and the House.

In the simpler of these two changes, racial attitudes came to play a major and consistent role in shaping a Republican vote. Racial conservatives were now Republican, racial liberals Democratic, and this was an evident reversal of the situation in the 1950s. Nevertheless, this change came to characterize all *six* available theaters: the presidency, the Senate, and the House, in more-black and in less-black areas for each. Note that this represented even more of a change for Congress than for the President, since the presidency had shown signs of moving this way in the 1950s whereas Congress had not, and thus the latter had much farther to go.

So, the common story involved race policy and public attitudes toward it. By contrast, racial *context* came to play a distinguishable role for each separate institution. This was the more complex and confounding of the changes that characterized the great transitional period of Southern politics:

- For the presidency, whites in blacker areas were now more Republican and whites in whiter areas more Democratic. The effect was small, but it was present among both racial liberals and racial conservatives, and it represented a clear shift from the 1950s.
- At the opposite extreme, with the House, whites in blacker areas remained more Democratic, with whites in *whiter* areas more Republican, again among both liberals and conservatives. This was the strongest relationship to racial context among the three institutions, and it had actually increased from the 1950s.
- The Senate, finally, fell in between, priming racial context in the manner of the House but much more weakly.

This second difference probably deserves emphasis. The congressional story for racial context remained in the pattern of the old South. Remarkably, it not only passed unchanged across the civil rights revolution, across a set of social changes that reworked the racial organization of Southern society; it actually increased in the case of the House. Yet the presidency moved in the opposite direction, and if the result was only a modest opposite tilt, it looked larger by comparison to the presidency in the 1950s, larger still by comparison to the House in its own time. The impact of a changed racial composition in the Southern electorate was thus registered with the presidency, but not with Congress.

And then this impact too was gone. For the world shifted again in the 1990s, to a simpler pattern, one that again characterized all three institutions. In this modern world, all three institutions for both racial contexts showed the same relationship to racial attitudes that had characterized the transitional period: conservatives voted Republican, liberals Democratic. Not only did this relationship continue, it grew stronger still. Yet now, the previous institutional difference by racial context, a hallmark of the previous three decades, had effectively disappeared.

For this most recent decade, Table 3.13 looks a little different, and is in one sense slightly less revealing. For there is a cell—whites in blacker areas who are racial liberals—that simply has no one left. Less than 3 percent of the sample is in this cell for the presidency and the Senate, less than 4 percent for the House, and therefore we have deleted it. This means that the summary numbers for the difference between liberals and conservatives or between whites in less-black versus more-black areas are just a single figure with all relevant respondents combined.

What remains is simply described. Racial attitudes have a large effect for all three institutions, having continued to grow in a major way, while racial context has sharply declined as an influence. Where racial context distinguished the presidency, the Senate, and especially the House in the three preceding decades, it now features only small and institutionally idiosyncratic differences among the three institutions. Within these, the ability of the House to shed all of its previously inverse relationship to the racial composition of electoral districts is nevertheless striking, and will require further comment in the next chapter. Here, the point is just the collapse of the previous priming effect by racial context.

In the end, after all of that, the racial South, like the economic South, was a different place. It was different in the racial organization of social life, merely by virtue of the coming of legal desegregation. But it was different in the organization of its partisan political life too, because legal desegregation brought a reconstituted politics of race. The demographics of race, by way of the racial composition of electoral districts, made its own contribution—actually two different contributions at different points in time—to the structure of a new Southern politics. Public preferences about racial policy, especially about governmental assistance to blacks, made a single, consistent, and massively growing contribution as well.

To put it differently, one piece of this new racial politics, the piece contributed by black Southerners, was massively Democratic when it arrived, and moved not at all during the succeeding decades. Yet the larger piece, the one contributed by Southern whites, required careful attention not just to racial identity but also to electoral context, policy preference, time period, and institutional setting. Nevertheless, in the end, there was a composite political world, simply described and still notably influenced by considerations of race, but strikingly different from the one that had lasted for so many generations before the civil rights legislation—and revolution—of the 1960s.

4

Class, Race, and Partisan Change

BY 1970, sweeping change was well under way in the political order of the American South. Economic development and an associated politics of class had arrived earlier and were moving inexorably, though also gradually, to change the nature of partisan politics. Legal desegregation and an associated politics of race had arrived later but with a rush, changing the nature of politics almost at a stroke. If scholars had long recognized both possibilities in the abstract, as incipient social forces that would remake Southern politics if they finally appeared, those scholars had no way of knowing when such change would come. Nor, on the basis of historical patterns, did they have any way of knowing what form it would take. Nor did they possess any means of knowing what the impact even of each individual change would look like, much less what the two might look like in combination.

Nevertheless, by 1970, both were vigorously present. Both were remaking Southern politics. And the direction of their separate and individual impacts was clear. Seen in isolation, these two grand social developments contributed a Republican accelerator in the form of economic development with its resulting politics of class, along with a more problematic Democratic brake upon this in the form of legal desegregation with its reconstituted politics of race. The latter looked to be stronger in the short run, the former to be stronger in the long term. Yet this comparison still depended to some unknown degree on the independent and additive effect of two social forces, where there was little reason in principle why these two forces should not have interacted as they evolved and much reason in practice to expect that they would.

In this chapter, therefore, we return to economic development and legal desegregation, and consider their joint impacts on partisan politics. At a minimum, this interaction contained the possibility that two great social forces, considered as simultaneous influences on partisan change, would not work in as simple and straightforward a fashion as they appeared to work when considered individually. In statistical terms, the multivariate relationships might look considerably different than two sets of bivariate relationships. One aspect of this reconsideration is thus to guarantee that an analysis built on investigating the two forces independently is not invalidated by a simultaneous investigation. Another, more forward-looking aspect is to fine-tune the resulting picture of comprehensive partisan change.

This is not, however, just a matter of revisiting previous analyses in a new format. Chapters 2 and 3 have already channeled this multivariate analysis in important ways:

- First, they have affirmed some findings that do not need to be revisited. In the lead example, they have demonstrated that the impact of legal desegregation and a politics of racial identity on the Southern black population was so powerful that it left no effective room for an additional politics of class. In that sense, race and class would *not* thereafter interact in this particular voting population.

- Second, those two chapters have highlighted other findings that now sit at the center of the argument. Race and class most definitely did interact within the Southern white population: this is what made economic development into a long-running partisan escalator and legal desegregation into such a problematic brake upon it. We have done some elementary checks on their interaction; we need to offer more.

- Finally, these two chapters have underlined the way in which different political institutions—differing institutional structures—mediated the impact of two great social forces in differing ways. Accordingly, a further check on the influence of a new politics of class and a revised politics of race needs to add political institutions back into the multivariate framework.

If the preceding analysis can indeed be affirmed and elaborated, there is still a major puzzle to be addressed: namely, the way a politics of race worked so differently for Congress than for the presidency. So far, we have highlighted the contours of this institutional puzzle but have left its explanation alone. Yet if this phenomenon—whites in more-black areas voting more Democratic for Congress, more Republican for President—survives a multivariate examination of a changing Southern politics, it is surely time to inquire into both its lengthy reign and its sudden disappearance.

When that inquiry is completed, the political *attitudes* associated with changing social forces—or sometimes impressively dissociated from them—can be put back into this comprehensive picture. The first part of such an analysis requires investigation of the way in which economic and racial ideologies themselves interacted across the postwar years. Only then is it possible to see their joint impact as an important elaboration of the structural changes that have impelled this story so far. When ideological preferences on class and race legislation not only survive their own multivariate analysis but prove to be a growing influence on the politics of the changing South, a new and different, composite political order will finally stand revealed.

All of which assumes, however, that an analysis framed in this fashion proves superior to the main alternative way of thinking about the course of partisan change in the postwar South. For the literature of Southern politics does in fact offer a common alternative perspective. This view introduces—and privileges—a further, internal, regional difference, between the Peripheral South and the Deep South, and that difference then serves for many of these authors as the main structural intermediary shaping the course of Southern politics. In an afterword to this chapter, we confront this alternative view directly.

A Politics of Class *with* a Politics of Race

The opening analysis for any simultaneous check upon the isolated impacts of social class and racial context needs, at a minimum, to demonstrate that the independent stories of economic development in Chapter 2 and of legal desegregation in Chapter 3 are not substantially changed when these two great social changes are considered together—considered, that is, in the way they actually occurred. The simplest way to do this is just to shift from bivariate to multivariate analysis, by way of a logistic regression of the Republican vote on both social class and racial context for the five complete decades of the postwar era, converted into a set of probabilities of voting Republican. The resulting pictures also provide a straightforward, data-driven way to summarize the story so far.

Figure 4.1 shows the marginal impact of each of these two great influences, economic development and legal desegregation, controlling for the other. For social class, the contrast is between the lowest and the highest income terciles, and the value is the difference in the likelihood of a Republican vote for a respondent living in a district with the region-wide average percentage black. For racial context, the marginal effect is calculated for a shift by white Southern voters from a district that is 10 percent black to one that is 30 percent black. Before the 1990s, about 25 percent of white Southerners lived in districts with 10 percent or fewer blacks while about 25 percent lived in districts with 30 percent or more, so this shift is effectively the interquartile range, a highly plausible contrast.[1]

Because the presence or absence of a Republican candidate was an essential precondition for a Republican vote, Figure 4.1A and B covers only contested seats for the House and Senate, those with both a Republican and a Democratic contender. The presidency always met this standard and thus its electorate is region-wide in both parts of the figure, but because the opening decades of this analysis already featured a serious Republican vote for President, we attempt to get at prior electoral change by breaking the presidential vote into old and new Republican areas—those which had Republican congressional contenders in 1952 versus those which did not—until this difference no longer has an empirical effect.

In the case of social class, the individual stories that result should by now be very familiar. That is, the same stories surface from this collective multivariate analysis as surfaced in the individual bivariate tables (Figure 4.1A). Dividing the presidential vote into old and new Republican areas for the immediate postwar years creates three and a half such institutional lines of partisan change. Their initial differences, their common resolution, and their differing paths to it all deserve comment.

With the House of Representatives, the relationship of Republican support to family income was modestly negative in the 1950s. That is, moving from the bottom to the top tercile actually reduced the probability of voting Republican by about 10 percent. The poor were modestly more Republican, the rich more Democratic. This relationship then shifted sharply in the opposite (the positive) direction, underpinning the changing fortunes of Southern Republicans in the House; this was the relationship that would resurface in every decade thereafter. In the 1960s, moving from the bottom to the top tercile *increased* the chance of a Republican vote by about 15 percent. The rich were now more Republican, the poor more Democratic. This class gap increased by a couple of points in the 1980s and by a further five or so in the 1990s, underpinning a final surge to majority status.

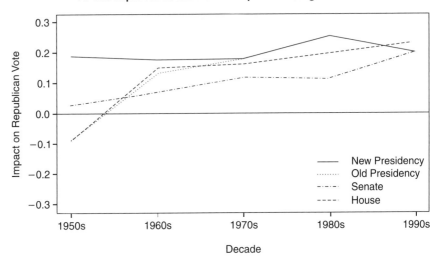

A. The Impact of Economic Development among White Southerners

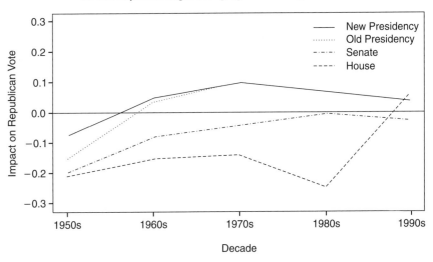

B. The Impact of Legal Desegregation among White Southerners

Figure 4.1   Social Class, Racial Context, and Partisan Change: 1950–2000.

The Senate version of the story was delayed by a decade and was a bit more modest when it came. Otherwise, it was the same story.[2] In the 1950s and into the 1960s, there was little or no linkage between income tercile and Republican vote. By the late 1960s and into the 1970s, the modern—in some sense, the "Northern" or national—pattern had arrived.

Now, that same move from bottom to top tercile was worth approximately a 10 percent Republican edge. This relationship then jumped up again in the 1990s, effectively doubling its impact at the point when the Senate and not just the House achieved a Republican majority in the South as a whole. As with the House and the presidency, moving from the bottom to the top tercile now increased the prospect of a Republican vote for the Senate by about 20 percent.

When the presidential vote is parsed into established versus new Republican areas for the 1950s, older Republican areas also showed a negative relationship to social class. That is, moving from the bottom to the top income tercile again reduced the likelihood of a Republican vote, by about 10 percent. This relationship, like that for the House, then moved sharply in the opposite (and positive) direction in the 1960s, while almost closing the gap with new Republican areas at the same time, at better than 15 percent. By the 1970s, the gap was closed. This new/old distinction was no longer consequential, and the class relationship to a Republican presidential vote continued thereafter in a unitary fashion, with about a 20 percent increase in the probability of a Republican vote as one moved up the class scale.

Newly Republican areas, by contrast, showed the strongest *positive* relationship of family income to Republican support for President at the start of this period. When this vote appeared, it featured a substantial increase in the probability of voting Republican as one moved from the bottom to the top tercile. These were, of course, the areas where the breakthrough that became a continuing class reversion first occurred, and that breakthrough proved to be strong, stable, and stereotypic: the rich were Republican, the poor Democratic, not the other way around. Moreover, having achieved this modern relationship pretty much from the start, these newly Republican areas more or less just sustained themselves thereafter on that (high) level of class alignment. Moving from the bottom to the top tercile increased the probability of a Republican vote by a full 20 percent, from the 1950s through the 1990s.

One further difference and one other similarity are inherent in these coefficients. The difference is in the timing of the effect: presidency first, House second, Senate last—not presidency, Senate, House, as an undifferentiated institutional argument might suggest. As in the bivariate analysis, the Senate in the multivariate analysis lagged a bit in its response to changing social conditions. Yet the similarity, more consequential as time passed and these lines moved forward, involves their apparent convergence nevertheless. By the 1960s, the presidency and the House had converged on the modern pattern. By the 1970s, despite its lag, the Senate had joined them. "Northern" class politics appeared to have come to the South.

In the case of racial context, all three individual stories—and this time, really only three, since old and new Republican areas always behaved in parallel fashion—should likewise seem familiar (Figure 4.1B). Yet here, the story of similarities and differences across institutions is more varied. That is to say: institutional structures contributed their own mediating influences to the impact of racial politics, producing differences that were not a simple matter of lag and arrival. If all three institutions ended up in the same general place, they neither started together nor traveled together on their way there.

In the case of the House, a strong negative relationship between racial context and Republican support characterized the opening years of the postwar era: whites in blacker areas were more likely to support Democratic candidates. Moving from an electoral context that was 10 percent black to one that was 30 percent black actually *reduced* the prospect of a Republican vote by about 20 percent. Remarkably, given the upheaval in the racial organization of Southern society, this relationship was unshaken by the civil rights revolution. It remained stable, showing only minor fluctuations through the 1970s. It actually gained strength in the 1980s, opening an expected gap of more than 25 percent. Only in the 1990s did it finally decline, essentially to zero.

The counterpart story for the Senate began in the same manner, with blacker areas more likely to provide white support for Southern Democrats and to resist emergent Southern Republicans. Indeed, it began with about the same 20-point gap. But as new black Democrats flooded into the electorate, this white relationship to racial context began a long, slow decline. It was still closer to the House than to the presidency in the 1960s, though it had already shed about half its original contribution to the partisan vote. It remained marginally closer to the House in the 1970s, while shedding half of its remaining vote impact. It became nearly zero in the 1980s. And it stayed there in the 1990s, as both the presidency and, especially, the House converged on it.

The presidency offered yet a third trajectory. Presidential contests also began the postwar years with a negative relationship between Republican vote and racial context: whites in blacker areas were more likely to vote Democratic, whites in whiter areas to vote Republican. Both old and new Republican areas for the presidency showed this effect less strongly than

for the two houses of Congress, but there was still about a 10 percent re-
duction in Republican prospects by moving from whiter to blacker areas,
and all "four" institutional arenas were in negative territory. Yet with racial
context—and very much unlike the situation with social class—there was
no real need thereafter to differentiate newly Republican from established
Republican areas.

Instead, the point is that the overall relationship moved clearly in the
opposite direction in the 1960s: whites in blacker areas were now more attracted to *Republican* candidates. If this effect was still quite modest—
moving from a 10-percent black to a 30-percent black district increased
the prospect of a Republican vote by about 5 percent—it was also sharply
different from the same effect for the House or the Senate, which de-
creased Republican prospects by 20 and 10 percent respectively. With the
presidency, this new if modest relationship then strengthened a bit in the
1970s, moving to about 10 percent, before weakening in the 1980s and
again in the 1990s, when it had effectively converged with the Senate and
the House.

Once more, all three institutions began in the realm of an old Southern
politics, with whites in blacker areas more reliably Democratic. But thereafter, the 1960s produced an institutional divergence: the same social forces
were obviously mediated very differently by three different institutions. As
a result,

- the House continued the old pattern for racial context, while simultaneously reversing its prior class allegiances;
- the Senate began an extended decline toward electoral irrelevance
  for racial context, while picking up the modern pattern on class only
  after an initial lag;
- and the presidency moved opposite to the House for one great social impact, reversing the influence of racial context, while leading
  the way on the other, strengthening the new—and also newly reversed—influence of social class.

Seen from above, Congress and the presidency actually primed the impact of racial context on white Southerners in opposite directions. Seen
from below, white Southerners chose to respond both to economic development and to legal desegregation in their voting for President, but only to
economic development (and its changing class politics) in their voting for
Congress. Seen either way, this relationship lasted from the 1960s through

the 1980s, by which time it possessed a neat—a nearly symmetric—institutional array in terms of racial context: presidency positive, House negative, Senate neutral and in between. All three institutions then moved toward contextual neutrality in the 1990s, finally producing convergence on race and not just class.

Class, Race, and Institutional Structure

Thus it appears that a focus on the interaction of economic development and legal desegregation, that is, on the interaction of a politics of social class and a politics of racial context, is sufficient to tell the postwar story of partisan change in the American South. A few relationships from the preceding bivariate analyses look modestly different at particular points in time when examined in a multivariate framework, but none such that the overall argument would shift. On the other hand, what emerges even more clearly—what derives further emphasis from the multivariate approach—is the mediating effect of differing institutional structures. And here, there is another way to tell this institutional story, one that is additionally helpful in highlighting the place of institutional intermediaries in shaping the partisan impact of social change.

This further approach involves graphing income terciles and racial contexts simultaneously onto the Republican vote, for each of these three institutions individually (Figures 4.2 through 4.5). Each separate plot is derived from a logistic regression of the Republican vote among Southern whites on income tercile and racial context. In each, the *vertical distance* under the line, either the upper-income or the lower-income line, is a measure of Republican success: the distance between these lines is then a measure of the impact of social class on the vote. The *slope* of these lines is a measure of the impact of racial context: the steeper the slope, the stronger the relationship. Plots are confined to the effectively relevant range, which is 0 percent to 50 percent black. Before the 1990s, almost no districts were majority black; in the redistricting of the 1990s, very few whites were left in majority-black areas.

With the initial exception of the 1950s, the resulting relationships are essentially linear throughout, notwithstanding the logistic estimation. Given the presence of this linearity, considering the problems of multicollinearity that come with interaction terms, and given our desire for clarity of presentation, we suppress interactions between income and racial context in the figures that follow, with that initial exception of Figure 4.2.

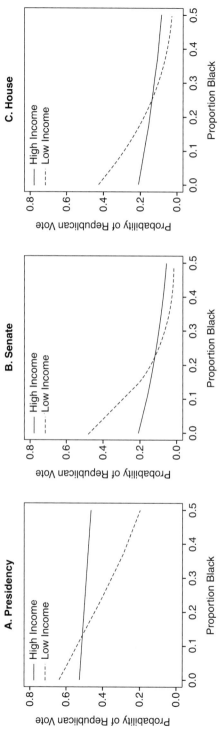

Figure 4.2   Social Class, Racial Context, and the Southern Republican Vote: The 1950s.

Otherwise, any non-parallelism between lines is strictly the result of the logistic setup. Relationships that are estimated using logistical regression are then converted to graphical form, to show the probability of a Republican vote depending on income level and racial context simultaneously.[3]

With the first set of these relationships, for the 1950s, the grand and gross contours of the presidency, the Senate, and the House are not dissimilar, though there are still details worth highlighting (Figure 4.2). Overall, the Republicans had begun to enjoy some success with the presidency— both the lower-income and the upper-income lines are higher in the presidential than in the congressional graphs—though no one could have been sure at the time whether this was a harbinger of anything. Beyond that, three effects stand out.

First, the class inversion characterizing the old South is still visible for all three institutions, though it was fast disappearing for the presidency. For the Senate and the House, the bulk of the area between the upper-income and lower-income lines is on the left-hand side of the plot and thus featured lower-income Southerners voting more Republican. By contrast, the larger area between these lines for the presidency is already on the right-hand side of the plot, so that it featured upper-income Southerners voting more Republican instead.

Second, upper-income Southerners clearly had begun, with the presidency, that migration toward the Republicans which would underpin the general class reversal of the 1960s, and which would reach the House so strikingly at the beginning of that decade. The upper-income line, while much closer to flat for all three institutions and thus essentially less responsive to racial context, is found considerably higher on the plot for the presidency than for the Senate or the House, delivering a half rather than a fifth of its total vote to the Republican candidate. This upper-income "migration," along with a lower-income resistance, would be the class story of postwar Southern politics for a very long time.

Finally, while it might appear that it is lower-income voters who were distinctively responsive to racial context in their balloting, showing a steeper slope to their line of Republican support, this probably just reflects the lingering contours of the old South. Or at least, this shows that its poorest areas—the Appalachian mountains of Virginia, Tennessee, and North Carolina—were also its whitest areas, where Republicanism had sustained its hold over all the years after Reconstruction, and that pattern still shows clearly for all three institutions in the 1950s. Lower-income whites remained distinctly more Republican in these less-black areas. If upper-income whites showed a more modest version of the same effect with Congress, their overwhelmingly Democratic support left little room for more.

The main plot of the postwar story then considers these three institutions during the extended transitional years from 1962 through 1990 (Figure 4.3). Obviously, a *comprehensive* reversal in class support for Republican voting had arrived. We know from Chapter 2 that it appeared during the 1960s. Yet an *institutionally differentiated* impact of racial context had also arrived, at the same time. We know from Chapter 3 that this differentiation then lasted through the 1980s. Accordingly, Figure 4.3 depicts the central summary picture of postwar Southern politics in operational terms.

The ability of changing social forces to break through earlier in the case of the presidency, producing an augmented Republican vote, is evident in this figure. That is, both the upper-income and the lower-income lines are considerably higher on the presidential plot than they are on the Senatorial or House plots. (We shall return to some of the contributing intermediary reasons for this difference in Chapter 5.) Republicanism had already arrived dramatically with the presidency in the 1950s. When it arrived for the House in the early 1960s and for the Senate in the late 1960s, the presidency still led them, as it would for a further twenty years.

Nevertheless, the three decades following this basic class reversal do show it characterizing all three institutions. That is, higher-income voters were more likely to vote Republican, for all three major elective institutions and across every level of racial context. The distance between the high-income and low-income lines then represents the strength of this effect, which was clearly weakest in the Senate and strongest in the presidency, with the House falling in between. On the one hand, social class had already become a major driver for voting behavior with regard to all three institutions, and in the modern—the "Northern"—way. On the other, it was still upper-income voters who showed the greatest variation across these institutions—and who thus contributed the bulk of the institutional difference by class.

The more striking differences among these three great elective institutions then concern the role of racial context. Recall that the main effect of racial context is captured in the degree of slope to the class lines—steeper slopes being a stronger relationship—along with their direction. Racial context lines slope clearly upward for the presidency, strongly downward

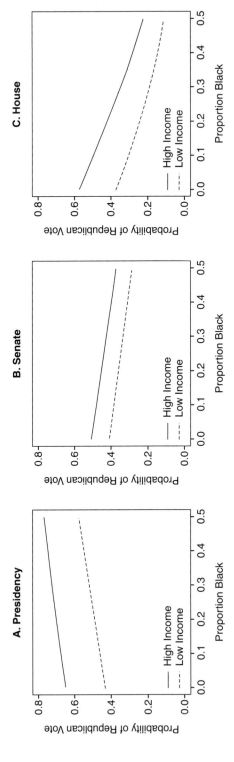

Figure 4.3   Social Class, Racial Context, and the Southern Republican Vote: The 1960s through the 1980s.

for the House, with the Senate tagging along. In other words, in the 1960s and for two subsequent decades, this main effect was actually opposite for the presidency and Congress. With the presidency, white voters in blacker districts leaned Republican; with the Senate, they leaned Democratic; and with the House, the "lean" became a "plunge."

One specific comparison with the 1950s brings all this into even sharper focus (Figure 4.4). As we know, the class reversal that characterized all three institutions from the 1960s through the 1980s was already in place among those newly Republican areas that represented the Eisenhower breakthrough for the presidency. In the bivariate format, this is just a tale of institutional lag, with Congress needing another decade "to get there." Yet when we switch to the multivariate format, two other points become equally and immediately striking.

The first is a further aspect of temporal sequence: the class breakthrough is utterly unaccompanied by a race breakthrough. Economic development precedes legal desegregation in shaping partisan change in the postwar South. Consideration of the bivariate tables in Chapters 2 and 3 has already indicated as much; multivariate consideration of the same material confirms it. From above, the party system for the country as a whole had already aligned the two parties in this fashion on welfare policy outside the South; it would be another decade before it realigned them on racial policy. From below, this welfare alignment was apparently recognized and accepted by Southern voters who were coming afresh to the Republican

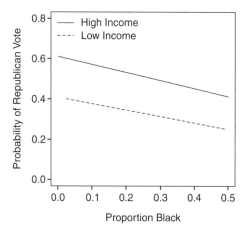

Figure 4.4   Social Class, Racial Context, and the Southern Republican Vote: New GOP Areas for the Presidency in the 1950s.

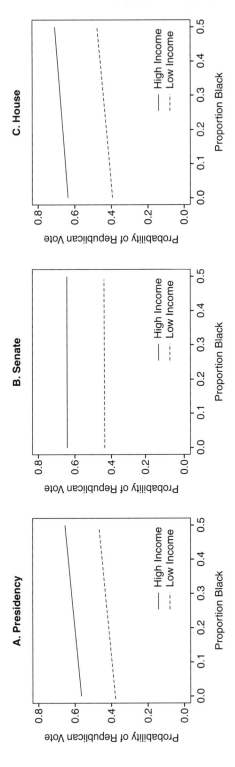

Figure 4.5   Social Class, Racial Context, and the Southern Republican Vote: The 1990s.

Party, while the subsequent racial alignment was neither anticipated nor demanded by them, even implicitly. In other words, both the party system nationally and social change within the region were eliciting partisan change on grounds of social welfare. Neither the party system nor social change was yet doing that with civil rights.

The second point is then an additional aspect of institutional difference in the impact of racial change when it did arrive. Uniquely among the institutions of national government, the presidency would undergo two major changes in succeeding decades: it would shift into a new class alignment in the 1950s, and it would shift again into a new racial alignment in the 1960s. Congress would follow quickly with the first of these changed alignments but not the second. To appreciate the distinction pictorially, note that newly Republican presidential areas from the 1950s (Figure 4.4), when considered for the joint impact of social class and racial context, look very much like the House picture for the next thirty years (Figure 4.3C).

Indeed, as we shall see below, it was arguable that Congress would never adopt the presidential pattern on race. Differential alignments for the presidency versus Congress on grounds of racial context were finally to decline in the 1990s, underpinned by the deliberate re-engineering of House districts. Viewed from the presidential side, this was the House being drawn suddenly and sharply toward voting patterns that had long characterized the presidency. Viewed from the House side, however, the important point is that this was convergence on effective neutrality. The sharp disjunction in the impact of racial context between President and House would finally disappear in the 1990s, but if the main movement in this convergence occurred with voting patterns for the House rather than the presidency, the convergence point was still effectively zero.

This further change in the impact of racial context, the second greatest change in the postwar period, arrived in the 1990s. Visually, the change looks like one more incarnation of the metaphorical "dog that did not bark." Plots of a logistic regression of the Republican vote for the presidency, the Senate, and the House are now close to interchangeable. Class gaps are nearly identical. Racial slopes are not very different. Major institutional differences are thus not much in evidence (Figure 4.5). Yet by comparison with the previous thirty years, this uniformity represented a very substantial change.

One part of this change was aggregate. Republicans were now fully competitive in Congress. That is to say, the presidency no longer offered a superior Republican performance overall. Moreover, underneath these aggregates, there was an increasingly uniform class effect. Both lower-income and upper-income lines were now impressively similar, so that residual differences should probably be treated more for their collective distinction from the preceding thirty years than for any marginal differences among the three institutions. In other words, the impact of social class had become much more consistent across all three institutions, and nothing in the aggregate level of Republican support required such an outcome. Class differences were now present everywhere, and strongly so.

More impressively still, the main visual difference among the three institutions across most of the postwar years, courtesy of the priming effect of racial context, had almost entirely disappeared. By the 1990s, the previously sharp—indeed, previously opposite—distinction between the presidency and the two houses of Congress was gone. The impressive ability of individual institutions to prime a major social force in different directions obviously disappeared with it. If the increasing uniformity of a class effect represented a real change worth noting, uniformity in the impact of racial context required a far greater shift for its realization. Nevertheless, not the slightest trace of the old, institutionally differentiated world remained.

This change in the priming effect of racial context appeared to represent a convergence from both directions. With the presidency, there was a continuing decline in the positive impact of racial context: whites in blacker areas were now only modestly more likely to vote Republican (though as we shall see in Chapter 5, the permanence of this shift may still depend upon the specifics of presidential politicking). With the Senate, there was only extrapolation of a gradual drift toward neutrality. But with the House, there was something much larger: an abrupt reversal of the negative priming effect of racial context. For thirty years, whites in blacker areas had voted more Democratic; in the 1990s, they voted modestly more Republican instead. In so doing, they changed a crucial contour of politics in the new South.

Congress and the Presidency as Institutional Theaters

What these composite multivariate pictures of Southern politics leave behind, after confirming the portraits sketched by the individual bivariate analyses in Chapters 2 and 3, are two questions. Why *did* the politics of race come to play out so differently, as between Congress and the presidency, from the 1960s onward? And why did this politics change again in the 1990s, effectively erasing that difference? At a minimum, any adequate answer requires two elements: a truly major change in the structure of politics, one anchored in those critical decades, along with an evident and powerful link between racial politicking and this change.

For the first of these impacts, the change into a differing racial politics for Congress versus the presidency, the leading candidate is obvious, and the puzzle is only why its reach did not extend farther. For the second, the change back to institutional uniformity in the role of racial context, the leading candidate is likewise easy to see, but its links to an altered politics of race are not so immediately self-evident. Before addressing either, however, it is worth emphasizing just how different the impact of racial context was in the crucial reshaping period from the 1960s through the 1980s, by contrast with the decade that preceded this period as well as with the decade that followed.

Table 4.1 combines two previous tables (Tables 3.5A and 3.7) to highlight the distinctiveness of this crucial thirty-year period. Those tables featured the margin in the vote by white Southerners for Republican candidates for the House and the presidency from districts that were more than 20 percent black versus less than 20 percent black. Note that (a) any difference *between* these two institutional margins was essentially nonexistent in the 1950s; (b) this difference ballooned to an average of more than 25 percent of the entire white Southern electorate from the 1960s through the 1980s; and (c) the difference then collapsed—it returned to being essentially nonexistent—in the 1990s.

Black racial politics, as we have seen, showed no such differentiation.

Table 4.1   **Presidency versus House? Racial Context**

Difference in Republican Vote among White Southerners between Less-Black (<20%) and More-Black (>20%) Districts

Decade	House	President	Difference
1950s	−6	-5	−1
(N)	(216)	(366)	
1960s	−17	+8	+25
(N)	(378)	(353)	
1970s	−12	+8	+20
(N)	(656)	(765)	
1980s	−31	+4	+35
(N)	(621)	(533)	
1990s	+6	+2	−4
(N)	(926)	(935)	

Black Southerners voted Democratic, institution by institution and year after year. But white racial politics most certainly did show this distinction (Table 4.1). White Southerners in blacker areas voted more *Democratic* both for Congress and for President in the 1950s. White Southerners in blacker areas voted more Democratic for Congress and more Republican for President from the 1960s through the 1980s. And white Southerners in blacker areas voted more *Republican* both for Congress and for President in the 1990s.

It is hard to miss a relevant stimulus event for the first of these changes, the reversal of presidential voting patterns by racial context in the 1960s. This was the decade of the civil rights revolution. Moreover, its impact was inescapably greater, for white as well as black Southerners, in those districts where black Southerners disproportionately lived. Black Southerners responded to this event by entering the electorate, in a flood, as Democrats. Clearly, they drew no institutional distinctions between the presidency and Congress in their newly practical partisanship. Just as clearly, white voters made one institutional change in their voting patterns in response to a sharply changed racial context—one institutional change, but not two.

Before the fact, it would not have been obvious that this white response would be differentiated by institution. Yet if white Southern voters were to pick one institution on which to focus their protests about enforced change in the racial structuring of Southern society, it certainly made substantive sense for that institution to be the presidency. President Lyndon Johnson, after all, had been the driving institutional actor behind the Civil Rights Act of 1964 and the Voting Rights Act of 1965. If opposition to those changes was to be the propelling force behind *one* change in the impact of racial context, then that change ought to surface among white voters in more-black areas with regard to the presidency—which in fact it did.

On the other hand, viewed retrospectively, what was equally noteworthy was the fact that this change reached the presidency but did not reach Congress, thus insulating the House to a remarkable degree. We believe that the same factor that ultimately led to the disappearance of this difference in the 1990s is sufficient to explain its advent in the 1960s as well: action by Democratic congressional candidates from the 1960s onward to prevent a parallel shift to that in the presidency, and their inability to sustain such action in the 1990s as a result of demographic redistricting. But before presenting the main evidence for that conclusion, it is important to acknowledge the most obvious alternative possibility, perhaps the leading candidate to explain both the appearance *and* the disappearance of this institutional difference in the impact of a changed racial context.

This other possibility is the mediating effect of incumbency. There were, after all, long-lived incumbents in Congress—and many of them—who managed to survive across this presidential shift in the impact of racial context, and to live well into the new era. By contrast, there were only short-lived incumbents (or none) in the presidency. Perhaps social forces were always taking all three institutions in the same—the presidential—direction? Perhaps it was just that resilient incumbents could stave off these forces for an incredible length of time, especially in the House? In the immediate postwar years, incumbent Southern Democrats did manifest a remarkable personal and institutional longevity (see Chapter 5). Was that all that needed to be understood?

The simplest way to check on this possibility is to examine the impact of racial context for the 1960s–1980s and for the 1990s among those districts that did and did not have established incumbents running for re-election. Table 4.2 does this, and the result is that *incumbency proves not to be the explanation*. Familiar incumbency effects are certainly present during all these years. Indeed, every comparison—Republican vote totals for the period of the 1960s–1980s versus the decade of the 1990s, Republican vote totals in less-black districts for the period of the 1960s–1980s versus the decade of the 1990s, and Republican vote totals in more-black districts for

Table 4.2 Open Seats, Incumbent Seats, and Racial Context: The House

Decade	<20% Black	>20% Black
A. Republican Vote in Open Seats		
1960s-1980s	54	41
(N)	(158)	(61)
1990s	53	55
(N)	(109)	(42)
B. Republican Vote in Democratic Incumbent Seats		
1960s-1980s	30	20
(N)	(386)	(525)
1990s	37	40
(N)	(350)	(63)

the period of the 1960s–1980s versus the decade of the 1990s—shows Republican candidates doing better in open rather than incumbent seats, as any analyst would expect (Hinckley 1981; Mayhew 1974).

Yet for the comparison that is central to this analysis, the fate of Republican candidates in more-black congressional districts in the two periods, incumbency is not an explanation. Republicans lagged in more-black districts in the first thirty years of the comparison for *both* incumbent and open seats. And Republicans caught up in more-black districts in the final decade of the comparison for *both* incumbent and open seats. For open seats, Republican candidates in more-black districts went from a lag of 13 percentage points to an edge of 2 between the 1960s–1980s and the 1990s. For incumbent seats, Republican candidates in more-black districts went from a lag of 10 points to an edge of 3 between the 1960s–1980s and the 1990s. The change was, in short, effectively the same.

By the same token, incumbency had a roughly equivalent repressing effect on the Republican vote in every cell of the comparison, between open versus incumbent seats. Yet incumbency had no differential impact—really none at all—in the more-black districts where the key change occurred. Incumbency had been massively insufficient to sustain an old *class* pattern in the Southern congressional vote at the time of the great reversal of that pattern, from the 1950s to the 1960s. Incumbency was totally insufficient to sustain a new *race* pattern in the Southern congressional vote at the time of the great reversal of this pattern, from the 1980s to the 1990s.

As a result, the answer has to lie in some further characteristic(s) of the institutions themselves, almost surely in a characteristic directly affecting their politics. And it has to lie, by definition, in some characteristic affecting racial context, for that is the relationship that actually changed. In other words, what is necessary is some key structural characteristic that was essentially stable from the 1960s through the 1980s, and then changed radically in the 1990s. What is then additionally necessary, if such an influence can be found, is some mediating implication from racial context which would lead to this particular shift—that is, to the continuation of a previous relationship between Republican vote and racial context for thirty years, and then to its annihilation.

The one obvious candidate for this role, a candidate possessing both necessary characteristics, is racial balance within congressional districts. Moreover, it offers a triggering event to cause the role of this balance to change: the widespread creation of so-called "majority-minority districts" after the 1990 census. The 1990s were indeed the decade when deliberate

reconstruction of Southern House districts on racial grounds came into being (Lublin 1997; Cunningham 2001). And the scope of the change they
produced was dramatic: there were three majority-black congressional districts after the 1980 census, seventeen after its 1990 counterpart.[4]

The scope of that change was also temporally focused. That is, the 1990
census, as channeled by the Department of Justice, triggered the change in
a single coordinated action. Moreover, the change occurred while the black
percentage of the South as a whole was essentially stable. The question,
then, really boils down to whether there was some further, triggering, racial
impact on political calculations that could have linked the priming effect of
racial context to the Republican vote. To us, the answer appears to be yes: if
Southern congressional districts are further subdivided by racial context, a
pattern does emerge. Three different types of district tell the story:

1. *Districts that were less than 20 percent black.* Many such districts were,
   of course, much less than 20 percent black—which is to say, much
   more than 80 percent white—but that figure will do for a division.
   These were districts where politics was a matter of striving for a majority of the white electorate. For Democratic candidates, black voters were undeniably valuable. Yet it was the fate of these candidates
   within the white electorate that mattered. Put differently, if efforts to augment black turnout raised any prospect that these efforts
   would alienate white voters, that was a bad trade-off.
2. *Districts that were more than 40 percent black.* At the other extreme in
   terms of racial balance, these districts were remarkably similar in
   strategic calculation: that is, they possessed the same *strategic logic* as
   those districts that were overwhelmingly white. For Democratic
   candidates, the key consideration was becoming the preference of
   black Democrats, and then turning out their vote. Any appeal to
   white voters that either lessened this preference or lowered that potential turnout was particularly disastrous, but all such appeals—assuming a preference among black voters—were effectively unnec-
   essary.
3. *Districts that were between 20 percent and 40 percent black.* These
   were, in effect, the districts whose apportionment required a biracial
   strategy, at least for Democrats. There was little evidence that a biracial strategy would do much for Republicans, since blacks in these
   districts continued to vote about 90 percent Democratic. Differences by social class did not provide a Republican opening; differ-

ences by racial context did not provide a Republican opening; differences by policy preference did not provide a Republican opening.
Yet for a Democratic candidate, successful strategies required the
twin necessities of a high black turnout and a substantial minority
of the white vote. These districts, accordingly, contributed the true
biracial strategic context.

Within that framework, what happened to the distribution of these
three types of districts for the entire South after the reapportionment of
the 1990s was abundantly clear:

- In the 1980s, most white Southerners already lived in the first category of districts, those that were more than 80 percent white. Yet
  this percentage managed to move up strongly in the 1990s (Table
  4.3). In the 1980s, only a quarter of Southern blacks lived in these
  mostly-white districts. Yet that percentage too actually went up, as
  indirect fallout from the creation of majority-minority districts.
- By contrast, in the 1980s, very few white Southerners lived in the
  (three out of one hundred twenty-three) districts that were more
  than 40 percent black. But then, with only three such districts, very
  few black Southerners lived in these districts either. In the 1990s,
  very few white Southerners still lived in districts that were more
  than 40 percent black. But now, after race-based reapportionment,
  37 percent of all black Southerners actually did.
- And the result for the middle category of congressional districts,
  those that were more than 20 but less than 40 percent black, followed ineluctably. In the 1980s, 35 percent of all white Southerners

Table 4.3   The End of Biracial Coalitions?

Racial Composition of Congressional Districts, 1980s versus 1990s (in percentages)

% Black	White Southerners		Black Southerners		All Southerners	
	1980s	1990s	1980s	1990s	1980s	1990s
<20	62	80	25	32	54	70
20–40	35	16	72	31	44	19
>40	3	5	3	37	3	11
[*N*]	[2348]	[2375]	[685]	[617]	[3033]	[2992]

had lived in such districts. In the 1990s, this figure was more than halved, to 16 percent. Likewise, in the 1980s, a full 72 percent of all black Southerners had lived in such districts. In the 1990s, this too was more than halved, to 31 percent. These were the districts that required a biracial electoral strategy. Within one iteration of the census, they were devastated.

Democratic candidates who refused to make the strategic adjustments required by a sharply revised racial composition were, at the very least, going to be additionally handicapped. In other words, sensible candidates should have been abandoning a biracial strategy, while candidates who would not or could not abandon this strategy ought to have been at increased risk. We have no individual-level data about *feelings* toward this specific arrangement. Yet in a careful deconstruction of the new districts, Petrocik and Desposato conclude that "the pro-GOP tide of the nineties followed a redistricting that left many Democratic incumbents with districts in which 40 percent or more of the constituents were new to the incumbent and 'unimmunized' by incumbency" (Petrocik and Desposato 1998, 619).

One implication of population shifts on that scale is that our statistics for the 1990s, comparing open versus incumbent seats in the U.S. House, surely overstate the effect of incumbency by comparison to previous decades. In the 1980s, an incumbent would still have been expected to be standing for re-election in a district roughly equivalent to the one that incumbent had previously held. In the 1990s, an "incumbent" could have been standing for re-election in districts that were 40 percent new. It should not be surprising, then, that the largest change from the period of the 1960s–1980s to the decade of the 1990s in our individual-level data (in Table 4.2) was precisely among white voters in *incumbent* seats in more-black districts: in these districts, the Republican vote literally doubled.

Regardless, the total impact seemed easily sufficient to erase a longstanding relationship between racial context and voting for Congress in the South. Since the previously opposite relationship had been gradually decaying for the presidency, the combination seemed easily sufficient to bring the two institutions, finally, into alignment on the impact of racial context. The key piece of institutional engineering behind this convergence was accomplished by way of the 1990 census. Yet its full impact can perhaps best be appreciated by putting that story back into the total sweep of postwar Southern politics (Figure 4.6).

The world of the 1950s had actually clustered its congressional districts in the key 20–40 percent range. If black Southerners were ever enfranchised, this was the area that would have to develop some biracial electoral strategy in order to sustain the Southern Democracy. For thirty years after enfranchisement, it did. Conscious reapportionment in the 1990s then pushed both black and white Southerners out to the extremes. In this modern world, a biracial electoral strategy no longer made much sense: there was no longer a serious social base for it. And the difference between the presidency and Congress in terms of the impact of racial context finally disappeared.

Policy Conflicts as Partisan Engine

Two questions are left hanging, after all of that. Both involve the policy conflicts accompanying a changing social structure as it shaped a shifting Southern politics. Each follows from earlier investigations of welfare policy (Chapter 2) and race policy (Chapter 3), in their relationship to social class and racial context. And both, inevitably, parallel the earlier questions in this chapter about the interaction of class, race, and political institutions:

- To what extent does the interaction of policy preferences on social welfare and aid to blacks work differently than each policy attitude

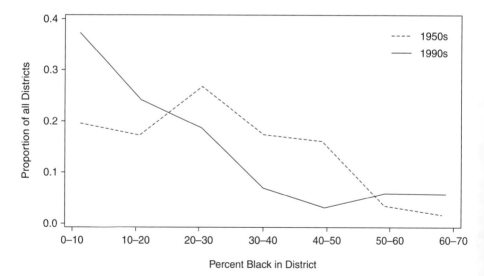

Figure 4.6   The End of Biracial Politics?

appeared to work when analyzed on its own, in their joint relationship to a partisan vote?

- And have the reversal of old class alignments, the institutional differentiation of new racial alignments, and then the disappearance of that differentiation brought additional changes to this joint policy relationship?

The pursuit of an answer to these questions, that is, the pursuit of a multivariate analysis of what were previously two sets of bivariate analyses, cannot proceed quite as neatly in the case of policy attitudes as it could in the case of social structures. The latter could be addressed by means of logistic regressions converted into probability plots, in Figures 4.2, 4.3, and 4.5, where the two key variables, income tercile and racial context, retained the same response categories across the entire fifty-year period. The same formal setup is available for Figures 4.7, 4.8, and 4.9, but here the underlying attitude measures vary in the available response categories: three in the 1950s, five in the 1960s, seven thereafter.

We believe that this variation has minimal impact on the substance of the resulting regressions, even though it was not possible to have complete uniformity in the underlying variables. The relevant interpretive logic is nevertheless identical. The *distance* between the liberal and conservative lines is a measure of the contribution of economic attitudes to the vote; the *slope* of these lines is a measure of the contribution of racial attitudes. Moreover, Figures 4.7 through 4.9 manage to summarize this story for all three nationally elective institutions in two ways: they show the evolution of joint policy impacts within each separate institution, and they permit an examination of these policy impacts across institutions for each succeeding period. Both stories are consequential.

Figure 4.7 begins with the presidency. For the 1950s, bivariate analyses had suggested a clear relationship between opinion on social welfare and presidential voting: liberals more Democratic, conservatives more Republican (see Table 2.5). And bivariate analyses had suggested a weak counterpart relationship between opinion on aid to blacks and presidential voting, again with liberals Democratic and conservatives Republican (see Table 3.9C). When the two attitudes are put back together and considered jointly, however, this picture does change (Figure 4.7A). For the 1950s, welfare attitudes still differentiated the parties, regardless of racial preferences. Yet once welfare attitudes were in the picture, racial attitudes made effectively no contribution to differentiating Republican from Democratic presidential voters.

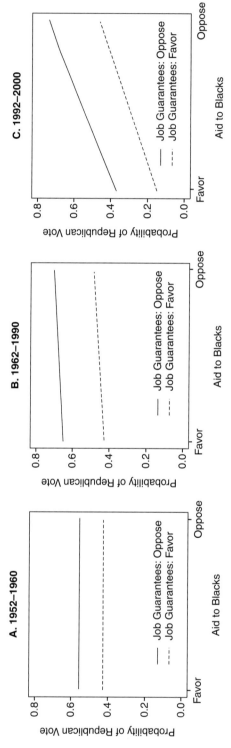

Figure 4.7   *Economic Attitudes, Racial Attitudes, and the Southern Republican Vote: The Presidency.*

In other words, welfare conservatives were already more likely to vote Republican for President than were welfare liberals, but aid to blacks was not yet on the policy dial for this presidential voting public. During the middle period of the postwar era, the 1960s through the 1980s, when a new Southern politics was being born, this relationship between policy preferences and presidential voting shifted (Figure 4.7B). Welfare attitudes expanded in their impact on the Republican vote, with liberals clearly Democratic and conservatives clearly Republican. And racial attitudes began to acquire a partisan attachment in the new—the modern—direction, with conservatives leaning Republican and liberals leaning Democratic, though this remained modest. Welfare preferences were still the main policy story.

Without knowledge of these relationships for the 1990s, this modestly increased role for racial attitudes would not deserve much emphasis. With that knowledge, it appears instead as an important evolutionary trend (Figure 4.7C). The partisan difference between economic conservatives and economic liberals—the distance between their two lines—remained roughly stable and very substantial during this successor decade. But the partisan difference between racial conservatives and racial liberals—the slope of their lines—increased strongly. As a result, by the 1990s, *both* policy domains were strongly related to a presidential vote. Yet the story of the decade for the presidency was the rising relevance of racial ideology. Where the 1950s had seen the coming of welfare ideology as a voting influence, and where the 1960s had seen the coming of racial *context* as an influence, racial ideology registered as a major voting influence only with the coming of the 1990s.

The great difference between this presidential story and the one that applied to the House of Representatives came at the very beginning. For the 1950s, in bivariate terms, welfare policy had shown no relationship to Democratic or Republican voting for the House (see Table 2.2). Racial policy, however, had shown a modest *inverse* relationship, with liberals more Republican and conservatives more Democratic (see Table 3.9A). When these two policy realms are considered together for the 1950s, the picture remains the same: no distance between the liberal and conservative lines on social welfare, an inverse tilt to liberalism and conservatism on race (Figure 4.8A). As a result, this time, the multivariate picture does not differ from the two previous bivariate pictures.

What needs emphasis instead is the degree of difference between the presidential and House pictures. Welfare attitudes were on the dial with

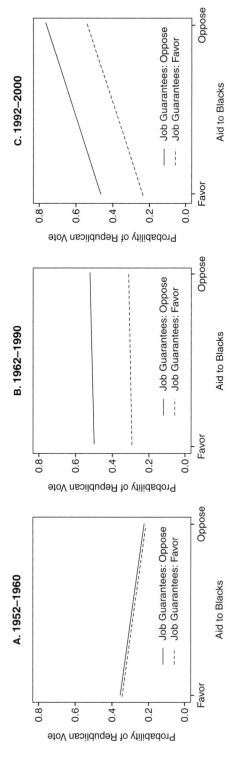

Figure 4.8   Economic Attitudes, Racial Attitudes, and the Southern Republican Vote: The House.

the presidency, off the dial with the House. Racial attitudes were neutral with the presidency, inverse with the House. From previous analyses, we know that the House pattern actually approximated the situation for established Republican areas in their presidential voting as well, so that the real difference was between attitudinal impacts on the House vote or attitudinal impacts on the presidential vote in established Republican areas *versus* attitudinal impacts on the presidential vote in newly Republican territory. Though it is worth remembering that this latter relationship was already sufficient by the 1950s to color the overall institutional relationship for the presidency.

In the great middle period of the postwar era, from the 1960s through the 1980s, these "pre-modern" relationships disappeared in both the House and the presidency. For the House, economic policy became central to the division between Democratic and Republican voters (Figure 4.8B). And this time, it ran in the national direction, with Republicans conservative and Democrats liberal. Indeed, the distance between economic liberals and conservatives expanded so much as to catch up with (and parallel) that for the presidency as a whole.

Race policy, on the other hand, was now nearly absent as a voting influence for the House. When racial ideology was examined in bivariate terms (see Table 3.9A), there appeared to be a modest positive relationship to the House vote during these years, trailing the presidency at a distance. When racial ideology is put into the multivariate framework, however, economic ideology absorbs all of this relationship. Race policy, in sharp contrast to racial *context,* had not yet come onto the policy dial for House voters. It had been on the dial in the 1950s, in an inverse direction. Yet it collapsed to neutrality in this middle period.

That situation could have implied a variety of evolutionary possibilities; what it actually implied was a long transitional period. For in the 1990s, the House brought racial policy back to an influence over actual voting, in the modern and not the inverse direction. As a result, both policy domains achieved substantial consequence (Figure 4.8C). As with the presidency, social welfare retained its influence—already a large one—by comparison to the 1960–1980 period. But now, racial policy acquired a strong relationship to the vote as well, likewise in the modern direction, with liberals voting Democratic and conservatives Republican. Indeed, in finally catching up with the presidency, the House achieved an effectively equivalent impact for racial ideology.

The Senate then managed to mix and match these relationships in a fa-

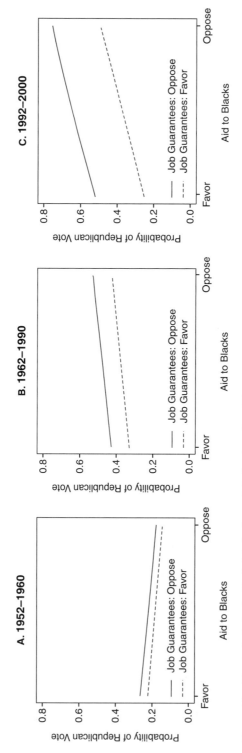

Figure 4.9 *Economic Attitudes, Racial Attitudes, and the Southern Republican Vote: The Senate.*

miliar but institutionally distinctive pattern. Overall, for the 1950s, the Senate approximated the pattern of the House. As with the House, bivariate analyses had shown no relationship between welfare attitudes and the vote (see Table 2.7), along with an inverse relationship to racial attitudes (see Table 3.9B). For the Senate too, this picture is essentially unchanged when presented in a multivariate format (Figure 4.9A). By comparison with the House, there was a trace more impact from attitudes on welfare, a trace less from attitudes on race. That was all.

For the 1960s through 1980s, by contrast, the Senate more closely approximated the pattern of the presidency. The Senate actually joined both other institutions in showing a clear but modest relationship to welfare preferences, the weakest of the three such relationships but still in the same positive direction: welfare conservatives going Republican, welfare liberals Democratic (Figure 4.9B). But where the House showed little additional relationship to racial attitudes, the Senate showed a modest but positive link there, looking much more like the presidency than the House during these decades: racial conservatives too were now more Republican, racial liberals more Democratic.

Finally, for the 1990s, the Senate joined—actually exaggerated—the common pattern of the other two institutions (Figure 4.9C). The relationship between policy preferences on aid to blacks and partisan voting became stronger; the link to racial ideology from the 1960s through 1980s had clearly not been a fluke. But the relationship between policy preferences on social welfare and partisan voting became notably stronger too. Indeed, this latter relationship was actually the strongest of the three institutions during the 1990s. Where the House had needed to pick up influence from racial attitudes in order to approximate the issue environment of the other two institutions, the Senate needed to pick up influence from economic attitudes. And it did.

Policy Preferences and the New South

From different directions and with different postwar histories, then, Southern voting patterns for the presidency, the House, and the Senate had come into apparent alignment during the 1990s. Policy preferences shaped partisan choice in a remarkably parallel fashion across all three institutions. Figure 4.10 merely reassembles Figures 4.7C, 4.8C, and 4.9C to reinforce that point.

First and most strikingly, all three institutions were now aligned in

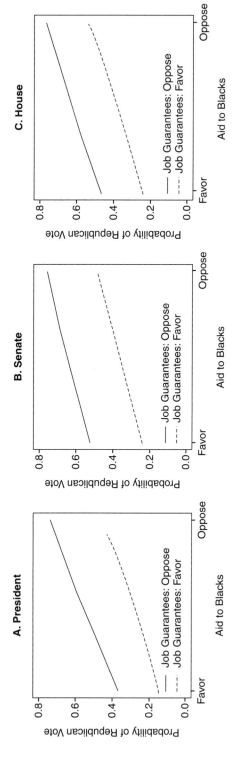

Figure 4.10 Economic Attitudes, Racial Attitudes, and the Southern Republican Vote: The 1990s Revisited.

nearly precise parallel with regard to the relationship between partisan voting and policy conflicts. For all of the preceding decades for which we have
survey data, for the 1950s through the 1980s, the impact of policy preferences on partisan choice had needed to be distinguished by institution.
Different issues affected voting for different institutions at different times.
They sometimes even affected that vote in different directions. In the newest Southern politics of the 1990s, all of this was no longer true.

Within this alignment, each major policy domain, social welfare and aid
to blacks, made serious contributions to the partisan composition of the
vote. In the 1950s, economic attitudes had trumped racial attitudes with
the presidency, while racial attitudes trumped economic attitudes with Congress. Then, for thirty years thereafter, economic attitudes had clearly led
racial attitudes as an influence on voting behavior. In the newest Southern
politics of the 1990s, none of this was true. Economic attitudes did not retreat, but racial attitudes clearly did advance.

Given such parallel patterns in major policy underpinnings to the
vote—especially as piled upon parallel developments in major demographic underpinnings, as seen in Figure 4.5—it should probably not be
surprising that the overall outcome looked remarkably parallel as well.
Both houses of Congress had now caught up to the presidency in their
overall level of Republican support. What resulted was an institutionally
common partisan phenomenon, driven initially by sociological change but
showing a growing role by the 1990s for policy preference, that is, for liberalism and conservatism on both economics and race.[5]

One last possibility is that this analysis still measures racial attitudes in
the wrong way, or that even if it does not, measuring those attitudes in a
different way would deny the commonality of an apparent new politics.
This is, once again, the possibility that it should be racial *feelings* rather
than racial policy preferences that were being registered in voting for public office, and thus that it is the interaction of welfare attitudes and racial
feelings that should really be examined. This proved not to be a particularly helpful perspective in the bivariate analyses of Chapter 3, but it is easy
enough to check on this possibility in a multivariate framework. The result
is once again negative.

By the 1990s, white ratings of blacks as a social group on the feeling
thermometer, when examined simultaneously with white preferences on
social welfare as an influence on Republican voting, no longer had any real
purchase, with any institution (Figure 4.11). As we have seen repeatedly,
welfare attitudes were strongly related to Republican voting for President,

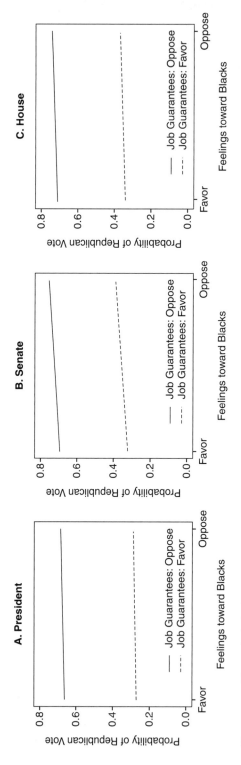

Figure 4.11 Economic Attitudes, Racial Feeling, and the Southern Republican Vote: The 1990s.

Senate, and House. As we can now see, racial feelings showed only the ti-niest hint of any relationship to that vote. Indeed, where racial *policies* had grown in their relationship to the vote for all three institutions, racial feel-ings had disappeared as a separable influence. Moreover, the pattern across institutions had become as close to identical as such data are likely to permit.

In the end, then, it was not just the social structure of the vote that con-verged across institutions in the 1990s; it was the ideological structure of that vote too. The change in social structure was the more dramatic. For thirty years beforehand, the interactions of social class and racial context had looked (and had been) different as between Congress and the presi-dency. In the 1990s, this ceased to be so. What ultimately appeared to eliminate an institutional difference, and bring the whole South into align-ment on what had once been the presidential and not the congressional pattern, was extensive, conscious racial redistricting after the 1990 census. At a stroke, the sociologically biracial districts were decimated. In the pro-cess, the need to build biracial electoral coalitions, the coalitions that had helped for so long in explaining why the influence of racial context did not change for Congress after the civil rights revolution, was sharply reduced. With it went that huge institutional difference in the impact of a politics of race.

Yet the change in ideological underpinnings was also substantial. By the 1960s, there was already a clear role for economic conservatism and an intermittent hint—harbingers—of a role for racial conservatism. In the 1990s these came together, similarly, for all three institutions, with a sharply strengthened role for economic conservatism and, this time, an in-disputable role for racial conservatism as well. In other words, like the eco-nomic South and the racial South, the ideological South too became a very different place. Once, within the lifetime of a goodly remnant of Southern politicians, economic ideology—attitudes toward public policy on social welfare—had been unrelated to partisan choice. At the same time, racial ideology—attitudes toward public policy on aid to blacks—had been in-versely related, with liberals going Republican and conservatives going Democratic.

As economic development and legal desegregation arrived, however, welfare attitudes came into alignment with partisan choice, and the old in-version between racial attitudes and party preference was destroyed. By the 1990s, the world had moved on additionally, such that economic conserva-tism and racial conservatism were both aligned with partisan choice in an impressive fashion. Neither set of policy attitudes appears to have been central to the original shift. Welfare attitudes lagged the class change in partisan attachment, and racial attitudes were unrelated to a changing racial context. Thereafter, however, both sets of policy attitudes augmented the impact of social change in major ways. Social structure had evolved as a partisan influence. Policy conflict had evolved as a partisan influence. And they had simultaneously converged across governmental institutions.

Afterword: One South or Two?

Our analysis of partisan change in the postwar South can be boiled down, so far, to a small set of summary assertions. Both economic development and legal desegregation, individually and together, were remaking the partisan character of Southern politics by the late 1960s. The impact of economic development had begun to arrive earlier. The impact of legal desegregation, when it came, was more insistent, more immediate, and more obvious. Once it became clear that the Republican Party would be on the growth side of the economic reorganization of Southern society—this required a complete partisan reversal—economic development became a partisan escalator for Southern Republicans. Once it became clear that the Democratic Party would be on the receiving end, overwhelmingly, of new black voters, racial desegregation became a countervailing brake, albeit more equivocal, on that same Republican progress.

Much of the literature of Southern politics, however, tells the same story in a related but clearly distinguishable fashion. Our approach treats economic development as the dominant engine for partisan change in the postwar South and legal desegregation as the more complex and conditional secondary influence, with their interaction effectively dictating the story of partisan change once both were let loose on the Southern political landscape. In the literature, by contrast, legal desegregation together with a politics of race is often the overwhelming influence on partisan change. And even when it is not, when it is merely the dominant influence as between two great social forces, economic development and a new politics of class usually serve as parallel reinforcements to the same result (see Lamis 1990, especially chaps. 2 and 3).

Either way, this literature then tends to introduce a third, major, separate, and distinct variable to mediate the partisan impact of social change. For this grand alternative, most authors adopt an analytic perspective that involves immersion in particular histories of regional life, rather than one drawn from the political science ordinarily used to study national politics.

What results is a focus on a distinction between the "Deep South" and the "Peripheral South" (the latter is also called the "Rim South" or the "Border South"), along with an insistence that this distinction matters. A fundamentally geographic variable, a kind of internal counterpart to the external distinction between South and non-South, thereby claims a central explanatory status.

Our approach provides little reason theoretically—and in truth, little room empirically—to expect an impact from this excursion into what is essentially cultural geography. Yet having introduced both economic development and legal desegregation into the analysis, and having examined them simultaneously, we are now in a position to address this third alternative as well. For V. O. Key, who did find this distinction helpful in eliciting sub-patterns to Southern politics, it was principally an epiphenomenon of race, that is, of racial concentration, the share of the total population contributed by black Southerners. For his disciples, this remained part of the equation, but the Deep South/Peripheral South distinction also acquired an overlay of regional culture (see Black and Black 2002, especially chaps. 2, 4, 9, and 10). The Deep South was viewed as closer to the core of "Southernness"; the Peripheral South was inevitably more distant, corrupted and compromised by proximity to Northern or Western cultural patterns.

The Deep South has traditionally comprised the states of Alabama, Georgia, Louisiana, Mississippi, and South Carolina, while the Peripheral South included Arkansas, Florida, North Carolina, Tennessee, Texas, and Virginia. Nothing in our analysis suggests any role for such a distinction. Yet that may be a result, so far, of failing to look for it. In any case, if the particular analysis remains undone here, its form is familiar, and the means for addressing it empirically are quite standard. This is a classic "container versus contents" assertion, and we should say a few words about the distinction:

- Geographic differences based on "contents" are those where two or more geographic areas differ by virtue of their social composition. The groups that contribute to this composition do not themselves differ additionally between one geographic unit and another. It is merely the *mix* that differs from unit to unit, creating a recognizable distinction between (among) the units as wholes.
- Differences based on the "container" feature the opposite situation: a dominant role for the geographic area. Social groups that live within the geographic unit may share some characteristics across

unit boundaries, but these are dominated, if not suppressed, by defining characteristics of the unit itself. Either a strong common culture or a sharply different historical trajectory is usually the explanation here.

Causal explanations that assert a relevant difference among the units in question, a difference that is not merely some compositional effect, are effectively asserting the importance of the container, of a geographic context. Otherwise there is no point—worse, there is real empirical confusion—in talking about, for example, the Deep South versus the Peripheral South. The usual way to pursue this distinction in the literature of Southern politics is to graph Republican progress onto maps that distinguish the Deep and Peripheral South. Lacking individual-level data, Key needed to proceed in this way, and what he squeezed from it remains impressive. His followers, proceeding in the same fashion, have been easily able to show that Republicans long did better in the Peripheral than in the Deep South, especially in voting for Congress.

If we were to proceed in the same fashion, we could quickly explain away this finding. Into the 1980s, the Peripheral South was distinguished from the Deep South in having far more white-collar congressional districts, and thus (in our analysis) far better Republican prospects. On the other hand, when the Deep South did generate white-collar districts, they tended to be captured by the Republicans, and when the Deep South finally enjoyed a white-collar surge in the 1990s, it experienced a Republican surge as well. Moreover, throughout this entire period, the Deep South was more black (less white), suggesting (again in our analysis) additional restraints on Republican opportunities. Indeed, out-migration by blacks and in-migration by whites actually caused this to be, if anything, more true as time passed, leading us to expect additionally repressed Republican gains in the Deep South until the racial reapportionments of the 1990s.

Yet what has distinguished our analysis so far, beyond a set of substantive conclusions, is a determined effort to escape anecdotal evidence, even in the form of mapped data with its great risk of ecological confusion, and to test assertions about the evolution of Southern politics through a complex dataset built around individual-level characteristics and behaviors but consciously including major aspects of political context. Accordingly, the first step in applying this dataset to the "Two Souths" argument involves comparing the *district demographics* of Republican success, stratified by location in the Peripheral or the Deep South, for the long period of the rise of a new Southern politics, the 1960s through the 1980s. When this is done, district demographics appear to eliminate the need for sub-regions in explaining partisan change.

The comparison is not perfect, since the Deep South lacked any substantial number of white-collar districts during this entire period. With fewer than five such congressional districts per decade, the behavior of a single district could move these percentages around in an extreme and idiosyncratic fashion. But for those districts that can be compared, that is, blue-collar districts which were more than 20 percent black or less than 20 percent black—districts that contributed more than three-quarters of the Southern total—the story is clear (Table 4.4). Republican success in parallel districts from the Peripheral South or the Deep South was effectively identical. There was no evident sub-regional contribution to the outcome at all.

This is still aggregate-level rather than individual-level exposition. Yet we are easily able to confront the alleged difference between Deep South and Peripheral South with individual-level data too. To repeat: both social class and racial composition do distinguish the two areas, with the Peripheral South being more white-collar in every decade, the Deep South being blacker in every period. The key question is whether the distinction between a geographic Peripheral South and a geographic Deep South makes these racial and class differences *work differently* in their impact on the rise of a Southern Republican Party; or whether the difference between Southern Republican prospects in the Deep versus Peripheral South is instead just a product of the differential distribution of these—more fundamental—racial and class differences.

A simple, reinforcing way to look for both sets of impacts, without

Table 4.4   The Distinctiveness of the Deep South? As an Influence on
Congressional Outcomes

Share of Congressional Districts Captured by Republicans, 1960s through 1980s

District Composition	Peripheral South	(N)	Deep South	(N)
>50% White-Collar, <20% Black	50%	(250)	**	**
>50% White-Collar, >20% Black	33%	(70)	**	**
<50% White-Collar, <20% Black	29%	(489)	29%	(86)
<50% White-Collar, >20% Black	16%	(295)	16%	(381)

**Fewer than five congressional districts per election during this period.

Table 4.5   The Distinctiveness of the Deep South? As an Influence on
Voting Behavior

Logistical Regression for Income Terciles, Racial Context, and a Deep
South Dummy on the Republican Vote, 1960s through 1980s

	House Contests		Senate Contests	
Income Tercile	0.75	0.73	0.39	0.39
	(0.14)	(0.14)	(0.13)	(0.13)
Percentage Black	−3.87	−4.54	−0.57	−0.66
	(0.44)	(0.52)	(0.41)	(0.46)
Deep South	—	0.40	—	0.06
		(0.15)		(0.15)
Constant	0.07	0.12	−0.41	−0.40
	(0.12)	(0.12)	(0.13)	(0.12)
Pseudo R^2	0.10	0.10	0.01	0.01
$-2l$ (LR)	1935.37	1928.55	1995.25	1995.07
N	1499	1499	1471	1471

the need to rely either on maps and their visual interpretation or on aggregation by congressional districts, is to run a logistical regression of the Republican vote on income terciles and racial contexts, once without a dummy for the Deep South and once with that dummy included. Table 4.5 does this for the same period, the three decades of the emergence of the new South. The coefficients in such logistical regressions are difficult to interpret in their own right, but that fact is not important here. The key point is merely that introducing a dummy variable for sub-region has almost zero effect on the relationship between Republican voting and either income tercile or racial context.

At bottom, then, a geographic distinction—the purported "Two Souths"—has nothing really to contribute: nothing to contribute to voting behavior for the House, and nothing to contribute to voting behavior for the Senate either.[6] In other words, the absence of much utility to a Deep South/Peripheral South division suggests that it is political change in the South as a whole that merits attention, rather than change within sub-regions. If there were any residual need for further evidence toward that argument, a final look at the comparative fates of those states classified as the Deep and the Peripheral South would certainly provide it.

At the time of the compromise of 1876, which restored the Southern

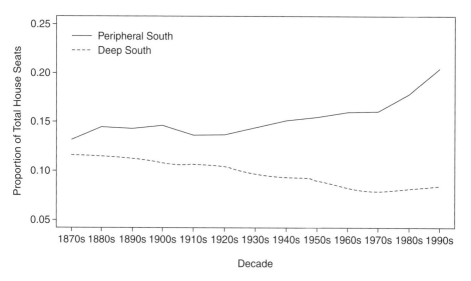

Figure 4.12   The External Consequence of the Deep South? Southern Sub-Regions in National Politics: Share of Total Membership in the House of Representatives.

Democracy while sending Southern Republicans into the wilderness, the Deep South and the Peripheral South were nearly equal in demographic consequence, with the Deep South claiming about 45 percent of the congressional seats from the Old Confederacy (Figure 4.12). The Deep South, however, began to decline with the census of 1900, and it was thereafter declining not just as a share of the Southern states but as a share of the nation as well. By contrast, the Peripheral South, already growing as a share of the Old Confederacy by 1900, actually began to grow as a share of the nation by the census of 1930, so that it was thereafter an increasing share both of the old South and of the world outside.

The Peripheral South began to grow even more explosively in the 1970s, a development captured by the census of 1980, as a share both of the region and of the nation. As a result, by 2000, Texas and Florida together were larger than the entire Deep South, and Texas plus North Carolina were actually equivalent to it. One can thus say four (pungent) things about this: The Peripheral South had become a huge and still-growing part of the region and the nation. The Deep South had long since gone into demographic, and consequent political, decline. The Peripheral South had thus *become* "the South" more generally. The Deep South had become a residual.

5

Social Forces and
Partisan Politicians

THE ANALYSIS TO this point has been one of structural shifts and partisan change. Economic development brought a new politics of social class to the American South. Legal desegregation brought a refreshed but altered politics of racial identity. And their interaction drove the partisan result. To the extent that this grand relationship has been mediated by explicitly political influences, these were contributed not by elite actors and their machinations, but by the organizational structure of governmental institutions. Social change has thus been joined by institutional structure to tell the story of partisan reconstitution. As such, this has remained a story of political change almost without human agency.

The story is thereby incomplete. At a minimum, there had to be a set of specialized political actors to register the impact of a new politics of class and a revised politics of race. Given the nature of the old Southern politics, these actors were destined to be Republican challengers and Democratic incumbents, plus their respective party leaderships. In part, we have kept them out of the story so far in order to keep sweeping social changes, the real causal agents, in the foreground of the analysis. Yet these specialized partisan elites were to do much more than merely register political outcomes; they *channeled* the effects of social change in major ways. It is to this process that we must now turn.

For there were other organized intermediaries between grand social forces and partisan electoral outcomes, in the form of political parties—a smothering Democratic and a nascent Republican party—and their denizens were hardly sleepwalking through history. They may not have pictured themselves as "critical buffers" between "social forces" and "partisan reconstitution." But they did see changes on the ground and they did respond aggressively, either to cope with or to benefit from those changes. In the process, they contributed—they became—major explanations for both the pace and the specifics by which structural shifts elicited partisan change. No individual actor in postwar Southern politics, nor any collection of them, really, could have been expected to stem the tide of economic development and legal desegregation. But the extent to which they could channel that tide would nevertheless prove impressive.

Some of this channeling was still a fairly direct reflection of the social forces driving the larger partisan story. In particular, much of the patterning in the appearance of Republican challengers could itself be reduced to the impact of major social changes, of economic development and legal desegregation as they created an opportunity structure for a nascent Republican leadership. More of this channeling was a reflection of the familiar disabilities inherited by these challengers—or, rather, of the familiar advantages retained by incumbents. Two generations of long-lived Southern Democratic officeholders did not intend to go quietly in the face of social change. They were to find themselves with the ability to realize their wishes for a very long time.

A second aspect of the collective response of these Democratic officeholders, however, has been largely invisible. This is the distinction between locals and cosmopolitans as the vehicles for this fight, a distinction that brought with it a clear strategic difference. Those who were born and bred in the relevant district appeared to concentrate on embodying its social characteristics; those who were attracted into the relevant district appeared to concentrate on representing its policy options instead. Not only were locals notably more successful than cosmopolitans in repressing a Republican vote overall; they also shaped the internal composition of that vote in notably different ways.

Both effects came as a surprise to us: this was not what the literature of Southern politics would have led us to expect. Nevertheless, a counterpart analysis could be extended all the way to the presidency. Southern Democrats as presidential candidates had many parallels to local Democrats as congressional contenders, and Northern Democrats to congressional cosmopolitans. Again, the locals fared better overall. Again, they also shaped the internal composition of the vote differently. Yet here, with the presidency, there was to be a second surprise. Both Southern Democrats and

Northern Democrats had major "coattails": they managed to project the differences between themselves as down-ticket influences on the congressional vote.

After allowing all these political actors back into the analysis, however, it will be necessary to close once again with an afterword, one that addresses the more usual way of telling the same story. This time, a final side-trip investigates the role of third-party candidates, the set of elite intermediaries who do receive considerable attention in the relevant literature. These individuals are often alleged to be human "bridges" between one political party and another, and thus between one political situation and another, and therefore ultimately between one political order and another. In the postwar South, Strom Thurmond in 1948 and George Wallace in 1968 stand forth dramatically as candidates for this role. A framework beginning with economic development and legal desegregation, once it has been supplemented with a more systematic picture of political elites in a changing South, will instead make them look not like bridges but like "dead ends."

The Provision of Challengers and the Resistance of Incumbents

In a longtime one-party region, where Democratic incumbents were omnipresent and where sporadic Republican candidacies had been generally hopeless outside of party strongholds left over from the days of the Civil War, the provision of fresh Republican candidates was obviously essential to capitalizing on any incipient voting potential, any putative partisan demand arising from underlying social change. Not surprisingly, then, the record of candidate provision is tightly entwined with the overall record of Republican successes. Changing social conditions helped to bring forth Republican challengers; Republican challengers were essential to harvest changing social conditions.

For the U.S. House of Representatives, there was only minimal provision of Republican candidates in the 1940s and 1950s, to go with a minimal Republican vote (Rohde 1991; Polsby 1997; Fenno 2000). Indeed, the party could manage an elite presence in only about 30 percent of all contests for the two decades at the opening of the postwar era (Figure 5.1). These were underpinned by reliable provision of candidates in the established areas of the Appalachian rim; by extension, they were additionally scarce elsewhere. In the 1950 election, for example, the one before Dwight

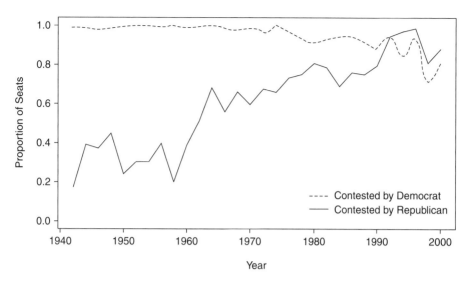

Figure 5.1   Change in the Provision of Republican Candidates: The House of Representatives, 1940–2000.

Eisenhower energized a Republican presidential vote in the South, his party could manage no House challengers at all in Arkansas, Georgia, Louisiana, and South Carolina. That was the situation in the old South.

There was then a sharp uptick in the addition of Republican candidates after 1960, in conjunction with an uptick in Republican voting by the general public. The year 1962 stands out in this regard, not just as the lead election in this uptick but also because it ran counter to the usual on-year, off-year dynamic, whereby the Republican Party attracted challengers in presidential years but shed them again in the following contest. This break was followed with a long, slow, but ineluctably upward trend of Republican candidacies from the 1960s through the 1980s, an extended period when Republicans could offer at least a token challenge in approximately two-thirds of all Southern House districts. Piece by piece, the new South was appearing. Then came a second substantial break, in the early 1990s, bringing the party close to saturation coverage (Connelly and Pitney 1994; Oleszek 1995).

Yet two separate processes were at work underneath the summary lines in Figure 5.1, and the first of these was explicitly political. As Figure 5.2 indicates, candidate recruitment was an entirely different exercise in the presence (or absence) of an incumbent officeholder. The overwhelming share of such incumbents were sitting Democrats, really up until the 1990s,

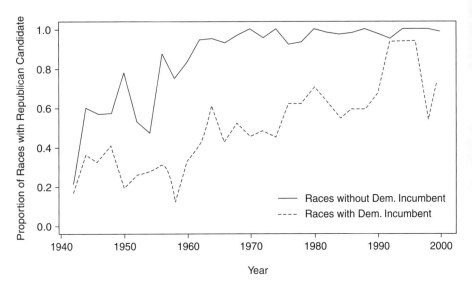

Figure 5.2   Democratic Incumbency and Republican Recruitment: The House, 1940–2000.

and thus their discouraging influence represents the other side of the drive to attract Republican challengers. Yet stated the other way around, from the early 1960s onward, whenever there was an open seat—whenever there was the *absence* of a sitting (Democratic) officeholder—there was likely to be a Republican challenger.

Open seats had always had somewhat greater attraction to incipient candidates, even in the era when Republican challenges were predictably hopeless. Yet after 1960, whenever there was an open seat, there was a Republican challenger for it. Open seats became, in effect, unfailing magnets. An uptick in Republican votes for the House in the 1960s did coincide with greater provision of Republican challengers even against incumbents. But into the 1970s, it was still possible to contest only about half of such incumbent races, and into the 1980s, only about 60 percent. From 1962, the counterpart number for open seats was effectively 100 percent.

Incumbency was an explicitly partisan influence on the prospect of electoral victory for any incipient challenger. Yet its power suggests that the main societal influences on the vote itself, namely economic development and legal desegregation, ought also to have shaped the appearance of challengers in those remaining districts (the vast majority) that did not offer open seats. Given the magnetic effect of open seats—whenever an incumbent was absent, a challenger appeared, regardless of the economic or racial composition of the district—a new politics of class or a revised politics of race could only have had further impacts on Republican recruitment in those districts that still had an incumbent officeholder. Yet unsurprisingly, social changes that were contributing a vastly changed voting potential in the South also directly affected the appearance of these Republican challengers.

In the case of economic development and a politics of social class, the coming of House districts with a white-collar majority became another powerful magnet for Republican challengers (Figure 5.3A). From 1962 onward, whenever a district acquired a white-collar majority, it was extremely likely to acquire a Republican congressional challenger. There were only two such districts in the 1950s, and they remained in short supply in the 1960s. Yet this near-saturation coverage was destined to serve the challengers well for the next twenty years, as the appearance of Republican candidates essentially rode up on the gradual growth of the white-collar South. By the time both white-collar districts and Republican candidacies were widespread, in the 1980s, the level of white-collar attraction actually dipped a bit. There were now some white-collar districts that also contained a large black population, an important counterpart repressor of Republican challenges. Yet the power of social class—of the class composition of congressional districts—was still a central part of the recruitment story for the House.

A more modest version of the same thing could be said of the racial composition of congressional districts (Figure 5.3B). For the 1940s and 1950s, the racial impact that did exist largely reflected the political order of the old South, where residual Republican strongholds were found in the less-black areas of the Appalachian fringe. Yet from the 1960s until the 1990s, this differential ease of candidate provision increasingly reflected the vast influx of new, black, Democratic voters in those more-black areas, with their inescapable (negative) implications for Republican prospects. As a result, less-black as opposed to more-black congressional districts continued to draw House candidates for their Southern Republican parties in what was a sharply changed electoral environment.

To treat the recruitment of challengers in this fashion, "recruited" more by a political situation or a social context than by personal choice or elite action, is not to dismiss the essential nature of their role. Such challengers provided a human presence for their party; they made social connections; they raised issues; above all, they campaigned. It is just that even more of

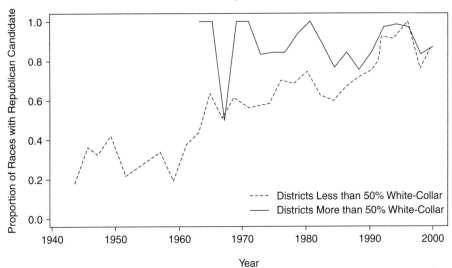

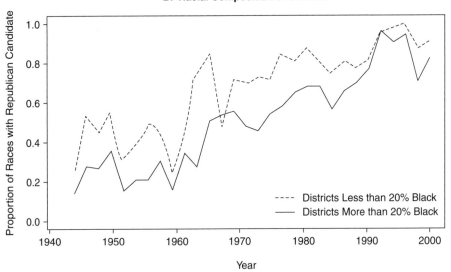

Figure 5.3   Republican Recruitment and District Characteristics: The House, 1940–2000.

the same could be said of incumbents (Jacobson and Kernell 1981; Fowler 1993). In other words, to treat the recruitment of challengers in this way *is* to emphasize the deterministic nature of their appearance:

- From the earliest point at which we can detect improved Republican prospects as a result of social change, open seats uniformly elicited Republican challengers.
- Among incumbent seats, white-collar majorities overwhelmingly elicited such challengers, and more-white constituencies provided disproportionate attraction.

Essentially the same story can be told for candidate provision to the U.S. Senate. We will present Senate figures duplicating House results only when the Senate differs in noteworthy ways *and* we are confident that the statistically choppier pictures from the Senate are not just artifacts of having too few contests divided in too many different ways. With the recruitment of Republican challengers, the Senate did begin further ahead, in part because it was easier to find 22 Senate candidates every six years than 100+ House counterparts every two (or 300+ every six!). This basic statistical fact gained social reinforcement from the fact that losing Senate contests were often regarded as more personally prestigious than losing House campaigns. The former were dignified, the latter merely idiosyncratic. Apart from this earlier start, however, the resulting trajectories were not impressively different.

The Senate could also provide more candidates earlier in incumbent districts than the House, yet this was really just another reflection of the greater prospect of recruitment to potentially hopeless seats in the Senate. For the Senate, there was a notable difference in the impact of emerging white-collar constituencies, because there simply were no Southern states with white-collar majorities until the 1980s, by which time the Republican Party had already achieved parity in candidate provision. Otherwise, exactly the same things could be said about the racial composition of Senate districts, that is, Southern states. Whiter states were easier, and drew Republican challengers earlier; blacker states were tougher, and elicited Republican challengers relatively late.

From one side, then, the *value* of candidate provision remained inestimable. An explicitly political situation, in the presence or absence of a Democratic incumbent, plus social change—economic development reliably pushing one way, racial desegregation usually pushing the other—

were the main engines eliciting Republican challengers, whatever these individuals believed their own motivations to be. Yet for a very long time, a
definitional condition also remained true: that social change could not result in partisan shifts unless and until there was an actual Republican challenger. That this elementary fact merits emphasis is one more measure of
how desperate the situation of the regional Republican Party was in the
immediate postwar years.

From the other side, however, the *power* of actual incumbency remained
immense, even in the presence of explicit challenges, even in the face of
sweeping social change. Incumbents—Democratic incumbents until very
late in the day—repressed challengers by their very presence. When they
failed to repress them, they beat them with monotonous regularity. Economic development might be a relentless Republican escalator; racial desegregation might be a highly conditional Democratic brake. Nevertheless,
both could be reduced in their impact on the vote, and neutralized in their
impact on the outcome, by the simple presence of an incumbent officeholder, at least until the 1990s (Rohde 1991; Rae 1994; Hood, Kidd, and
Morris 1999).

Probably the simplest way to put this entire picture back together is just
to turn the preceding portrait around. Rather than looking at the key intermediary result, voting behavior stratified by candidate provision and incumbency status, this approach looks at the ultimate outcome instead—at
wins and losses stratified in the same way. Figure 5.4 does this for the
House, and Figure 5.5 for the Senate. In the process, the distribution of
elections among categories, the evolution of categories across time, and the
Republican success rate within these contests all emerge as important facets of the resulting picture.

Many things stand in sharper relief when this is done, and the most obvious is not necessarily inconsequential for that fact. Obviously, when there
was no Republican candidate, there could be no Republican winner. Likewise, though it hardly merits mentioning in the early years, there could be
no Republican *loser* when there was no Democratic candidate. Yet the related point in Figure 5.4 is the sharp drop in the number of Southern congressional districts without a Republican candidate after the 1950s, and its
nosedive in the 1990s. Conversely, the number of districts without a Democratic candidate stepped up once this process was under way, after the
1960s, and stepped up again in the 1990s—when there were more empty
districts among Democrats than among Republicans.

On the other hand, when the focus is the share of Republican winners,

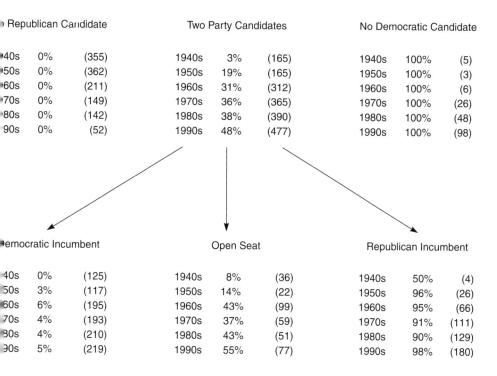

Republican Candidate			Two Party Candidates			No Democratic Candidate		
40s	0%	(355)	1940s	3%	(165)	1940s	100%	(5)
50s	0%	(362)	1950s	19%	(165)	1950s	100%	(3)
60s	0%	(211)	1960s	31%	(312)	1960s	100%	(6)
70s	0%	(149)	1970s	36%	(365)	1970s	100%	(26)
80s	0%	(142)	1980s	38%	(390)	1980s	100%	(48)
90s	0%	(52)	1990s	48%	(477)	1990s	100%	(98)

Democratic Incumbent			Open Seat			Republican Incumbent		
40s	0%	(125)	1940s	8%	(36)	1940s	50%	(4)
50s	3%	(117)	1950s	14%	(22)	1950s	96%	(26)
60s	6%	(195)	1960s	43%	(99)	1960s	95%	(66)
70s	4%	(193)	1970s	37%	(59)	1970s	91%	(111)
80s	4%	(210)	1980s	43%	(51)	1980s	90%	(129)
90s	5%	(219)	1990s	55%	(77)	1990s	98%	(180)

Figure 5.4   The Power of Incumbency: The House. Note: percentages are the share of contests won by the Republican; numbers in parentheses are the total number of contests.

the larger story occurs in those districts that did possess candidates from both parties. In the 1950s, Republicans were already showing some gains in these districts, but from a miserable base. Much of this was merely a return to the pre–New Deal situation. In the 1960s, however, their share of wins stepped up sharply, even as the share of contested seats almost doubled, and it continued upward in every decade thereafter. The Republican escalator had obviously begun to move.

Nevertheless, whenever there was a Democratic incumbent in these districts, from the 1940s to the 1990s and without interruption, the district *stayed Democratic*. For the Republicans, the only redeeming factor in this was that the same had become true for them by the 1950s—whenever they possessed an incumbent, that individual won too—so the crucial fact was that the number of such incumbents began to rise for the Republican Party as the increased wins of the 1960s were reflected in increased Republican incumbencies thereafter.

Accordingly, once districts attained both Democratic and Republican congressional candidates, most further combat was focused in those districts which had open seats. That is to say, the social forces that were driving the larger story were overwhelmingly likely to be registered in seats with two major-party candidates where an incumbent did not run for reelection. For these seats, the open seats among two-party candidates in Figure 5.4, the jump for the Republicans really did occur in the 1960s, in tandem with an expanded vote, and stayed around 40 percent until a second, lesser jump occurred in the 1990s, when the Republican majority arrived.

Nevertheless, the dominant economic dynamic could still break through in the ultimate sense of wins and losses only when Democratic incumbents removed themselves from the contest—and an established generation of senior Southern congressmen managed to live a very long time in such an environment. As time wore on, some of these retirements were surely themselves motivated by the prospect of increasingly vigorous Republican challenges. Yet incumbent Democratic Congressmen, most especially, remained the great firewall against the Republican surge.

Figure 5.5 recasts the same record of wins and losses for the Senate, again with the distribution of elections among categories, the evolution of categories across time, and the Republican success rate within these contests as important facets of the resulting picture. The overall story of incumbency does look much the same for the Senate as it did for the House. That is, the same overall impacts appear, apparently colored by the somewhat greater contribution of individual Senate contests to the aggregate outcome.

Districts without a Republican candidate were of course never won, but the important point remains that they were extremely common in the 1940s and 1950s, sharply reduced in the 1960s and 1970s, and effectively eliminated in the 1980s and 1990s. Likewise, districts without a Democratic candidate were always won, although here, there is a difference from the House: only in the 1980s, and then only twice, were there Senate elections that lacked a Democratic candidate, so that this effect, at least as of 2000, has never been consequential.

What was and is consequential for both bodies was the fate of those districts with both Democratic and Republican nominees. The jump to Republican victories in these seats was delayed in the case of the Senate, appearing as a flicker in the 1960s and gaining full strength only in the 1970s. Once it did, however, these districts became the story of Republican progress in Southern Senate seats. Moreover, as with the situation in the House, despite the jump in the Republican vote during the 1960s, Demo-

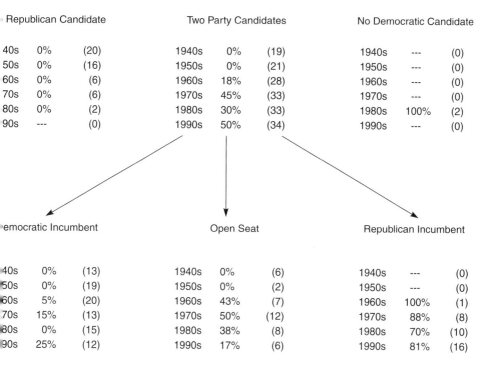

Republican Candidate			Two Party Candidates			No Democratic Candidate		
40s	0%	(20)	1940s	0%	(19)	1940s	---	(0)
50s	0%	(16)	1950s	0%	(21)	1950s	---	(0)
60s	0%	(6)	1960s	18%	(28)	1960s	---	(0)
70s	0%	(6)	1970s	45%	(33)	1970s	---	(0)
80s	0%	(2)	1980s	30%	(33)	1980s	100%	(2)
90s	---	(0)	1990s	50%	(34)	1990s	---	(0)

Democratic Incumbent			Open Seat			Republican Incumbent		
40s	0%	(13)	1940s	0%	(6)	1940s	---	(0)
50s	0%	(19)	1950s	0%	(2)	1950s	---	(0)
60s	5%	(20)	1960s	43%	(7)	1960s	100%	(1)
70s	15%	(13)	1970s	50%	(12)	1970s	88%	(8)
80s	0%	(15)	1980s	38%	(8)	1980s	70%	(10)
90s	25%	(12)	1990s	17%	(6)	1990s	81%	(16)

Figure 5.5   The Power of Incumbency: The Senate. Note: percentages are the share of contests won by the Republican; numbers in parentheses are the total number of contests.

cratic and Republican incumbents in the Senate were still disproportionately likely to be re-elected, so that the core of this story inhered in open seats, those without an incumbent from either party.

On the other hand, unlike the situation in the House, once the Republicans began their rise in Senate elections, they did gain the potential to knock off the occasional Democratic incumbent. The 1970s and 1990s were particularly kind in this regard. Likewise, and again unlike the House, Republicans could not be sure of holding all of their own incumbents. They did give a few back as time passed, once they had some to surrender. These differences are probably a testament to the importance of individual candidacies within a subset of contests subject to the peculiar concerns of a particular year.

Nevertheless, the main plot line still inheres in those open seats, and there, the Republican line of success began earlier, in the 1960s, and rode up not so much on an increase in the share of such seats captured, as just on the increase in the number of such seats available. Only in the 1990s, as Republicans began themselves to hold an equal share of Southern Senate seats—and thus perhaps had harvested their own most serious prospects—did the share of open seats being picked off by Republican challengers decline again. By then, on the other hand, there were more incumbent Republican than incumbent Democratic Senators from the South as a whole.

What also can be glimpsed from within these figures, but cannot be captured in data as crude as wins and losses per se, is the way that the coming of changed social conditions, capped by the appearance of Republican challengers, could change the calculations of incumbent Democrats. In the old South, an initial contest, sometimes with one serious challenge thereafter, determined the fate of House and Senate seats for the lifetime of many incumbents. In the postwar years, however, what was once effectively an entitlement became a situation demanding some campaign activity and then a situation threatening a real contest, potentially including the ultimate risk.

Although we have no interview data from fifty years of incumbent decisions, regarding the decision to stand for re-election or not, it is possible to know *how* an incumbency was terminated, that is, by defeat, by retirement, or by death. And here the Senate, with its small number of seats yielding statistical difficulties in many analyses, does make it easier to do the total calculation, while the ability to aggregate by decade removes some of the year-by-year annoyance of Senate numbers (Figure 5.6).

What this Senate calculation reveals is the shift from a world of overwhelming Democratic incumbency, where incumbents were largely successful in repressing even the appearance of Republican challengers, to one of widespread Republican insurgency—where challengers were still not generally successful in overthrowing those incumbents, but were now reliably willing to push them. What stands out is the sea change in the means of *terminating* an incumbency:

- In the 1940s and 1950s, the main route by which a Senate incumbent left the institution was death. Given the power of incumbency and without electoral challenge, there was little reason to leave under your own power. Few did.
- In the 1960s and 1970s, the main route to leaving the Senate was retirement. Incumbency was still a source of security—deaths still outnumbered defeats—but aging officeholders did have to face the prospect of electoral contests.
- In the 1980s and 1990s, the prospect of actual defeats finally arrived. Deaths had become an accidental factor, and departing Sena-

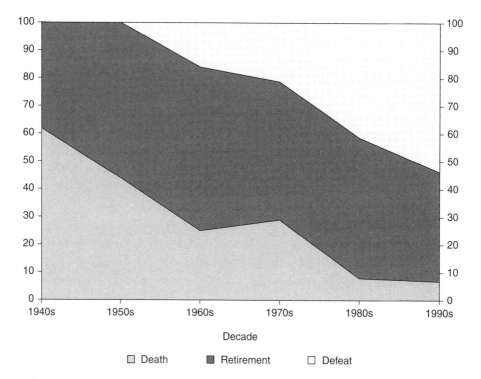

Figure 5.6   Exit Routes for Incumbent Senators, 1940s through 1990s.

tors either retired of their own free will or were put out to pasture by the competition.

"Local" Democrats as a Barrier to Change

Outside the South, the conventional way to carry such an analysis further would be to move on and divide the challengers—Republican challengers, in our story, for a very long time—according to what is now widely recognized as "candidate quality" (Jacobson and Kernell 1981; Jacobson 1987, 1990). As social change altered the character of electoral districts, and/or as incumbents retired, the "out" party could expect to prosper in direct proportion to the quality of its challengers. Yet in the case of partisan change in the postwar South, this approach has little to offer. For in the case of the key measure of candidate quality, political experience—time spent in prior political office—Democrats had it, Republicans did not, and that was really all there was to say (Jacobson 1990, 46–48).

Republicans began with a candidate recruitment base among public officeholders that was effectively exiguous. When they nevertheless began to win, they did so initially at higher, not lower, levels. Into the 1990s, then, Republican challengers were of reliably lower "quality": they lacked officeholding experience, and they did not come up through the ranks. Candidate quality could neither be the means by which a serious Southern Republican Party came to be born, nor could it even, ordinarily, be expected to elaborate those social changes—most especially economic development—that did potentially constitute such a means. For the Republicans, a challenger was a challenger was a challenger.

Therefore, the story of intermediary elites and their strategies for the postwar South must focus instead on incumbent characteristics. And right from the start, these Democratic incumbents did offer a large and consequential, internal distinction. That is, not all incumbents were created equal, either in their impact on the total vote or in their impact on its internal composition. Yet among them, the key distinction proved to be an old and apparently outdated, rather than a contemporary and fashionable one: the difference between "locals" and "cosmopolitans." This is a distinction not so often connected up to electoral politicking; yet it proved to be highly consequential.

The notion was originally isolated and formalized by Robert K. Merton:

> The chief criterion for distinguishing the two is found in their *orientation* toward Rovere. The localite largely confines his interests to this community. Rovere is essentially his world. Devoting little thought or energy to the Great Society, he is preoccupied with local problems, to the virtual exclusion of the national and international scene. He is, strictly speaking, parochial.
>
> Contrariwise with the cosmopolitan type. He has some interest in Rovere and must of course maintain a minimum of relations within the community since he, too, exerts influence there. But he is also oriented significantly to the world outside Rovere, and regards himself as an integral part of that world. He resides in Rovere but lives in the Great Society. If the local type is parochial, the cosmopolitan is ecumenical. (Merton 1968, 447)

"Rovere" was a pseudonymous Northeastern city, but the translation is easily made to, say, the State of Georgia or the Seventh District of North Carolina:

All other differences between the local and cosmopolitan influentials seem to stem from their difference in basic orientation. The group-profiles indicate the tendency of local influentials to be devoted to localism: they are more likely to have lived in Rovere for a longer period, are profoundly interested in meeting many townspeople, do not wish to move from the town, are more likely to be interested in local politics, etc. Such items, which suggest great disparity between the two types of influentials, are our main concern in the following sections. There we will find that the difference in basic orientation is bound up with a variety of other differences: (1) in the structure of social relations to which each type is implicated; (2) in the roads they have travelled to their present positions in the influence-structure; (3) in the utilization of their present status for the exercise of interpersonal influence; and (4) in their communications behavior. (Merton 1968, 448–449)

For our purposes, the Mertonian formulation has the dual advantages of being easily carried both from place to place and from institution to institution, as well as allowing application in a manner that is not a direct epiphenomenon of either the social changes that were sweeping the postwar South or the partisan changes that followed from them. For Congress, this implied translation into a pair of simple indicators. We classified all Democratic candidates for the House (or the Senate) between 1952 and 2000 as to: (1) whether they were born inside or outside the state from which they eventually ran for office; and (2) whether they were educated inside or outside the state from which they subsequently ran. Those who were both born and educated in the state where they pursued a political career were classified as "locals." All others became "cosmopolitans."[1]

With that as background, the tasks of the two sets of regional party leaders were inherently different during the postwar years in the South, at least up until the 1990s. Republican leaders needed to find candidates, period. The additional characteristics of these individuals, for the longest time, were quite secondary to the presence of a Republican *body*, available to capitalize upon social changes tending in a Republican direction. Democratic leaders, by contrast, though they would not necessarily have articulated this as their role, needed to find and support candidates who were best able to prevent social change from replacing incumbent Democratic officeholders with emergent Republican challengers.

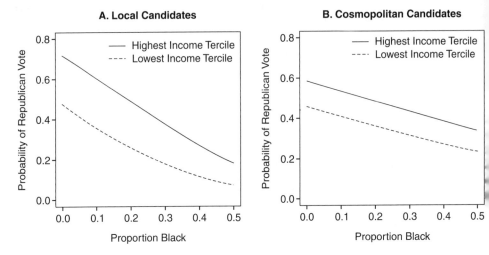

Figure 5.7   Locals, Cosmopolitans, and the Democratic Resistance: The House, 1960s through 1980s.

In the 1950s, in truth, the job of these Democratic Party leaders was still just to manage any internal competition over what was likely to be a sure ultimate election. By the 1990s, their hold on the formerly solid South had been broken, and the ability to make this recruitment choice between local and cosmopolitan candidates would itself be fading fast. But for the 1960s through the 1980s, the crucial period when a new Southern politics was being created, the job of Democratic Party leaders was in fact—whether or not they so conceived it—to deal with social changes that would otherwise facilitate Republican gains. And the ability to find (and nominate) local rather than cosmopolitan candidates was to be central to their success.

Figure 5.7 looks at the contribution of cosmopolitan versus local Democratic candidates to the success of this effort with regard to the House. Figure 5.7A is taken from a logistic regression of the Republican vote among white Southerners on their social class and racial context for House contests in the period 1962–1990, for all contested races that possessed a "local" Democratic candidate. Figure 5.7B is the same regression for all those that featured a "cosmopolitan" Democrat instead. Both are converted to percentage distributions for easy interpretation.[2] What emerges is simple, striking, and inescapable:

- For thirty years across the entire South, local candidates were vastly more successful at repressing an emergent Republican vote than their cosmopolitan counterparts. The Republican vote among low-income Southerners—the area under the low-income line—was substantially larger when there was a cosmopolitan rather than a local Democratic candidate. And the same could be said of the Republican vote among high-income Southerners. In other words, locals retained a huge vote that cosmopolitans gave away.

• Moreover, the class difference among House voters—the distance between the top and bottom income lines—was greater across the board for local candidates than for their cosmopolitan counterparts. That is, local Democratic candidates probably emphasized, but certainly benefited from, a class cut to politics to a considerably greater degree than cosmopolitan candidates. And since they were already doing better overall, the damage to Republican prospects which this represented among lower-income whites was especially noteworthy.

• Perhaps surprisingly, the race difference among House voters—the comparative slope of the two lines of racial context—was likewise greater for local candidates than for cosmopolitans. As with class, so with race: local candidates reflected this demographic characteristic of their districts more than cosmopolitans. Yet because these locals were already doing better overall by the time a district was 10 percent black, the sharper fall-off among white voters as districts got blacker was, again, a particular injury to potential Republican gains.

• Finally, the sole exception to all of this—the only further twist requiring comment—came among high-income voters in the very whitest areas, where cosmopolitan Democrats actually outpolled their local counterparts. Otherwise, local Democrats outperformed their cosmopolitan colleagues across the board, a dominating performance and a serious additional brake on Republican prospects.

Why should this be so? The obvious hypothesis is that local candidates simply represented a better overall "fit" to their respective districts.[3] But why should local candidates for the House fare so *differentially* better than cosmopolitan candidates at holding back an incipient Republican tide? That is, why should they offer a further patterning within their overall superiority? One powerful suggestion can be gleaned by regressing the Republican vote against local versus cosmopolitan Democratic candidates not just on social class and racial context, but also on the two main policy attitudes that ought logically to be associated with them, namely social welfare and civil rights.

Figure 5.8 does this, again using logistic regression converted into prob-

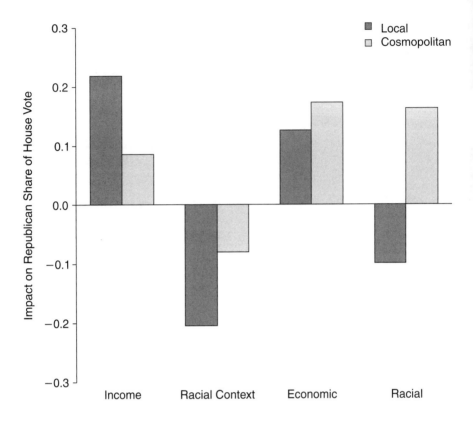

Figure 5.8   What Gets Primed by House Candidates? Demographics versus Ideology, 1960s through 1980s.

abilities. In the translation of logit coefficients into this visual depiction, the impact of income is estimated for a 0 to 1 shift from bottom to top tercile; for racial context, for a 0 to 1 shift from 10 percent to 30 percent black; and for economic and racial attitudes, for a 0 to 1 shift from liberal to conservative. When this is done, one huge difference among the impacts of these variables stands out. The vote for and against local Democratic candidates is more powerfully responsive to the social backgrounds of the voters. The vote for and against cosmopolitan Democratic candidates, by contrast, is more powerfully responsive to the policy preferences of those voters. That is to say:

- The vote in contests featuring a local Democrat was more tightly re-lated to the income tercile of the voter than was the vote in contests featuring a cosmopolitan Democrat, by a factor of two to one. And the same can be said for the racial context of the voter. Apparently,

local Democratic candidates were better at representing the *social background* of their constituencies. It is as if the local candidate's theme was "Vote for me because I am one of you."
- Conversely, the vote for contests featuring a cosmopolitan Democrat was more tightly tied to the economic *ideology* of the voters than was the vote in contests featuring a local Democrat. And the same can be said for racial ideology. Indeed, with the latter measure, local Democrats actually managed to break the relationship with liberalism or conservatism entirely, doing modestly better among those who were racial conservatives. It is as if the cosmopolitan theme was "Vote for me because I stand for what you want."[4]

In any case, the implication for change over time—for partisan change—in this differential impact of locals versus cosmopolitans as Democratic candidates proved additionally relentless. Gradually but ineluctably, locals were being replaced by cosmopolitans among Democratic candidates across the postwar era, and that effect itself removed an intermediary barrier to Republican progress (Table 5.1). In the House of the 1950s, genuine cosmopolitans were in short supply, while locals were the story everywhere. During the period when the new South came into being, however, from the 1960s through the 1980s, this balance shifted gradually but inexorably in the direction of the cosmopolitans.

The Senate would tell roughly the same story as the House during these crucial decades, with one further twist of immense incipient potential. Yet this is also an instance where the "small *N* problem" of Senate contests—an average of seven contests per election, often featuring only two cosmopolitan contenders, within what was a national and not a regional sample—would make it difficult to interpret this result on its own, that is, before the presidential results had been added to the composite record. Accordingly,

Table 5.1   The Decline of Local Candidates: The House, 1950s through 1990s

Share of Seats by Candidate Type			
Decade	% Locals	% Cosmopolitans	[N]
1950s	77	23	501
1960s	71	29	466
1970s	65	35	433
1980s	60	40	509
1990s	53	47	511

we shall defer attention to the cosmopolitan/local division in the Senate until the impact of that division has been investigated for the presidency as well as the House. This will provide either a common or a divergent pair of institutional patterns with which to compare Senate results.

"Southern Democrats" as a Barrier to Change

Those are impressive contributions from two different types of incumbent Democrat to the impact of social forces on partisan change. But is it possible that these empirical contributions seem even more impressive, conceptually, because the distinction is not usually cast in this way? If we had instead begun by referring to the locals as "Southern Democrats" and the cosmopolitans as "National Democrats," the resulting difference in their impact on partisan change might have seemed less striking. And indeed, we shall translate these notions to presidential candidates in terms even more closely analogous to that usage.

In extending this analysis to the presidency, there is little point in a mechanical transfer. House nominations guaranteed that the ultimate nominee would, at a minimum, reside within the district in question. Presidential nominations gave no such guarantee. They were never necessarily rooted in Southern districts, Southern states, or even the South as a region. The candidate was imposed instead through a national struggle, the bulk of which was guaranteed to occur outside the South. Moreover, candidates who could manufacture sufficient appeal to mount a successful national campaign were very unlikely to be true parochials—born in the region, educated in the region. By our measure, Lyndon Johnson, the Democratic nominee in 1964, would still qualify as a local Southern candidate. No one after him would—not Jimmy Carter nor Bill Clinton.

On the other hand, it is less necessary to extend the analysis in this formulaic way because the relevant analogy is so easy to recognize. It requires no careful delineation of a local versus cosmopolitan sociology to isolate Southern Democrats and Northern Democrats as nominees for President. And this is indeed the relevant difference. In analogous terms, Southern Democrats were presidential nominees who had acquired their political careers in the states of the Old Confederacy; Northern Democrats were those who had not. Indeed, Southern Democrats as presidential nominees were often justified—by their supporters or, of course, by themselves—as bringing a local attachment to the American South as one of their prime assets for a general election campaign. Northern Democrats, again by definition, brought no such attachment, despite their occasionally tortuous attempts to connect with purportedly "Southern" values.

Either way, the key measure with regard to national public office was just whether a candidate had the appropriate regional background or not. Southern Democrats met this test; Northern Democrats failed it. By those standards, it is easy to regress the white vote for Republican presidential nominees on income terciles and racial contexts for elections during these same transitional decades, the 1960s through the 1980s. Figure 5.9A1 does this for all years when Southern candidates secured the Democratic nomination for President. Figure 5.9A2 does the same for Northern (non-Southern) candidates. When this is done, three developments stand out:

- Unsurprisingly, Southern Democrats ran better than Northern Democrats against the Republican candidate for President in the South. That is, they did a better job of repressing the overall Republican vote. But in fact, they ran better in all income terciles and in every racial context. The worst-performing sector for Southern Democratic candidates for President was still marginally better than the best-performing sector for Northern Democrats.
- Moreover, Southern Democratic candidates exaggerated the effect of social class by comparison to Northern Democrats. The distance between the bars showing a Republican vote for the upper versus the lower income terciles was evidently larger in the case of Southern Democratic than Northern Democratic candidates for President. In other words, Southern Democrats managed to prime class, in common with their "local" counterparts in contests for the House.
- By contrast, it was Northern Democratic candidates who exaggerated the impact of racial context. The slope of the lines showing a Republican vote for both upper and lower income terciles was evidently steeper in the case of Northern Democratic than Southern Democratic candidates for President. In other words, Northern Democrats managed to prime race, in a manner opposite to both cosmopolitan *and* local candidates for the House.

For purposes of comparison, Figure 5.9A uses the same time period as Figure 5.7 (and 5.11), the 1960s through the 1980s. Yet in the case of the presidency, it is worth worrying about whether this pools a different number of Southern and Northern Democrats, as indeed it does, while reach-

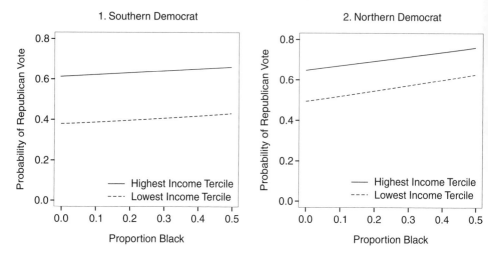

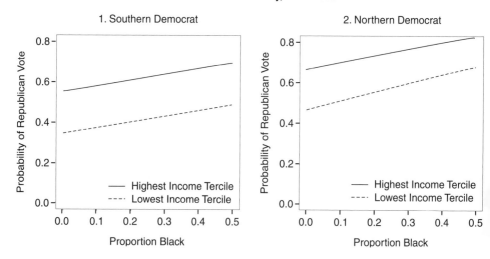

Figure 5.9   Southern Democrats, Northern Democrats, and the Democratic Resistance.

ing back to an era when the presidency was only on the cusp of change, as it might be argued to do. Accordingly, Figure 5.9B features an equal number of Southern and Northern candidates from the national Democratic Party, the ones nominated *after* the civil rights revolution, with partisan change well under way in the American South: Jimmy Carter in 1976, Carter in 1980, Bill Clinton in 1992, and Clinton in 1996, versus Hubert Humphrey in 1968, George McGovern in 1972, Walter Mondale in 1984, and Michael Dukakis in 1988.

Perhaps surprisingly, this change in period (and candidate composition) makes little difference to the main comparison. The list of candidate names, by itself, suggests that Southern Democrats remained better than Northern Democrats at repressing a Republican vote in the South, as indeed they did. More to the point, Southern Democrats still primed class more substantially than did Northern Democrats, at least among white Southern voters—just as Northern Democrats still primed race more than Southern Democrats. With the passage of time, it was no longer possible for Southern Democratic nominees to tamp down the impact of racial context as much as they had a few years earlier. But that was only a residual difference; the resulting pictures were still essentially interchangeable.

The same key analytic questions recur here as occurred with the House. Why should this local-cosmopolitan difference be so powerful overall? And especially, why should Southern Democratic candidates for the presidency fare so *differentially* better than Northern Democratic candidates at holding back an incipient Republican tide? The answers prove to be similar as well, with the exception of racial context, which Chapter 4 has shown to be a very different story for the House versus the presidency during these key transitional decades.

With the presidency rather than the House as a focus, the "locals"—Southern Democratic candidates for President—drew a vote more tightly tied to the social class of their voters than did the "cosmopolitans," the Northern Democratic candidates (Figure 5.10). This is a result precisely analogous to the comparison of local versus cosmopolitan aspirants for the House. In the same way, *Northern* Democratic candidates for President drew a vote more tightly tied to ideological preferences—on both economics and race—than did Southern Democratic candidates. This too is precisely analogous to the comparison of cosmopolitan versus local House candidates. So far, then, everything is effectively parallel.

The difference came in the comparative relationship to racial context, a difference growing out of the way in which Northern Democrats primed race. Recall that it was locals who primed the relationship to racial context with the House (see Figure 5.8). With the presidency, it was Northern Democrats, the "cosmopolitans," who primed this relationship. Yet they primed it in the opposite direction—whites in more-black areas being more Republican rather than more Democratic (Figure 5.10). Remarkably, not only did Southern Democratic candidates for President now show a weaker relationship to racial context than did their Northern counterparts, but with attitudes as well as demographics in the picture, that relationship was actually negative, if only very modestly so. That is, Southern Demo-

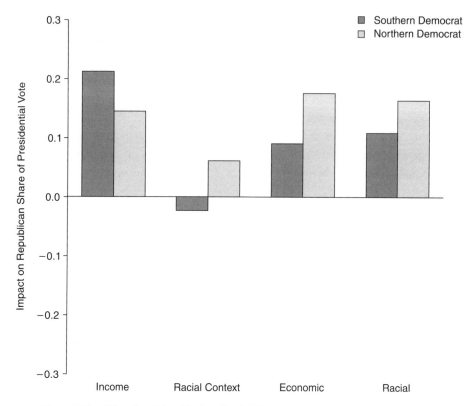

Figure 5.10   What Gets Primed by Presidential Candidates? Demographics versus Ideology, with a Twist, 1960s through 1980s.

crats still managed to draw a slight edge in their presidential vote from blacker areas, unlike the result for Northern Democratic nominees but echoing the result for both locals and cosmopolitans in the House.

These results for the presidency also make it possible to return to a parallel analysis for the Senate, in ways that now seem substantively interpretable rather than statistically idiosyncratic. Indeed, now the difference between the fortunes of local versus cosmopolitan Democratic candidates for Senate seats appears to reside largely in the way that locals follow the pattern typical of local candidates for the House, whereas cosmopolitans had already begun to follow the pattern typical of "cosmopolitan"—that is, Northern Democratic—candidates for the presidency. Figure 5.11 offers this parallel comparison, and produces another, equally remarkable disjunction between locals and cosmopolitans.

Once again, as with the House, local Democrats managed to magnify the class difference within their vote, the distance between the upper-income and lower-income lines. But this time, cosmopolitans were not just outdone by the locals. These Senate cosmopolitans actually saw this class difference collapse—and since locals and cosmopolitans were doing roughly as well among upper-income voters, the effect of this collapse on the lowest income tercile, where Republicans always did their worst, was devastating. We are looking at a 15-point gap gained by locals or lost by cosmopolitans in their resistance to Republican inroads within this bottom tercile (Figure 5.11).

At the same time, however, while local Democratic candidates for the Senate suggest the same racial story as local Democratic candidates for the House, cosmopolitan Democratic candidates for the Senate instead suggest the racial story characterizing Northern Democratic candidates for the presidency. Local Democratic candidates for Congress, both House and Senate, primed race inversely: whites in blacker areas were more likely to stay Democratic. The Senate relationship was not as strong in this regard, but it was clearly parallel. However, cosmopolitan Democratic candidates for the Senate primed race in the *opposite* direction, with whites in blacker areas voting more Republican—like the situation with Northern Democratic candidates for President, and utterly unlike the situation with cosmopolitan Democratic candidates for the House.

All three institutions would ultimately align their votes this way in the 1990s. Yet during the crucial transitional decades, Northern Democratic

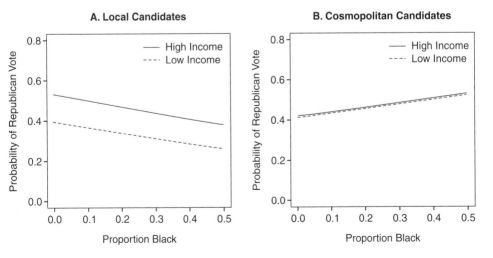

Figure 5.11 Locals, Cosmopolitans, and the Democratic Resistance: The Senate, 1960s through 1980s.

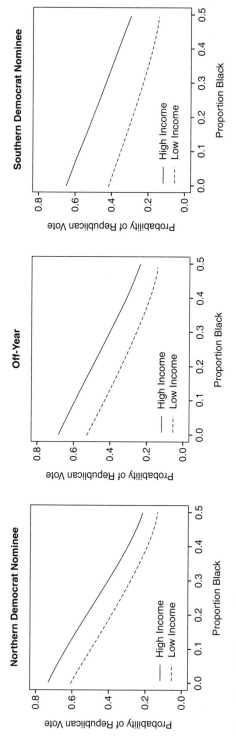

Figure 5.12   The Power of Coattails: The Presidency and the House, 1960s through 1980s.

candidates for President, the "cosmopolitans," achieved this pattern strongly, while Southern Democratic candidates showed only the slightest trace of it (Figure 5.9A). Local *and* cosmopolitan Democratic candidates for the House resisted that pattern, with the locals even more resistant but both sets of candidates clearly aligned in the opposite direction (Figure 5.7). And the Senate was split, with local candidates showing the same relationship to their voters as locals in the House, but cosmopolitan candidates showing the same relationship to their voters as cosmopolitan (Northern) Democratic candidates for *President* (Figure 5.11).

In the end, then, analogous applications of the notions of local versus cosmopolitan appear to offer every bit as much power with the presidency, the Senate, and the House. Yet this is an analytic realm with the potential for much more than formal comparison. For in fact, all House elections occur at one and the same time as the election of a President every four years. Accordingly, it is possible to look for the effect of Northern or Southern Democratic candidates for President on *House* elections in their years, just as it is possible to look at those off-year House elections that cannot be shaped directly by a (nonexistent) presidential ballot. Accordingly, the point of Figure 5.12 is to compare voting patterns for the House in years with a Southerner at the head of the ticket, years with a Northerner at the head, and, of course, years with neither—the off-years in congressional elections.

In some sense, the off-year elections, those without a presidential candidate at the head of the ticket, form a kind of congressional baseline, free of any direct contamination from a presidential contest. And in fact, the voting pattern in these off-year elections fell between on-year contests under a Southern Democratic nominee and on-year contests under a Northern Democrat candidate (Figure 5.12). That is, they primed class less than Southern-Democratic presidential years and more than Northern-Democratic presidential years, just as they primed race less than Northern-Democratic presidential years and more than Southern-Democratic counterparts.

One important methodological implication of these patterns should be noted. If off-year elections were merely compared with on-year elections, these pictures would look nearly identical, and there would be nothing further to explain. In the process, the possibility of presidential coattails would be dismissed. And this would clearly be wrong. Because Southern-Democratic presidential years and Northern-Democratic presidential years *flank* off-year congressional elections in the role of both social class and racial context, presidential years cannot be blended in a congressional comparison without destroying the institutional realities of voting behavior.

But then note the more important, further substantive finding: Southern-Democratic candidates for President managed to expand the influence of social class and reduce the influence of racial context *in congressional elections* during their on-year. Conversely, Northern-Democratic candidates for President managed to expand the influence of racial context and reduce the influence of social class, again in congressional elections, during their on-year. In other words, it was not just that Southern versus Northern Democratic nominees for President had this effect with regard to each other; they also spread the effect down-ticket.[5]

Political Elites as an Autonomous Influence

Social change was remaking partisan politics in the American South across almost the entire postwar era. Economic development was already doing so by the 1950s, though the effect would have been at best debatable in its own time. Likewise, racial desegregation was remaking partisan politics from the 1960s onward—and this time directly and obviously, by means of a vastly expanded black electorate, followed closely by white reactions to it. What differed additionally in the impact of racial desegregation as opposed to economic development was that the latter, for a full thirty years, had an institutionally specific impact: voting patterns for the presidency were changed sharply; voting patterns for Congress were hardly altered at all.

Chapters 2 through 4 have emphasized the power of these two great social changes, singly and together, separately or converging, by time-period and by institution. In contrast, this chapter has emphasized the role of political elites in mediating between these social forces and partisan change. Societal change on this scale could hardly escape having major political implications, and the scale of these reverberations was such that no political actor—no Congressman, no Senator, no President, no party leader—could hold them back. The most skillful could capitalize upon, or parry, the partisan implications of social change. But that was all.

On the other hand, regardless of the power of these social forces, political actors on the ground had to *try* to mediate their partisan impact. This was the role that history left them; it was the means by which they could hope to have individual influence. What this implied, however, was completely different as between two sets of local party leaders. For emergent

Republican elites, mediating the impact of social forces meant fostering candidacies in previously neglected areas, to capitalize on the underlying drift of social change. For entrenched Democratic elites, even more crucially, it meant husbanding incumbencies and searching out the best possible successors when an incumbent was not available, so as to channel those incipient forces.

Once again, both sets of efforts differed additionally by institution. The recruitment of challengers was a strategic imperative for Congress, a guaranteed outcome with the presidency. The resistance of incumbents was a strategic given with Congress, a practical irrelevance with the presidency. Regardless, the character of the result could be expected to matter in both institutions, albeit in a very different way:

- With the recruitment of challengers, the crucial consideration for Congress was merely having someone to undertake the role. All else was secondary, given a history of non-candidacy throughout the region, a lack of available political experience, and the power of emergent social forces. In turn, the combination of one key political factor, the presence or absence of a Democratic incumbent, plus the state of two changing social forces, economic development and legal desegregation, were largely sufficient to explain the presence or absence of these challengers.

- Given the guaranteed presence of a Republican candidate for President, by contrast, the more crucial consideration was the nature of his Democratic opponent. Long into the postwar era—still, indeed, as this is written—a Southern Democrat, an arguable "local," could count on repressing the Republican vote. Moreover, Southern Democrats appeared to do this by priming class, in contrast to Northern Democrats who specialized in priming race. Lines of conflict drawn on class made Democrats at least competitive. Lines of conflict drawn on race offered a clear (Republican) winner.

- Yet with only the slightest amount of translation, the same could actually be said of Congress. True locals, those born and educated in the state from which they ran, could likewise repress the vote for successfully recruited Republican challengers, and in an even more sophisticated fashion. On the other hand, for an institution more likely to reflect enduring partisan change—that is, less amenable to the electoral volatility associated with national contests—the job became increasingly difficult. Gradually but ineluctably, locals gave way to cosmopolitans as congressional candidates in the postwar South.[6]

In all these effects, there remained an element of individual autonomy. That is, the identity of individual candidates mattered, over and above the drift of social change. Better candidates could channel—not overcome, but channel—the impact of social forces on the congressional or presidential vote. Those with the best "fit" to Southern districts, Southern states, or the Southern region—the locals rather than the cosmopolitans—did better, but also differently, with the Southern electorate. In the process, they either repressed or facilitated Southern Republican progress. If they could not prevent a partisan change that would ultimately reshape all of American politics, they could (and did) channel it for a very long time. Or at least, they did so during the long and crucial period of the 1960s through the 1980s, when the old Southern politics was being replaced by something new.

Afterword: Third-Party Candidates as Bridges?

This way of proceeding, by emphasizing social change as the engine of partisan politics while categorizing the elites who responded by their relationship to a changing society, is intended to keep social forces, the real causal agents, in the foreground of the analysis. At the same time, these elite categories—challengers and incumbents, but especially locals and cosmopolitans—can be analyzed in a way that individual idiosyncrasies, real or only alleged, cannot. This way of proceeding simultaneously locates famous individuals from postwar Southern politics in the actual operating environment of their time, implicitly denying them the ability to substitute personal characteristics—good ads, a winning smile, the "killer instinct"—for more enduring influences on the outcomes of politics.

This is not to deny a veritable parade of distinctive individuals in the pantheon of postwar Southern politics, each with their champions for ostensibly autonomous—and critical—influence on the shape of partisan change. We think that an analysis built around social forces, institutional structures, and elite categories implicitly dismisses most of these individuals, and puts sharp limits on the possible impact of even the most consequential. So we are not inclined to spend time dismissing them further, one by one. Yet there was a real theoretical argument for the influence of a different subset of specific individuals in the literature of Southern politics.

As with the arguments about the "Two Souths" at the end of Chapter 4, our analysis does not leave much room for this effect either. But once more, perhaps this is because we have not tried to find such an effect.

In any case, the best alternative argument for a regionwide impact from individual actors is easily summarized. At its center are third-party—independent—candidates for President, who are said to serve as a "bridge" between the old and the new political orders. They are the ones who "crack" an established party system. That is, they provide established identifiers with an opening opportunity to vote for a specific candidate rather than having to go all the way to the *other* party, which they have never previously supported. Having done that, these independents can flame out, leaving incipient major-party change in their wake. Former party loyalists, having committed a first act of apostasy, can feel much freer to cross to the other party, their new party, once their independent candidate is gone from the scene.

This argument has two great incarnations in the postwar South, Strom Thurmond and George Wallace (see Frederickson 2001; Carter 1995). Thus some further attention to each of them, by way of what we regard as the relevant data, should make a contribution to the simple historical record. Yet this analysis is much more than informed antiquarianism, and not just because these men represent the major "evidence" for a theoretical argument about bridges to partisan change. Both are also putative major vehicles for the transforming influence of race. Accordingly, if that is an accurate categorization and if they *did* manage to perform this bridging role, then they might provide a backdoor route for augmenting the influence of race rather than class in the transformation of Southern politics.

The first version of this argument involves the Thurmond candidacy of 1948. Governor Strom Thurmond of South Carolina joined the bolt by rebellious Southern Democrats from the Democratic National Convention in that year, where a major civil rights plank in the national party platform broke open the race issue for the first time in the postwar era. Emerging as titular leader of these party-bolters, Thurmond, the "Dixiecrat" candidate for President in 1948, then served (in this line of argument) as a bridge to Dwight Eisenhower, the Republican candidate for President in 1952—where a substantial minority of Dixiecrat supporters lived happily ever after.

The generic argument is even more commonly made about the Wallace candidacy of 1968. Governor George Wallace of Alabama mounted an independent candidacy for President in that year, asserting that there was "not a dime's worth of difference" between the Republican and Democratic nominees, Richard Nixon and Hubert Humphrey, and gathering a variety of issues under his banner: public order, support for the war in Vietnam, traditional social values, and most especially, a defense of racial segregation. As the American Independent candidate for President in 1968, Wallace thus served (again, in this argument) as a bridge to Richard Nixon, the Republican candidate for President in 1972—and on into the future.

Despite the absence of individual-level data, the effect of racial context on (white) Southern voters remains clear enough in the Dixiecratic ballot of 1948. Governor Thurmond actually carried the more-black states in the South, while losing less-black counterparts—just as he carried the more-black districts within each group of states, while losing their less-black brethren. Moreover, for 1948, it is possible to know that this effect was not an ecological fallacy, since blacks were not enfranchised generally in the South and were particularly scarce as voters in these more-black areas. Even though we were forced to use only district aggregates, then, we are looking at an almost uniformly white electorate.

Summary statistics can be made to give a certain, further, surface plausibility to the Thurmond-as-bridge argument. In 1944, in the South, the Democrats carried 103 congressional districts for President, the Republicans exactly 2. In 1948, however, the Democrats held only 68 of their previous total; the Republicans crept up a bit—their apparent "natural" gain— to 8; and the Dixiecrats secured the remaining 29. And in 1952, Democrats were left with almost exactly the same number, winning 67 congressional districts, while Republicans picked up all 38 of the remainder.

Once the Dixiecrat outcome of 1948 is disaggregated and connected more precisely back to 1944 and forward to 1952, however, any evident contribution to the subsequent vote for Republican presidential candidates is not only invisible but, if anything, inverse. What is essential even to this ecological analysis is to trace the evolution of presidential outcomes by congressional district across the three elections of 1944, 1948, and 1952, as shown in Figure 5.13. For 1944 and 1948, this requires no further calculations: district boundaries were stable, even if voting outcomes were most definitely not.

The continued comparison to 1952 does fall across the 1950 census, in which five of the eleven Southern states gained or lost a seat, while Florida gained two. Accordingly, Figure 5.13 maintains comparability by imposing the same district boundaries on the 1952 vote as prevailed throughout the 1940s. In later years, after the Supreme Court imposed the "one man, one

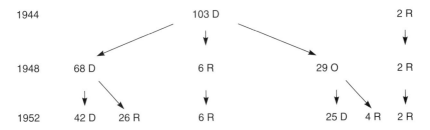

Congressional Districts Carried by
Democrats, Republicans, and Others

1944		103 D		2 R
1948	68 D	6 R	29 O	2 R
1952	42 D 26 R	6 R	25 D 4 R	2 R

Figure 5.13   The Role of the Dixiecrat Revolt.

vote" standard on intrastate apportionment, this would become a more difficult calculation. But for 1952, only one county (Orleans Parish in Louisiana) was subdivided, and that trivially, so that county election statistics
make these recalculations simple and straightforward.

This makes it easy to trace the evolution of district outcomes, and the
story of the move from 1944 to 1948 is indeed the story of the Dixiecrat
revolt. Democrat Harry Truman managed to lose a third of the congressional districts that Franklin Roosevelt had carried for President in 1944,
but this loss was overwhelmingly to the independent challenge by Strom
Thurmond and not to the major-party candidacy of Republican Thomas
Dewey. Yet the more important point is the fate of these districts in the
1952 election, theoretically "cracked" by the independent Thurmond and
therefore ready to go with Republican Dwight Eisenhower.

Of the 29 congressional districts that Governor Thurmond had pulled
away from the Democrats in 1948, those districts which had been carried
by President Franklin Roosevelt in 1944 and were carried by Thurmond
in 1948, the overwhelming majority—25 out of 29—returned to Democrat Adlai Stevenson in 1952. By contrast, of the 68 congressional districts that had ignored Thurmond and stayed with Harry Truman in 1948,
all of which had voted for Franklin Roosevelt in 1944, almost 40 percent abandoned Stevenson in 1952 and went to the Republican candidate,
Dwight Eisenhower. In other words, Dixiecratic districts remained overwhelmingly Democratic. Loyalist districts were more likely to go Republican. Thus if the bridging metaphor had any validity, it was Truman, not
Thurmond, who was the bridge to enhanced Republican prospects!

In our terms, this picture is fully consistent with the hypothesis that legal desegregation and a politics of race were a powerful stimulus to Demo-

cratic defection in 1948. Yet when there was instead a powerful Republican surge in 1952, one that did prove lasting, we already know that it was instead underpinned by economic development and a politics of class. Figure 5.13 is a picture much more consistent with this analysis. By 1952, in this picture, the former Thurmond districts—more-black but less-white-collar—were actually the *most* Democratic. It was some of the former Truman districts—the ones that were less-black but more-white-collar—that became more Republican.

Much the same story can be retold in 1968, but with better data (Figure 5.14). Once again, the presidential vote as measured by aggregate congressional outcomes would confirm that Governor George Wallace of Alabama, the nominee of his own American Independent Party, carried the more-black and lost the less-black states of the Old Confederacy, while carrying the more-black and losing the less-black districts within those states. And once again, the overall result can be made to yield superficial support for the Wallace-as-bridge argument. In 1968, the Republicans held almost exactly the same number of congressional districts as they had in 1964: 41 versus 44. Yet the Democrats hemorrhaged hugely, dropping from 61 to 16, while Wallace surged (from 0) to 48.

Presidential 1972 is useless for further comparison, since Richard Nixon, the Republican nominee, carried all but two Southern congressional districts for the Republican ticket. And 1976 features a possible, putative, Southern restoration, courtesy of Jimmy Carter as a Southern Democrat.

**Congressional Districts Carried by
Democrats, Republicans, and Others**

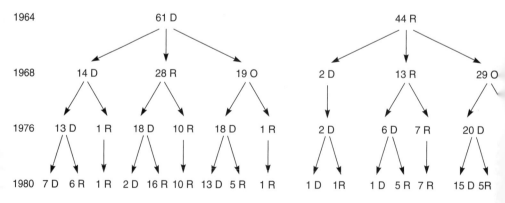

Figure 5.14   The Role of the Wallace Revolt.

But by 1980, when Carter was defeated even within the South by Ronald Reagan as the Republican candidate, the original distribution of wins and losses from a generation before—61 Democratic and 44 Republican districts in 1964—had been converted to an opposite majority: 39 Democratic and 66 Republican. Once more, those who were sufficiently determined to believe it could argue that George Wallace was the crucial wedge, shattering the old Democratic order.

Yet once again, disaggregation of these district outcomes along with more precise connections backward and forward in time give the lie to this argument, even before consideration of the individual-level data (Figure 5.14.) Note that even at the start of this reanalysis, the Wallace victories of 1968 were actually harder on the Republicans than on the Democrats. Wallace carried a much higher percentage of districts that had gone Republican in 1964 (66 percent) than he did of districts that had gone Democratic (31 percent). To use the bridge metaphor, more traffic was running away from (rather than toward) the Republicans, courtesy of the independent presidential candidacy of George Wallace.

Jimmy Carter, in his first run for the presidency in 1976, was then hard on Republican prospects all across the board, though he did pick up heavier majorities of those districts that had gone for Wallace (at 79 percent) than of those that had gone for Nixon (at 59 percent). Yet four years later, when Carter ran for re-election and his electoral magic was gone, the South had clearly evolved in a fashion utterly opposite to Wallace-as-bridge. In 1980, the Republicans were indeed in possession of nearly all those districts which they had carried in 1968, at 93 percent. And they were actually in possession of half, 50 percent, of those districts that the *Democrats* had held in that disastrous year. The only districts that retained a majority in Democratic hands were those that had gone for Wallace, where Democrats were still worth 58 percent of the total.

If the focus were not on the longer-term role of the Wallace candidacy, it would be possible to say the same thing in even more provocative fashion. First, the Republican candidate for President in 1968, Richard Nixon, did better in districts carried by Lyndon Johnson (the Democrat) in 1964 than by Barry Goldwater (the Republican): 46 percent versus 30 percent. In that sense, if anyone was a "bridge" to Republicanism in 1968, it was Johnson, not Goldwater. Likewise, if the focus were instead on the shape of the partisan world in the longer run, then Ronald Reagan, the Republican candidate for President in 1980, *still* did far better among districts carried by Richard Nixon in 1968 than in those carried by Barry Goldwater in 1964:

93 percent versus 61 percent. If there was a lasting impact from earlier Republican successes, it came by way of Nixon, not Goldwater—which is unsurprising if further Republicanism was to be built on class rather than race.

These district-level results are not, by themselves, as definitive for the Wallace adventure of 1968 as they were able to be for the Thurmond candidacy of 1948. By 1968, black Southerners constituted a significant minority of the electorate in most of these congressional districts, so that the record of wins and losses is no longer purely a white record. Moreover, the need to compare 1968 with 1980 does involve the translation of district lines across a national census that split more counties than its counterpart in 1952. For many grand and gross purposes, this still does not matter. Given the availability of voting statistics by cities within counties, only Florida presents a serious challenge to recalculations across this census divide, and because all that matters is the winner in a congressional district (rather than the vote percentages), we are reasonably confident of the Florida results. In any case, even in the face of these constraints, it is very hard to make Wallace a bridge to anywhere other than oblivion when his vote is embedded in real physical locations.

Yet by 1968, we do have individual-level data, which means that we are not dependent on aggregate outcomes, however decisive they may appear. Most fundamentally, this means that we can stratify individuals to find white voters only. And these voters, possessing actual congressional districts, do not require any district "translation." To cut to the chase: they tell the same story. The data are still not ideal, because they are not panel data: we cannot have the *same* white voters from 1964 through 1980. But we do know what the Democratic and Republican electorates looked like in previous and, especially, subsequent years, so that we can see whether the Wallace electorate of 1968 is even a plausible successor or precursor to either.

For 1968, we can ask both about racial context and about class background for individual white voters in the Southern states. Figure 5.15 is a multinomial logistic regression converted to a probability distribution, where the vote for the Democratic nominee, Hubert Humphrey, is used as the basis of both comparisons since the drift away from the Democrats is what is at issue here. In fact, the probability of voting Republican—the Nixon vote—looked almost exactly as it would for the entire 1960s and, for that matter, the 1970s: a modest edge for the Republicans in more-black

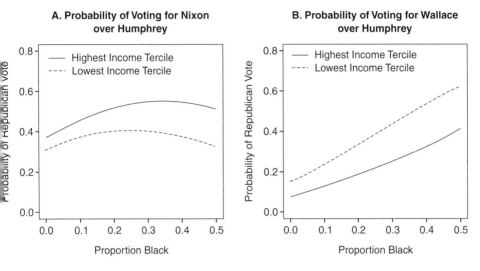

Figure 5.15   George Wallace as a Bridge to Nowhere.

districts, on top of a clear class differentiation to the vote, with the bottom tercile Democratic and the top tercile Republican (Figure 5.15A). This is a Republican vote for President that would be recognizable for the next thirty years.

Like Thurmond before him, Wallace did indeed attract a racially based white vote: the probability of voting for Wallace over Humphrey was sharply higher among whites in more-black districts (Figure 5.15B). Yet what is equally striking about Wallace's vote, and what made it very unlikely to become a bridge to subsequent Republicanism, was its class composition. There was also a powerful class basis to the choice between Humphrey and Wallace, but it was inverse to the usual Democratic pattern: lower-income voters were more likely to go with Wallace, higher-income voters to stay with Humphrey, and this was even more true among whites in more-black areas. To put it differently: the Humphrey vote looked more like subsequent Republican votes for President than did the Wallace vote. A "bridging" candidate cannot have that profile.

This was, of course, precisely parallel to the situation involving Truman and Thurmond twenty years earlier, at least as measured by congressional district outcomes: the Truman vote looked more like subsequent Republican votes for President than did the Thurmond vote. Both Thurmond and Wallace did pit social class against racial context as voting influences. Both also represented the triumph of race over class among white voters. But the point is that these were the two main times in the entire postwar period when that triumph occurred. Both Thurmond and Wallace were otherwise unavailable as bridges to subsequent Republicanism because the latter would be built so centrally around social class, where both independents drove in the wrong direction. In that sense, neither was a bridge to partisan change. Each was instead an obvious dead end.[7]

6

Old South, New South, No South?

BY THE TIME OF the 2000 census, there was a new politics in the American South, one simple in its outlines yet drastically different from its predecessors. The marker for this new politics was the place of a Southern Republican Party. By 2000, a party that had been operationally absent in the South for nearly all of the century after formation of the modern two-party system nationwide, and that was often an anti-competitive shell when it did appear, was arguably the majority party. Yet the real changes in the structure of Southern politics were underneath this marker:

- Race remained hugely consequential to the new (as to the old) Southern politics. In particular, black Southerners had shifted to the Democratic Party and represented the lead population that had been almost completely unresponsive to an overall Republican trend.
- Among white Southerners, social class was tightly aligned with support for the Republican (or Democratic) Party, and this too was a major change. Wealthier whites now leaned Republican by overwhelming margins, while poorer whites remained stubbornly unresponsive, though their margins were smaller than those for black Southerners, and could occasionally be breached.
- There were traces of a racial effect within this white population too. White voters in areas with a large black population, having trended Republican for the presidency but not for Congress, were now marginally more likely to vote Republican overall. But as the 2000 cen-

sus approached, these were traces only. It was the class background of white citizens, not the racial composition of their electoral surroundings, that was underpinning Republican gains.

- Racial attitudes, by contrast, were strongly aligned with support for the Republican (or Democratic) Party. Those who were supportive of aid targeted specifically to black Americans were more likely to stay with the Democrats, those opposed to such aid to move to the Republicans—and the bulk of Southern whites were strongly conservative on these grounds.

- Even more tightly aligned with partisan choice were economic attitudes. Those supportive of governmental subventions for social welfare were likely to stay with the Democratic Party, those opposed to move to the Republicans. Since the 1930s, this would not have seemed strange outside the South. Now it was true, and strongly so, within the region as well.

- And in the end, after all of that, the two Southern parties looked remarkably like a reversal of their previous selves. Where once there was a minority party based on concentrations of poor whites plus blacks everywhere, there was *still* a minority party based on concentrations of poor whites plus blacks everywhere. It was just that once this party had been the Republicans, and now it was the Democrats.

It is hard to overstate the distance between this modern world and the old world of Southern politics. The latter had been even simpler in its outlines, with contours that had already lasted nearly a hundred years when the postwar era began. We now know that change was imminent. Yet these older outlines could still be easily recognized in political data—survey data, census data, electoral data—from the 1950s. The marker for partisan politics within these data was still the (moribund) state of a Southern Republican Party. But once again, the critical differences lay in the structural characteristics that sustained its morbidity:

- Economic development was famously lacking—over 40 percent of the region remained in subsistence agriculture—and social class, to the extent that it showed any alignment with partisan choice, was inversely aligned by the standards of the modern era. The rich were more Democratic, the poor more Republican, though this was largely an epiphenomenon of where Republicans and Democrats had been concentrated since the time of the Civil War.

• Race managed to be both omnipresent and absent—massively relevant to the structure of a political order—in that the region of the nation with the largest black population had almost no black voters, thanks to systematic legal discrimination. In that sense, racial differences were fundamental, yet at the same time they were almost completely missing (along with potential black voters) from the behavioral data of politics.

• In a key secondary instance of the political role of race, white voters in blacker districts were more likely to vote Democratic, and this fact would fuel scholarly expectations about the impact of a purported "racial threat" if legal desegregation ever arrived. But again, this was still more a reflection of where Republicans and Democrats had resided for almost a hundred years than it was the precursor of any given partisan change.

• Economic attitudes were effectively unrelated to Southern partisanship—not inversely related, just unrelated. A national party system in which welfare liberals were Democratic while welfare conservatives were Republican was combined with a regional party system in which lower-income Southerners leaned Republican while upper-income Southerners leaned Democratic. Policy confusion at the grass roots was the logical product, and any connection between economic policy preferences and the vote was a logical casualty.

• Finally, racial attitudes *were* aligned with partisan preference, in a pattern that looks inverted from a modern perspective but followed naturally from the history of racial politics: that is, racial liberals were Republican, racial conservatives Democratic. This was presumably the attitudinal backdrop to racial politics in the era of Reconstruction, the years immediately after the Civil War. Remarkably, it was still a backdrop to Southern politics in the years immediately after World War II.

The three decades from the 1960 to the 1990 censuses were to tell a much more mottled story, as seems almost inevitable, given the scope of the change between the old South and the new. Elements of change—sociological elements initially, but then also attitudinal elements—did not arrive in a linear and coordinated fashion. Neither, as a result, did partisan change. Nevertheless, this transitional world was an extended time period with its own distinctive political contours:

- Economic development and a consequent realignment of class relationships began to arrive in the 1950s. Their arrival did differ initially by institution, arriving in the 1950s with the presidency and the 1960s with Congress, and in the House before the Senate in the latter body. Thereafter, however, the story was really just one of catching up, and then of moving forward strongly and in tandem among these institutions.

- Legal desegregation and a revised politics of race relationships arrived in the 1960s, in a much more concentrated and dramatic fashion. The inescapable register of their arrival was the appearance of black Southerners as members of an actual voting electorate. From the first, these members were undivided partisan Democrats; they arrived in huge numbers; and those two facts would not change from the interim to the modern political order.

- Among whites, however, the story of the arrival of a revised politics of race—of legal desegregation with racial contexts that had practical consequences this time—was far more institution-sensitive than the story of a changed politics of class. The old racial order in which whites in blacker areas were more Democratic changed immediately in the case of the presidency but continued unbroken in the case of Congress, most especially in the House. This institutional disjunction was perhaps the clearest marker characteristic of the transitional era.

- Yet this was also the period when economic attitudes, in their relationship to partisan choice, changed massively. At first, attitudinal change lagged the shift in class relationships. Then, economic ideology became aligned in the modern fashion with partisan choice—liberals voting Democratic, conservatives Republican—but at different speeds within different institutions. Ultimately, these attitudes emerged as powerful and powerfully parallel influences in their own right.

- The same could be said, only more so, about racial attitudes: early lag, differential impact by institution, then strong movement forward. What was additionally noteworthy here, however, was the way that racial ideology remained a separable influence from racial context for a very long time. Contextually, more-black areas were more Republican for the presidency and more Democratic for Congress. Attitudinally, however, racial conservatives were always more Republican, racial liberals more Democratic.

Seven Myths and a Method

This hugely compelling portrait of social change and partisan impact is surprisingly misaligned with expectations derived from the existing literature of Southern politics. We attribute the differences to distinctions in the way analytic questions have been formulated, both here and there; to differences in judgments—in particular, about what actually constitutes the relevant data; and, by extension, to differences in the application of these data to those propositions. In this concluding chapter, two points require special attention.

First, we think that our data-driven picture is particularly at variance with what we have come to regard as the "seven myths" of Southern political change—though we do not assert that any given work within that literature offers all seven, nor that there may not be others deserving of similar systematic contestation. We do think, however, that a concluding chapter ought to return briefly to these myths, rather than just summarizing an argument that, by now, must surely stand or fall on its own.

At the same time, a concluding chapter ought to say something about a mode of analysis that has produced major shifts of substantive nuance in the overall story, when it does not stand that story on its head. Note that it is easy to miss an important further aspect of this second argument, about proper data and respect for its implications. For proceeding in this fashion is also an argument that a social science relevant to political life cannot be divorced from its context—that abstracted propositions divorced from time and place are bootless when applied to any real society.

But first, the myths:

- that the engine of partisan change in the postwar South was legal desegregation, black enfranchisement, and white reaction to it;
- that economic development and a politics of social class were at best secondary to these influences, at worst just a secondary correlate of them;
- that the politics of race, whatever its place in the funnel of causality, was a reliable and consistent contribution to the rise of a new Republicanism;

- that the resulting collapse of the old Democracy began in one distinctive sub-region, the Peripheral South, and culminated in another, the Deep South;
- that such change was simultaneously registered "from the top down," with the presidency dragging other institutions in its wake;
- that third-party candidates for president played an especially critical role, as bridges to a new partisan world;
- and that incumbent candidates for Congress otherwise featured resistance as their central function, and intransigence as their main strategy.

In one sense, the impact of legal desegregation and a politics of race dominate our story, as they have dominated most of the stories in the professional literature preceding it. Yet even here, it is extremely important to note in what sense that is true. In the case of black Southerners, racial identity became such a dominant—and altered—influence on partisan politics that nothing else among our grand structural influences mattered: not social class, not racial context, not economic ideology, not racial ideology. However, where racial identity once led Southern blacks to the Republican Party, after desegregation it led them massively and unerringly toward the Democratic Party instead. In other words, this is the population for which the politics of race is the story of postwar change in the American South.

For the white South, on the other hand, the story as told here clearly privileges the impact of economic development and an associated politics of class. There was to be a changed politics of race among white Southerners as well, yet economic change arrived earlier and, for most purposes, was consistently larger in its impact. Accordingly, if the white South still represents by far the larger share of Southern voters, as it does, and if it represents the entire population of those shifting to the Republican Party, given the monolithic partisan character of black Southerners, then it must be economic development and class politics that claim the lead role in transforming the political order of the old South.

This is not to say that there was not also a *white* politics of race in the new South, though it is very much to say that this was a more nuanced politics than the relevant literature allows. We have addressed part of this necessary nuance at the beginning of this chapter: class politics in the modern form not only came to the white South before race politics in the modern form, but it thereafter shaped Southern politics in a far more consistent fashion across time. Yet for much of the postwar era, this white politics of race was also critically conditioned by the institutional theaters in which it could be registered. To state the difference as starkly as possible: the coming of legal desegregation had little evident impact on the way racial context—the presence or absence of large black populations—affected partisan choice for Congress, whereas it literally reversed old relationships for the presidency.

For Congress, whites in more-black areas voted more Democratic before desegregation, and whites in more-black areas voted more Democratic after desegregation. For the presidency, whites in more-black areas likewise voted more Democratic before desegregation, but more *Republican* thereafter. As a result, it is possible to believe that white voters focused their response to racial change on one institution rather than another, and we do believe this. It is possible to believe that partisan elites stalled off the forces of racial change with one institution and fostered it with another, which we also believe. But it is not possible to believe that the forces of racial change worked in an undifferentiated manner, across time or across institutions, nor that they dominated the forces of economic change overall.

One evident collateral casualty of these data-based arguments is the distinction between the Deep and the Peripheral South, a distinction useful in organizing much of the existing literature but one that is often given a spurious causal impact in the associated stories. In the taxonomic sense, the distinction holds: the Peripheral South had a larger share of white-collar Southerners early on, while the Deep South had a greater number of black Southerners throughout. As causal engine, however, the distinction disintegrates completely in the face of disaggregated data. The *reason* the Peripheral South offered early gains for Republicans was that it was more white-collar. The *reason* the Deep South held the line on Republican gains was that it was more-black. Yet more-black districts in the Peripheral South or white-collar districts in the Deep South—and their denizens—did not behave appreciably differently from the same districts in the opposite sub-region.

If the Peripheral South/Deep South distinction essentially collapses as a causal part of the postwar story, the presidency/Congress distinction—so important in the period of the 1960s through the 1980s—needs much more careful handling in the face of a multifaceted dataset than it often receives in the existing literature. Perhaps the leading example of this problem is the argument for "top down" change, led by the presidency, subsequently infecting Congress, and presumably moving further down from there. It is right to note that the earliest inklings of what would become the general pattern for a new Southern politics were registered with the presidency, specifically in the Eisenhower vote in the 1950s. This is, after all, an important part of the evidence for the dominant impact of economic development and social class.

What is not right is a mechanical—an under-nuanced—projection from that story, across time and across institutions. From one side, what the presidency gave, the presidency could take away: Kennedy and Johnson reclaiming Eisenhower, Carter reclaiming Nixon, Clinton, more modestly, reclaiming Reagan and Bush. From the other side, what Congress received, it largely held. The line of House or Senate progress for a Southern Republican Party is much smoother, and hence more relentless. From either side, however, the main point is that massive change was *welling up from Southern society*, falling across both the presidency and Congress. Differences in institutional structure did condition its impact. But neither institution—certainly not in their Southern incarnations—was actively pulling these forces out of society. That relationship was running the other way around.

Where the nature of presidential candidates did matter consistently, by contrast, was in their local versus national character. Southern Democrats as opposed to Northern Democrats at the head of the Democratic ticket not only did a better job of repressing Republican gains overall, they also skewed the vote in notably different ways. Southern Democrats privileged class, the old bedrock of the New Deal order, whereas Northern Democrats privileged race. Moreover, these effects were felt down-ticket, as Southern Democratic candidates for President not only repressed Republican totals but pulled the congressional vote toward class, while Northern Democrats endured larger Republican totals while pulling the congressional vote toward race. Thus in an era where presidential coattails are widely thought to have shrunk nearly to the vanishing point, presidential candidates had substantial coattails in the new South.

Independent candidates for President, that is, third-party rather than major-party candidates, also mattered, though not in the fashion most commonly offered. Such candidates usually appear in the existing literature as Republican facilitators, serving as a bridge away from Democratic partisanship. Third-party candidates did flare to prominence in the postwar South, most notably Strom Thurmond in 1948 and George Wallace in 1968. When they did, they were obviously relevant to the tension between class and race as influences on the vote. Moreover, both of these candidates were motivated by the threat of racial change—Thurmond prospectively and Wallace concurrently—and both secured a powerful racial cast to their vote. Yet both also drew a poor-white rather than a rich-white electorate in the process, so that both candidates became side routes—dead ends, really—rather than bridges in the progress of a new Southern Republican Party.

Congressional candidates, by contrast, are often treated as having little more than resistance as their main operative characteristic after legal desegregation, so that they end up being classified on some implicit scale of intransigence. Some did fit this characterization, especially in the short run. But in the longer term, it was an incentive structure that conduced toward biracial campaigns (and then its collapse) that mattered more. The reason this racial context appeared to work so differently as between Congress and the presidency, for open seats and not just for standing incumbents, was that the biracial composition of many congressional districts imposed an institutional logic of its own, demanding biracial campaigns. When this incentive was sharply reduced after the 1990 census, those campaigns became much rarer—and the racial disparity between Congress and the presidency disappeared.

Yet what distinguished congressional candidates additionally, and especially what distinguished incumbent congressmen from each other, was a different characteristic. True sociological locals, candidates who were born and educated within their home states, proved much better at repressing Republican progress than did sociological cosmopolitans, those with greater ties to the outside world. Like Southern Democrats with the presidency, local Democrats with Congress not only restrained Republican gains but actually structured the vote in different ways. They were particularly good at emphasizing social class as a voting influence, an emphasis that could still benefit Democrats for a very long time. But they were also good, by comparison to the cosmopolitans, at emphasizing shared social identifications rather than issues or policies, in an era when the positions of their national party were often a Southern difficulty.

These strike us as seven major myths about Southern politics, and in the preceding paragraphs we have offered our own corrections. Yet an attack on these "myths" in the existing literature is simultaneously an assertion about the proper—methodological, empirical—way of proceeding. At one and the same time, it is an assertion:

- about the need to *formulate propositions* about political change, rather than accept the surface drift of political history as having resolved them;
- about the need to *assemble appropriate data* for those propositions,

that is, individual-level data for individual-level propositions, contextual data for contextual propositions, and systematic elite data for propositions about elite actors; in the process, cross-level analysis becomes possible as well;

• and about the need to *treat the result seriously*, when it does but especially when it does not accord with the anecdotal evidence that comes from headline events.

The course of headline events in social change for the postwar South is as dramatic as any in American political history. The scope of the Southern economic miracle that coincided with partisan change is legitimately described as "dramatic": a region having many of the distinguishing characteristics of the contemporary third world at the beginning of the postwar era managed to rejoin the rest of the nation economically within two generations, even while the rest of that nation enjoyed explosive growth.

Nevertheless, for drama as the notion is conventionally understood, the civil rights revolution overwhelmed the economic miracle. From the bus boycott in Montgomery, to lunch-counter sit-ins in Greensboro, through the murder of civil rights workers in rural Mississippi, to confrontations on the Edmund Pettis Bridge during the march to Selma—and on and on and on—the truly incendiary incidents of those two political generations were forged in the attempt to end legal segregation in the American South.

Yet surface drama cannot by itself demonstrate that political behavior followed from these events in any one-to-one fashion. Such a demonstration requires a different kind of analysis. We have found the existing literature of Southern politics, from V. O. Key onward, to be hugely useful in getting a purchase on the relevant hypotheses about this political change. We have also found bits of data scattered throughout this literature, some useful and some not, along with the occasional extended analysis, which we have borrowed gratefully.

Beyond that, it has been necessary to construct a comprehensive dataset, with systematic mass, elite, and contextual elements. When these intendedly relevant data are then applied to hypotheses drawn from the original literature, we have found a picture of partisan change in the postwar South that should remain familiar in its main elements but with fresh contours and a different balance. We think that this picture of the partisan transformation of Southern politics retains enough difference from prior portraits to contribute substantially to our understanding of the larger changes in American national politics during the modern era.

Yet there is a second methodological point inherent in all this. From one side, we have forced the ethnographic and historical literature on a particular region to confront empirical (even statistical) propositions of more general application, usually developed outside that region. We hope that this is a contribution to the study of Southern politics, over and above the specific substance of our own findings. From the other side, however, we have forced an opposite confrontation, and this is the second methodological point. For we have definitely not abstracted our findings from the temporal and social context, the time and place, where they in fact occurred—nor have we ever attempted to do so. Indeed, we have self-consciously deployed the social and institutional contexts of various participants as variables in their own right—sometimes as causal agents, more often and more critically as conditioning factors—to help explain political behavior.

This may seem so obvious as not to need emphasis. But the point should not be missed that most political behavior is "law-like" only in a highly conditional sense. From this point of view, much—indeed most—political analysis is underspecified. Effects can seem weak, but only because of their conflation with opposite effects. Given the powerful contrasts between congressional and presidential voting, what would we have found had we focused on a rather abstract disposition such as party identification rather than on the multiple, concrete arenas in which behavior is actually exhibited? Party identification might well conflate these arenas.

Likewise, relationships posited as invariant, or at least as emblematic, often rest on unstated conditions. What if we had settled on House elections as adequately diagnostic by themselves? We certainly started there for good and obvious reasons. House elections are the most susceptible to statistical treatment, given their frequency, the sheer number of districts, and the decentralized and statistically well-behaved pattern of candidate recruitment (Shafer and Johnston 2001). If we had stopped there, we would have gotten the larger picture of racial contexts wrong. Moreover, it was the institutionally mottled impact of racial context that actually drove us to look more closely at the impact of racial redistricting, as a reason why these contexts might work differently across time, and then to search for some critical distinction among the candidates for public office that might make racial contexts work differently at the same point in time.

Our subsequent discovery of the power of the distinction between locals and cosmopolitans makes the larger point even more neatly. For in the end, this search did lead us to something approaching a unified theory of localism versus cosmopolitanism as it applied to all three arenas. But we never would have started down this path had we not extended the original analysis to the whole system. To get to a general proposition, we first had to specify conditions particular to institutions, not to mention times and places. All of which ends up being a plea for mid-range analysis as an intellectual strategy, since this is where that specification can most reasonably occur.[1]

It is also a plea for modesty in measurement. The indicators in this book are almost embarrassing in their simplicity: the simplest imaginable indicator of social position, a handful of census quantities, two very low-budget characterizations of candidates. The same might be said, only more so, about our outcome indicators, namely, whether the respondent voted Democrat or Republican, by arena. No attempt is made to get at some more fundamental disposition. In practical terms, the only evidence we have about dispositions are the measures tapping preferences on welfare policy and race policy, each a single-item measure.

Elsewhere, we have moved evidentiary mountains to get beyond single indicators (Claggett and Shafer 2002, 2004). Here, the need to have the precise same measures across fifty years in all regards has forced us back onto one item only in each domain. Even then, this indicator moves around a bit in the early years, so that we have been forced to discard some otherwise useful information—such as the seven-point metric that came into use in 1972—in order to level the playing field as between decades. What is nevertheless striking, in the face of what must be massive random measurement error, is that the story these indicators tell remains simple and powerful. To emphasize the same point once again: clarification has come not through measurement manipulation but through due consideration of social and institutional context.

Other substantive implications follow as well. For example, having demonstrated the growing influence of social class on partisan choice, we still have no basis for projecting further growth in this influence. Even more to the point, having demonstrated the *shifting* influence of racial context on partisan choice, we have even less reason to expect that if one revisited these data in another fifty years, the current relationship would reappear. Indeed, here, a contextual variable itself warns us against such hubris.

To put it differently, all political events have a context. If we have explicitly criticized old approaches to political change in the postwar South as amassing details instead of formulating and testing arguments, we have implicitly criticized newer approaches that appear to believe that the context can be lost on the way to political understanding. Old approaches rarely got beneath such a context; new approaches too often ditch it. In this regard, the proper use of context is precisely to motivate and facilitate the search for law-like statements.

Such statements can only emerge from situations that exhibit, in the relevant methodological vocabulary, conditional independence and unit homogeneity (King, Keohane, and Verba 1994). If we believe in the layered nature of social and political reality, and if we believe that many key relationships within it do not run in only one direction and are often not linear, then fulfillment of these conditions is possible only when critical elements of *context*—in our case, class, race, institutional theater, and candidate characteristics—are controlled.

Convergence on a New Political Order?

In any case, a new Southern political order was in place by the 1990s. Its power was affirmed by the ease with which it could be boiled down to a few simple propositions about social class, racial context, economic ideology, and racial ideology. That power was reaffirmed by the difference between this structure and the structure of politics in the old South. Yet such a summary still understates the force of change. For not only had the world sketched so meticulously by V. O. Key been transformed in its details, but there had also been a remarkable, further convergence within it: across institutions, across states, and, just as remarkably if more conditionally, across large political regions.

This theme of convergence had already surfaced when the focus was institutional politics, where the presidency and Congress had primed social change in different ways during the long transition from the 1960s through the 1980s but where these patterns had come back into alignment during the 1990s (see Chapter 4). There is no need to repeat that analysis here. Yet the power of the convergence at its core can be simply emphasized by showing the same result "the other way around," featuring convergence among white voters across time where the focus is first racial context and then economic context.

Figure 6.1 regresses the Republican vote among white Southerners on the proportion black of each congressional district for the presidency, the Senate, and the House, first for the 1950s, then for the 1960s through 1980s, finally for the 1990s. In the old order of the 1950s, there was a rough parallelism to this vote across institutions. Republican voting for the presidency was already stronger. Republican voting for the House was

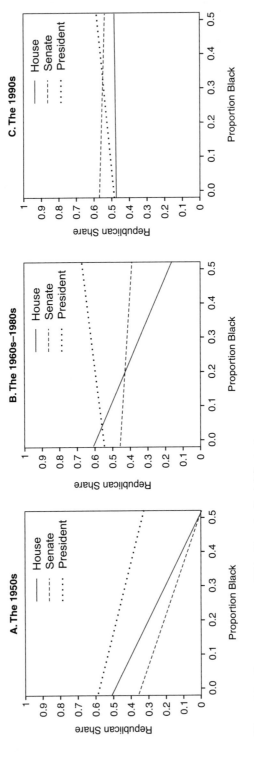

Figure 6.1 Convergence among White Voters by Racial Context.

more responsive to racial context. But by and large, the institutional lines of voter support were roughly gathered, while running parallel across institutions.

During the transitional decades of the 1960s, the 1970s, and the 1980s—the period for the coming of a new Southern politics—this rough homogeneity was shattered. The presidency continued to outperform both houses of Congress for the Republicans; that did not change. But the pattern of Republican voting for the presidency versus the House actually responded to racial context in opposite ways. As a result, the lines of support were no longer even roughly parallel. Indeed, the differences at the more-black end of the continuum approached 50 percent, half the electorate!

This situation continued until the 1990s and the apparent institutionalization of a new order, when patterns of voting support reconverged with a vengeance. Now, there was almost no difference in the level of Republican support among the presidency, Senate, and House. And now, the small amount of difference in voting response to racial context was indeed residual, not just far smaller than this difference in the transition period of the 1960s through 1980s, but far smaller than the situation of the 1950s as well. When the focus was Republican votes and racial context, one story could encompass all three institutions in the 1990s.

The story of convergence among voters by *class* context was simpler, beginning in diversity but converging early and actually tightening thereafter (Figure 6.2). When districts are arrayed by their white-collar shares, the old order of the 1950s featured very different impacts for class composition by institution. Wealthier voters were actually more Republican for the presidency, more Democratic for Congress, and became more so as the white-collar share of the district increased. We know, however, that this difference was rooted in the way that an impending change had registered earlier with the presidency, so that by the time of the transition to a new South, from the 1960s through the 1980s, this divergence had evaporated. Republicans did better for the presidency than for the two houses of Congress, but relationships to class context were otherwise identical. For the 1990s, as this new order became institutionalized, voting patterns for the three institutions were still parallel and even more tightly clustered.

Suffice it to say that individual voting behavior had converged by the 1990s to operate not just in parallel but in nearly identical fashion across the presidency, the Senate, and the House. What may appear more surprising is the convergence across Southern *states* that occurred during this same extended period (Figure 6.3). In principle, individual voters could

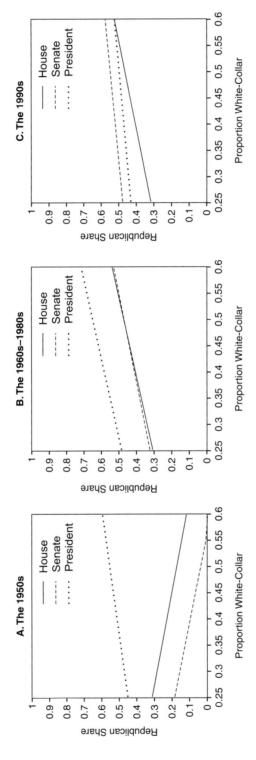

Figure 6.2   Convergence among White Voters by Class Context.

move in parallel or divergent directions, while their aggregate state electorates remained in more or less parallel relationships—in similarity or
in difference—to each other. In practice, this was most definitely not the
case. The South as a political region became ever more homogeneous in-
ternally.

This is one of those cases where the "*N* problem" that is always in the
background of statistical calculations for the Senate becomes impossible.
Senate figures by state for any given decade include only three or four contests. Beyond that, a three-contest decade often includes a re-election for
the same incumbent, thereby converting aggregate statistics back into individual idiosyncrasies. Yet for the House and the presidency, the problem is
at least eased. The House, aggregated by state per decade, always offers at
least twenty contests within its aggregate, and sometimes as many as a
hundred and fifty. The presidency is even better, since the *same* contest is
offered in every state, facilitating comparison.

For the House of Representatives, Southern states varied tremendously
in the earliest years in their levels of Republican support—and here, using
aggregate data, we are able to reach back into the 1940s (Figure 6.3A).
Then, some states offered a recurrent Republican minority; others produced nearly nothing at all. By the 1960s, the level of this state support
pattern had begun to rise, but the rise itself was still roughly uniform. That
is, states still differed tremendously in the attractiveness of a nascent Republican Party, and in roughly the same way that they had differed in the
1940s. The decade of the 1990s, however, was a different world. By the
1990s, the level of support was not just vastly higher; it had also leveled
out to an impressive degree. Interstate differences in their partisan support
for Republican congressional candidates had declined sharply. In partisan
terms, previously individual states had become effectively one political region.

In the case of the presidency, there is only one twist to the same repeti-
tive story (Figure 6.3B). The 1940s featured even more divergent levels of
general support for the presidential candidates of the Republican Party, as
among the eleven states of the Old Confederacy. Yet by the 1960s, movement into a rough conformity across these states—the same general "flat-
tening" of the line—had already occurred. Unlike the House, the old numbers did not simply move up with a rising Republican tide. Instead, they
moved additionally into alignment with the modern pattern. Unsurprisingly, then, the 1990s merely continued the story of the 1960s. If the presidency led in registering regional convergence, both institutions, presidency

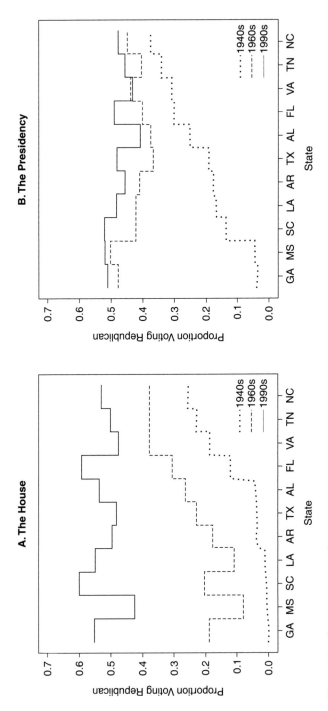

Figure 6.3   Convergence across States.

and House, attested to the diminishment of state (inter-South) differences and to the emergence of a common regional politics.

The final element of convergence in the pattern of Southern politics was, however, the most remarkable of all. For at varying points during the transition to a new Southern politics, depending on the measure and the institution in question, the South as a political region actually came into conformity with the rest of the nation. In the process, what had been a defining *regional* difference in national politics, from the 1850s through the 1950s, threatened to disappear. And the possibility arose that the rhetorical question posed by the title of this chapter—Old South to New South to No South?—could be answered in the affirmative.

Partisan statistics for the House of Representatives are, as ever, a good introduction. When the focus was candidate provision, for the North versus the South, the regional gap began to close sharply during the 1960s, at the point when Southern politics began its transformation (Figure 6.4A). This closure continued gradually during the next twenty years. The gap then disappeared in the 1990s: there were as likely to be Republican congressional candidates in the South as in the rest of the nation. This was a situation never before encountered in American political history.

Given that candidate provision followed closely upon electoral promise, it is not surprising to find that this first aspect of regional convergence is intimately related to regional closure in an actual Republican vote (Figure 6.4B). Before the 1960s, Republicans (like Democrats) were entitled to roughly half of the non-Southern vote for the House, while they secured a miserable 10-plus percent in the old South. When change began in earnest, this gap was quickly cut in half. By the 1980s, it was marginal. By the 1990s, it had not only disappeared, but the South actually showed a modestly better vote for Republican congressional candidates than the North.

Moreover, when this Republican vote is considered not for all congressional seats but only for seats that possessed candidates from both major parties, one aspect of the story of regional convergence can be shown to have been gathering force below the surface considerably earlier (Figure 6.4C). Seen this way, the gap of the 1940s actually narrowed a bit in the 1950s and then declined nearly to the vanishing point in the 1960s. On the other hand, it is important not to overstate this finding. While the gap between the South and the North in Republican voting when there was a Republican candidate had effectively closed by 1965, the provision of candidates still shadowed the prospects for a good Republican vote. If more candidates could somehow have been forced into less-promising districts,

A. Candidate Provision

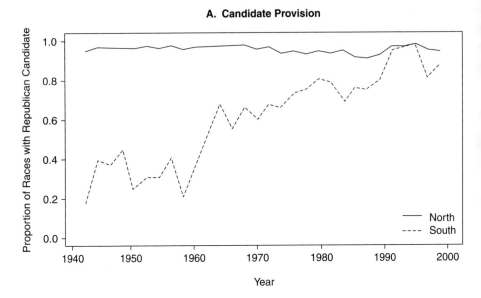

B. The Republican Vote

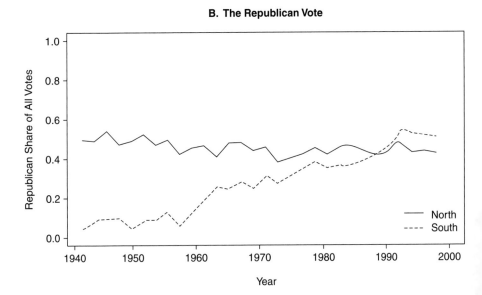

Figure 6.4   Convergence across Regions: The House.

C. The Republican Vote, Contested Seats Only

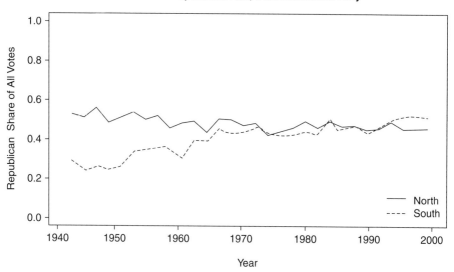

D. Republican Victories

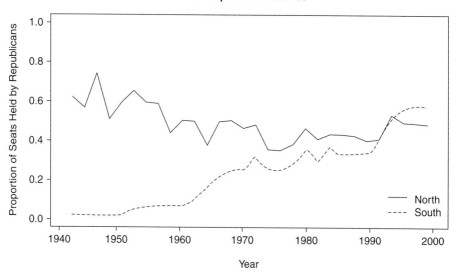

Figure 6.4   (continued)

the voting gap might well have closed later rather than earlier. Either way, it was largely closed by the 1980s.

Last but in most senses most consequentially, the gap in wins and losses for regional Republicans naturally tracked the progress of this Republican vote (Figure 6.4D). As before, the line of Southern Republican victories for the House jumped up sharply in the 1960s, edged up over the next twenty years, and then jumped again in the 1990s. Because the Northern Republican line of victories for the House was actually declining across the 1950s, the gap between these two lines closed notably in the late 1960s and narrowed further in the 1970s, before seeing the South actually move past the North in the 1990s. By then, seen by way of the U.S. House of Representatives, the old partisan difference between the South and the rest of the nation had apparently disappeared.

The Senate had always done better than the House in generating Republican challengers. As a result, the Senate came near to closing the regional divide over candidate provision in the late 1960s and early 1970s, and did close it in the early 1980s (Figure 6.5A). As ever, candidate provision and the prospects for a Republican vote were intertwined, so that a huge gap in the share of the Republican vote, South versus non-South, also began to close rapidly in the late 1960s (Figure 6.5B). The Northern Senate vote was remarkably stable across the postwar years, at about 50-minus percent Republican. But the Southern vote jumped from about 35-plus percent in the 1960s to 40-plus in the 1980s, and then actually edged not just into majority territory but above the North in the 1990s.

The record of wins and losses by regional Republican (and Democratic) parties then completes this Senate picture (Figure 6.5C).[2] The Republican rise in Southern seats lagged its vote in the earlier years, since that vote, while growing, was still normally under 40 percent. But a Republican rise was still evident by the 1970s, blossoming in the 1980s and forging into majority territory by the 1990s. Because Northern Republicans suffered major losses in the late 1950s from which they never fully recovered, the regional gap was actually closing by 1970, did close temporarily by 1980, and then not only closed again but drove in the other direction, with a Southern lead, in the early 1990s. The same logic that once caused Republican seats to lag Republican votes, when the latter were still not a majority, now provided a bonus for majority standing.

The presidency, finally, can be seen to tell the same story, on a somewhat accelerated calendar. To begin with, candidate provision was never an issue with the presidency. Moreover, the gap in Republican voting, South versus non-South, was itself closing rapidly by the 1950s (Figure 6.6A). Eisenhower ran better in the North than the South, but not all that much better. This regional difference wobbled from the mid-1960s to the mid-1980s, with sometimes the North but sometimes the South offering a slightly larger Republican vote. And the South actually led the North, albeit again not by much, from the mid-1980s onward.[3]

The Electoral College, being winner-take-all by state, merely exaggerated this voting story (Figure 6.6B). The South lagged the North in Electoral College results in the old order of the 1940s and 1950s. Yet it essentially closed with the North in the interim decades, from the 1960s until the middle 1980s; and it actually ran ahead of the North from the mid-1980s onward. In the process, the old divergence between the South and the rest of the country, built upon the peculiarities of politics in the former, had once again comprehensively disappeared.

Or had it? Presidential outcomes, especially as registered through the Electoral College, were much more volatile than congressional outcomes, so that results for the presidency from the mid-1980s onward just might be foreshadowing a different story. The South was undeniably in transition from an old order, reaching back to the 1870s but captured in our data only in the 1950s. It had undeniably arrived at a new order by the 1990s, one that aligned demographics and attitudes, institutions and states. Yet its presidential results might be read to suggest that this transition was not from exceptionalism to integration, but rather from one incarnation of exceptionalism to another.

In this view, the presidency, by overstating the partisan fundamentals, showed the demise of the old South, followed by a period of North-South convergence which was more apparent than real. For what this transitional period really represented was the shift to a world in which the South was now disproportionately Republican, as it had once been overwhelmingly Democratic. Indeed, with these presidential results as a goad, it is possible to read the House and Senate results in the same light: beginning with a huge Democratic edge; evolving across the national partisan mean, which made convergence look plausible; yet headed not toward cross-regional uniformity but toward a new Republican edge—not just an edge over Democrats within the region, but a greater partisan edge than the Republican Party could generate in the non-South.

Every story of political change, even one for what was previously the

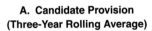

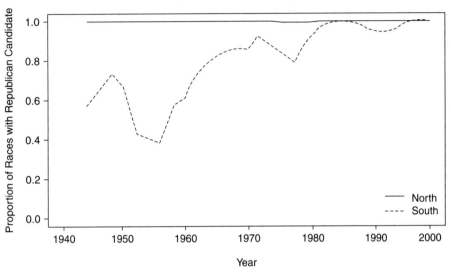

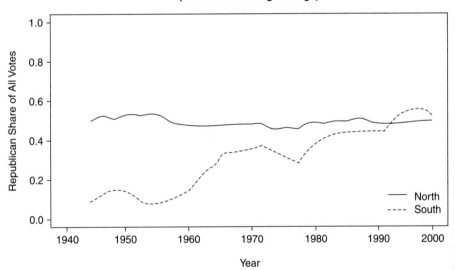

Figure 6.5   Convergence across Regions: The Senate.

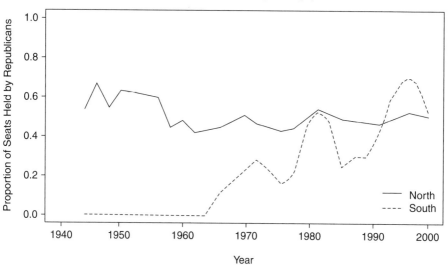

Figure 6.5   (continued)

"changeless" region of American politics, has to stop somewhere. This one stops at the end of the 1990s—at 2000—with what is still overwhelmingly a story of convergence. In that sense, the story also stops with the end of Southern distinctiveness. In the vocabulary of social change, the last available data present convergence as reflecting a set of reinforcing structural changes in Southern politics. The new world is not only here, but likely to endure.

Yet an analysis of the breakup of one of the great and enduring political orders in all of American history can hardly rest content by replacing one static portrait with another. Indeed, if there is any larger moral to the story of partisan change in the postwar South, it is that politics is always open-ended, even in this apparently enduring order, even in this apparently changeless region. Thus convergence among Southern voters, Southern institutions, and Southern states could continue, but to a point that represents *divergence*, once again, from the rest of the political nation. In this view, the South would just be on its way from one distinctive incarnation to another, with passage past the national mean representing a mere transition in its larger trajectory. Without another decade of data, we cannot know.

We can, however, say three things about this possibility. We can say that its confirmation or disconfirmation would require the same sort of analy-

A. The Republican Vote

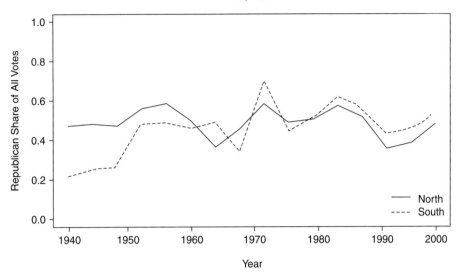

B. Electoral College Results

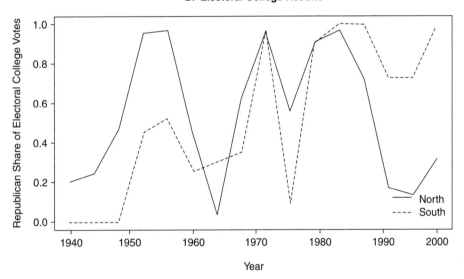

Figure 6.6   Convergence across Regions: The Presidency.

sis—propositions, data, testing—to see whether this is the reassertion of Southern exceptionalism or just the logical product of a different social mix in the North versus the South. We can say that incipient new directions for Southern politics, many of which will prove to be false portents but some of which will be harbingers of further political change, do appear with almost every election—like the appearance in 2000 of the first Southern Republican candidate for President in all of American history. And finally, we can say that no serious analyst who has spent an entire volume studying the breakup of an old and enduring order should want to end by assuming that its successor is static rather than dynamic, ossified rather than evolutionary, or fixed rather than open-ended.

❧ Notes

1. The Nature of the Puzzle

1. *National Election Studies, 1948–2000 Cumulative Data File* (Ann Arbor: University of Michigan, Center for Political Studies, 2002).
2. *Congressional District Data Book* (Washington, D.C.: U.S. Department of Commerce, 1961, 1973, and supplements); *Congressional Districts in the 1970s, 1980s, and 1990s* (Washington, D.C.: Congressional Quarterly Inc., 1973, 1983, and 1993).
3. *Candidate and Constituency Statistics of Elections in the United States, 1788–1990,* 5th ICPSR ed. (Ann Arbor: University of Michigan, Center for Political Studies, 1995); *Guide to U.S. Elections,* vols. I and II (Washington, D.C.: Congressional Quarterly Inc., 2001); Jerrold G. Rusk, ed., *A Statistical History of the American Electorate* (Washington, D.C.: CQ Press, 2001); *America Votes* (Washington, D.C.: Congressional Quarterly Inc., various years); *The Almanac of American Politics* (Washington, D.C.: National Journal, various years). *America Votes* initially had a series of short-run publishers before becoming institutionalized at Congressional Quarterly; *The Almanac of American Politics* was first published privately and then by E. P. Dutton before becoming institutionalized at *National Journal.*

2. Economic Development and a Politics of Class

1. And, fatally for us, with no way to distinguish South from non-South among the respondents.
2. In our analysis, decades are grouped from the year "2" through the year "0," to keep them in line with the decennial census and, especially, with the congressional districting that followed from it. Thus the 1950s run from 1952–1960, the 1960s from 1962–1970, and so on. This has the added advantage of *not* pooling on the basis of particular partisan outcomes; partisan change must register within analytically neutral time-periods if it is to register at all. On those occasions where a division into census decades threatens to introduce a substantive distortion, as in Table 2.6 below, we address the problem in context.
3. It might seem that a further shift of substantive consequence occurred between the 1950s and 1960s, as the marginals became more conservative overall. We believe that this is an artifactual shift, rooted in measurement reform rather than social change. Part of it must be traced to available item responses: these were broadened substantially after the 1950s, removing a kind of forced choice of the extremes. More of it, we think, is due to the way in which question referents in the 1950s involve aspects of social insurance ("a job," etc.), whereas referents af-

ter 1960 all feature economic redistribution ("a good standard of living"). Majorities of Americans have always been much more supportive of the former than
the latter (Jaffe 1978; Shapiro and Young 1990; Cook and Barrett 1992). This
interpretation is reinforced by the fact that the same shift in the marginals occurred at the same time in the non-South, thereby guaranteeing that the relevant
influences are not diagnostically Southern.

4. As in Tables 2.6 and 2.7, "the 1950s" for the Senate encompass the years 1952–
   1966, while "the 1960s–1980s" are actually 1968–1990.
5. Because Table 2.10 is a cross-tabulation of two bivariate relationships for each
   institution, drawn from Tables 2.1 and 2.2, 2.3 and 2.5, plus 2.6 and 2.7, there is
   some inevitable attrition of the sample in demanding both income tercile and
   welfare attitude. It is a simple matter, however, to take those who appear in Table
   2.10 and rerun the previous tables with this particular, slightly smaller sample.
   When this is done, none of the previous class or attitude marginals change in
   substantial ways, and no overall relationships change at all.

3. Legal Desegregation and a Politics of Race

1. It may seem that any effect from racial context would require a greater concentration per congressional district—say 40 percent—in order to surface in behavior (and in these data). Yet until the 1990s, less than 5 percent of Southern blacks
   lived in districts that were more than 40 percent black.
2. This was also the decade of the creation of self-conscious "majority-minority"
   districts, the point when Southern congressional districts were deliberately—racially—reconstituted. We shall return to this fact, and to its centrality to this
   change in the relationship between racial context and partisan voting, in Chapter 4.
3. As in fact we have already done in Table 3.3A.
4. It is worth noting that these were essentially the areas that had once *been* majority black.
5. This way of proceeding gains reinforcement from parallel concerns with welfare
   policy in Chapter 2, note 3.
6. Once again, because Table 3.13 is a cross-tabulation of two bivariate relationships for each institution, drawn from Tables 3.5, 3.6, 3.7, and 3.9, there is some
   attrition of the sample in demanding both racial context and racial attitude. Yet
   it is a simple matter to take those who appear in Table 3.13 and rerun these other
   tables with this particular, slightly smaller sample. When this is done, none of
   the previous class or attitude marginals change in substantial ways, and no overall relationships change at all.

4. Class, Race, and Partisan Change

1. Shifts were computed with CLARIFY software (Tomz, Wittenbeg, and King
   2003), appended to STATA, which generates both point estimates and con-
   fidence intervals for effects.
2. For Figure 4.1, we have followed the practice of Chapters 2 and 3 in periodizing
   the Senate vote. See Chapter 2, note 4, for specifics.
3. This same derivation applies to similar figures throughout Chapters 4, 5, and 6.
   Underlying coefficients, standard errors, and equation statistics are available
   from the authors.

4. This change also generated substantial scholarly debate over a variety of further impacts, most of which are only indirectly related to our concerns here. McKee 2002 is closest to our concerns, but see also Hill 1995; Cameron, Epstein, and O'Halloran 1996; Epstein and O'Halloran 1999; Lublin and Voss 2000.

5. There is a substantial literature on welfare policy attitudes (gathered helpfully in Shapiro and Young 1989; Cook and Barrett 1992), a substantial literature on racial policy attitudes (gathered in Schuman et al. 1997; Krysan 2000), and some argument about their linkage (Sniderman, Tetlock, and Carmines 1993; Sears, Sidanius, and Bobo 2000).

Our work on Southern politics addresses these only obliquely, but three aspects seem relevant. First, given the face content of the items we use to measure welfare and race attitudes, it would be surprising if they were unrelated. In fact, our two items are always correlated, and the correlation grows stronger across the postwar years. On the other hand, our multivariate analyses for each policy realm are reported controlling for the other, so that all results exist in the presence of that control. Moreover, the two attitude domains rarely collapse. In the earlier years, they do not even work in tandem. In the later years, each gets stronger. It would be hard to argue that they were tapping the same thing.

Yet we have pursued these questions a bit further, by modeling welfare attitudes, racial attitudes, and racial feelings in the presence of income terciles and racial contexts. So we know that welfare attitudes are not very responsive to racial feelings, nor are they much affected by racial context. They are strongly related to income, and this link only strengthens over time. Racial attitudes are clearly affected by racial feelings, and have a varying but only modest relationship to racial context, being unrelated in the 1960s, rising a bit thereafter, and becoming unrelated again by the 1990s. They are essentially unrelated to income.

For our purposes, the important fact remains that welfare and racial attitudes appear together in enough of our analyses that when they are appearing together, the effect of one controls for the presence of the other. This simple setup seems to suffice for the purposes of this book, especially given its temporal reach, and manages to produce some impressively strong relationships to both attitudes.

6. Congress is the focus of the "Two Souths" argument in the relevant literature, as well it should be. The class and race arguments run parallel for Congress, opposite for the presidency, so that they make no clear and testable predictions for a presidential vote. In the case of the presidency, white-collar concentrations (and thus the Peripheral South) predict stronger Republican support, but black-voter concentrations (and thus the Deep South) also predict stronger Republican support, so that it is impossible to say what a confirming (or disconfirming) outcome would look like. But in the case of Congress, white-collar concentrations (and thus the Peripheral South) predict a greater Republican vote, while black-voter concentrations (and thus the Deep South) predict a greater *Democratic* vote, so that contrasting predictions are testable.

5. Social Forces and Partisan Politicians

1. Lest this seem an unduly restrictive definition of local, we should note that a substantial majority of all Democratic candidates from the South within this fifty-year period could indeed meet its strictures for both the House and the Senate, and hence were by our standards "locals." Note that for candidates who

completed several higher degrees, we use the final one to register in-state versus out-of-state education.

2. For a fuller description of the derivation of Figure 5.7 and others like it in this chapter, see the text of Chapter 4 at note 3.

3. The great student of district fit in our time has been Richard F. Fenno, Jr., beginning with Fenno 1978 and pursuing the notion through books like Fenno 1998 and Fenno 2003. But could our analysis not turn instead on a masked difference between districts with or without an incumbent Democrat, such that it is not localism and local "fit" but simple incumbency that is at issue? The answer appears to be clearly no. Splitting the file into presence or absence of a Democratic incumbent and then running the same analysis for both halves produces very close to the same result. The constant is in a different place, since Republicans do better when there is no Democratic incumbent. Otherwise, incumbents induce only a very slightly increased slope on racial context, and there is no difference at all in the income coefficient.

4. Could this difference have been washed away by other aspects of the analysis? That is, could it have been the simple result of a problem of endogeneity, in which wealthier and whiter districts not only proved more attractive to cosmopolitans but then gave them a vote more like the cosmopolitan archetype? The parallelism between congressional and presidential results makes this most unlikely: the social characteristics of Southern congressional districts could have only extremely modest impacts on the identities of presidential nominees in most years, and the presence of a Northern or Southern Democrat for President could have nearly no effect on the presence of a local or cosmopolitan candidate for Congress.

Nevertheless, we have modeled the process of candidate recruitment to the House—the differential recruitment of locals versus cosmopolitans—using our basic background variables. District characteristics are, as one would expect, related to candidate recruitment. But the influence of the cosmopolitan-local distinctions does not go away with more extensive controls. Rather, it is inconsequential in the 1950s and inconsequential again in the 1990s, but remains statistically significant during the key intervening period, the 1960s through the 1980s. We suspect that its disappearance in the 1990s is the product of extensive redistricting to create majority-minority districts.

5. As with Figures 5.9A and 5.9B, it is possible to check a more recent and more consciously balanced time-period to search for different results as between Northern and Southern Democratic nominees for President. Yet here, comparisons of coattail effects on the House, 1962–1990 versus 1968–1996, are so effectively identical that we have not presented the second set of figures. Off-year results for 1968–1996 still fall between Northern Democratic and Southern Democratic presidential years, in terms of their relationship to both social class and racial context; Southern Democrats still prime class by comparison to Northern Democrats; and Northern Democrats still prime race by comparison to Southerners. The lone element of difference is that Southern Democratic nominees appeared to prime class even a bit more during this later period.

6. Did the difference between locals and cosmopolitans matter to *Republican* candidates for Congress? Our attempt to extract the relevant data from the historical record was not just a statistical challenge but a further comment on the structure of politics in the postwar years. To wit: before the 1980s, it proved extremely

difficult to have even our simple indicators of local or cosmopolitan status, where the candidates were born and educated. In fact, we lack one or both indicators for a majority of all Republican House candidates before this date, and what we do have is additionally compromised by the fact that it comes disproportionately from the winners: unsuccessful challengers had a hard time making it into this part of the dataset.

This difficulty, of course, emphasizes the desperate state of the Southern Republican Party until quite late in the period. Nevertheless, we can say that for the 1980s, when the Republican data too are of high quality, the powerful impact on the vote of the distinction between locals and cosmopolitans among Democrats is not being biased by the same distinction among Republicans. This seems the most important contribution of our GOP data to Chapter 5. Republican candidates were more likely to be cosmopolitans than locals for the South as a whole, on a 60/40 basis, but *Democratic* locals and cosmopolitans were equally likely to be facing Republican locals or cosmopolitans among them.

Likewise, we know for the 1980s that Republican cosmopolitans and locals did not differ substantially in the relationship of their vote to either demographics (income tercile and racial context) or attitudes (on welfare or race policy). This powerful effect among Democrats, whereby locals primed demography and cosmopolitans primed opinion, had no counterpart among Republicans. Among candidates, apparently, a Republican was a Republican was a Republican, and the important thing was just to hold the party symbol and benefit from social change. There is, however, a tendency for Republican locals to run better than Republican cosmopolitans across all categories of voters. The Democrats certainly helped themselves for a long time by having a pool of sociological locals on which to draw. Apparently, Republicans too would have benefited had they had more.

7. There was to be one other serious independent candidate for the presidency in the postwar years, namely, H. Ross Perot in 1992 and then again in 1996. And there were, at least in 1992, analysts who believed that he might serve as a bridge *away* from the Republicans. The South was ultimately to be less responsive to Perot than the rest of the nation, giving him just 13 percent of its vote versus 21 percent in the non-South. But while it was impossible to use congressional districts to tell the story of his impact since he failed to carry any, his vote was large enough to register in the Southern part of the NES, and thus we were able to take at least an impressionistic look at its composition.

For 1992, there was only a negligible difference in the Perot vote among whites in more-black versus less-black districts, although there was a clear differentiation by income, with wealthier whites more attracted to the independent. In that sense, Perot shared no parallels with Strom Thurmond or George Wallace; his vote was a class and not a race vote. In principle, that did subtract from the Republican electorate, and in fact, the Republican nominee that year, George H. W. Bush, showed a weaker class alignment than usual in his support. Even on its own terms, however, this pattern made Perot an extremely unlikely bridge back to the Democrats.

Yet in 1996, two things happened to annihilate that possibility. In the first, the Perot vote in the South fell to 7 percent, making any lasting impact—as a bridge to anywhere—unlikely. And in the second, among those who stayed with Perot, the previous class profile evaporated. The wealthy were no longer disproportionately Perotistas, so that this 7 percent residual contained no promise for either Republican or Democratic gains when Perot was gone. As if to reinforce that impression, the vote for Robert Dole, the Republican nominee in 1996, showed a sharply restored class profile, one typical of Republican presidential candidates over time.

6. Old South, New South, No South?

1. An eloquent prior statement in the same tradition is Fenno 1986. The current statement of "best practice" in this regard is King, Keohane, and Verba 1994.
2. The fact of the Senate's much better record than the House at providing Republican challengers also meant that there was no need, after the 1950s, to provide a separate picture of the Senate for contested seats only. Such a picture narrows the partisan gap a bit, especially in the early years, but that is really all. On the other hand, the fact that controls for contested seats do not matter with the Senate may be another way of emphasizing the importance of candidate provision, and thus may suggest that the House actually would have shown additional early gains if it could have provided additional early candidates.
3. If the voting comparison is confined to the two-party vote, in an attempt to minimize the impact of independent presidential candidacies, then this entire change—the closure of a North-South gap in presidential voting—appears to arrive a bit earlier in a more permanent fashion. This difference reflected the Wallace (independent) vote in 1968, but it was not really very large; the two pictures remain essentially identical.

❧ References

Abramowitz, Alan I. "Issue Evolution Reconsidered: Racial Attitudes and Partisanship in the US Electorate." *American Journal of Political Science* 38 (1994), 1–24.

Aistrup, Joseph A. *The Southern Strategy Revisited: Republican Top-Down Advancement in the South.* Lexington: University of Kentucky Press, 1996.

Aldrich, John H. "Southern Parties in State and Nation." *Journal of Politics* 62 (2000), 643–670.

Aldrich, John H., and Richard G. Niemi. "The Sixth American Party System: Electoral Change, 1952–1992." In Stephen C. Craig, ed., *Broken Contract? Changing Relationships between Americans and Their Government.* Boulder: Westview Press, 1996.

Bartley, Numan V. *The New South, 1945–1980.* Baton Rouge: Louisiana State University Press, 1995.

Bartley, Numan V., and Hugh Davis Graham. *Southern Politics and the Second Reconstruction.* Baltimore: Johns Hopkins University Press, 1975.

Bass, Jack, and Walter DeVries. *The Transformation of Southern Politics: Social Change and Political Consequences since 1945.* New York: Basic Books, 1976.

Beck, Paul Allen. "Partisan Dealignment in the Postwar South." *American Political Science Review* 71 (1977), 477–498.

Berard, Stanley P. *Southern Democrats in the U.S. House of Representatives.* Norman: University of Oklahoma Press, 2001.

Black, Earl. "A Theory of Southern Factionalism." *Journal of Politics* 45 (1983), 594–614.

——— "The Newest Southern Politics." *Journal of Politics* 60 (1998), 591–612.

Black, Earl, and Merle Black. *Politics and Society in the South.* Cambridge, Mass.: Harvard University Press, 1987.

——— *The Vital South: How Presidents are Elected.* Cambridge, Mass.: Harvard University Press, 1992.

——— *The Rise of Southern Republicans.* Cambridge, Mass.: Harvard University Press, 2002.

Bond, Jon R., Cary Covington, and Richard Fleisher. "Explaining Challenger Quality in Congressional Elections." *Journal of Politics* 47 (1985), 510–529.

Brattain, Michelle. *The Politics of Whiteness: Race, Workers, and Culture in the Modern South.* Princeton: Princeton University Press, 2001.

Brodsky, David M., and Robert H. Swansbrough, eds. *The South's New Politics.* Columbia: University of South Carolina Press, 1988.

Bullock, Charles S., III, and Mark J. Rozell, eds. *The New Politics of the Old South.* Lanham: Rowman & Littlefield, 1998.

Bureau of the Census. *Statistical Abstract of the United States.* Washington, D.C.: Government Printing Office, various years.

Butler, David, and Donald Stokes. *Political Change in Britain: Forces Shaping Electoral Choice.* London: Macmillan, 1969.

Button, James W. *Blacks and Social Change.* Princeton: Princeton University Press, 1989.

Cameron, Charles, David Epstein, and Sharyn O'Halloran. "Do Majority-Minority Districts Maximize Black Representation in Congress?" *American Political Science Review* 90 (1996), 794–812.

Campbell, Bruce A. "Patterns of Change in the Partisan Loyalties of Native White Southerners: 1952–1972." *Journal of Politics* 30 (1977a), 730–761.

——— "Change in the Southern Electorate." *American Journal of Political Science* 21 (1977b), 37–64.

Carey, Robert T., Bruce W. Ransom, and J. David Woodard. "Growth in Party Competition and the Transformation of Southern Politics." *The American Review of Politics* 23 (2002), 93–121.

Carmines, Edward G., and James A. Stimson. "Issue Evolution, Partisan Replacement, and Normal Partisan Change." *American Political Science Review* 75 (1981), 107–118.

——— "On the Structure and Sequence of Issue Evolution." *American Political Science Review* 80 (1986), 901–920.

Carter, Dan T. *The Politics of Rage: George Wallace, the Origins of the New Conservatism, and the Transformation of American Politics.* New York: Simon & Schuster, 1995.

——— *From George Wallace to Newt Gingrich: Race in the Conservative Counterrevolution, 1963–1994.* Baton Rouge: Louisiana Sate University Press, 1996.

Cash, W. J. *The Mind of the South.* New York: Alfred A. Knopf, 1941.

Claggett, William J. M., and Byron E. Shafer. "The Pure Politics of Policy Choice: Issue Evolution, Policy Preference, and Voting Behavior in Postwar American Politics." Paper presented to the annual meetings of the American Political Science Association, 2002.

——— "Policy Substance in the Public Mind: The Issue Structure of Mass Politics in the United States during the Postwar Era." Paper presented to the annual meetings of the American Political Science Association, 2004.

Clark, John A., and Charles Prysby, eds. "Grassroots Party Activists in Southern Politics, 1991–2001: The Deep South." *American Review of Politics* 24 (Spring 2003).

——— "Grassroots Party Activists in Southern Politics, 1991–2001: The Rim South." *American Review of Politics* 24 (Summer 2003).

Cobb, James C. *Industrialization and Southern Society, 1877–1984.* Lexington: University of Kentucky Press, 1984.

——— *The Most Southern Place on Earth: The Mississippi Delta and the Roots of Regional Identity.* New York: Oxford University Press, 1992.

——— *The Selling of the South: The Southern Crusade for Industrial Development, 1936–1990.* Champaign-Urbana: University of Illinois Press, 1993.

Congressional District Data Book. Washington, D.C.: U.S. Department of Commerce, 1961, 1973, and supplements.

Congressional Districts in the 1970s, 1980s, and 1990s. Washington, D.C.: Congressional Quarterly Inc., 1973, 1983, and 1993.

Congressional Quarterly Weekly Report, vols. 52, 54, and 56. Washington, D.C.: Congressional Quarterly Inc., November 12, 1994; November 9, 1996; and November 7, 1998.

Connelly, William F., and John J. Pitney. *Congress' Permanent Minority? Republicans in the U.S. House.* Lanham: Rowman & Littlefield, 1994.

Converse, Philip E. "On the Possibility of Major Political Realignment in the South." In Angus Campbell, Philip E. Converse, Warren E. Miller, and Donald M. Stokes, *Elections and the Political Order.* New York: John Wiley, 1966.

Cook, Fay Lomax, and Edith J. Barrett. *Support for the American Welfare State: The Views of Congress and the Public.* New York: Columbia University Press, 1992.

Cowden, Jonathan A. "Southernization of the Nation and Nationalization of the South: Racial Conservatism, Social Welfare, and White Partisans in the United States, 1956–1992." *British Journal of Political Science* 31 (2001), 277–301.

Cunningham, Maurice T. *Maximization, Whatever the Cost: Race, Redistricting, and the Department of Justice.* Westport: Praeger, 2001.

Epstein, David, and Sharyn O'Halloran. "Measuring the Electoral and Policy Impact of Majority-Minority Voting Districts." *American Journal of Political Science* 43 (1999), 367–395.

Eulau, Heinz. *Class and Party in the Eisenhower Years: Class Roles and Perspectives in the 1952 and 1956 Elections.* New York: Free Press of Glencoe, 1962.

Fenno, Richard F., Jr. *Home Style: House Members in Their Districts.* Boston: Little, Brown, 1978.

—— "Observation, Context, and Sequence in the Study of Politics." *American Political Science Review* 80 (1986), 3–15.

—— *Congress at the Grassroots: Representational Change in the South, 1970–1998.* Chapel Hill: University of North Carolina Press, 2000.

Forbes, H. D. *Ethnic Conflict: Commerce, Culture, and the Contact Hypothesis.* New Haven: Yale University Press, 1997.

Fowler, Linda L. *Candidates, Congress, and the American Democracy.* Ann Arbor: University of Michigan Press, 1993.

Frederickson, Kari. *The Dixiecrat Revolt and the End of the Solid South, 1932–1968.* Chapel Hill: University of North Carolina Press, 2001.

Geer, John G. "New Deal Issues and the American Electorate, 1952–1988." *Political Behavior* 14 (1992), 45–65.

Giles, Micheal W. "Percent Black and Racial Hostility: An Old Assumption Revisited." *Social Science Quarterly* 70 (1977), 820–835.

Giles, Micheal W., and Melanie A. Buckner. "David Duke and Black Threat: An Old Hypothesis Revisited." *Journal of Politics* 55 (1993), 702–713.

Glaser, James M. "Back to the Black Belt: Racial Environment and White Racial Attitudes in the South." *Journal of Politics* 56 (1994), 21–41.

—— *Race, Campaign Politics, and the Realignment in the South.* New Haven: Yale University Press, 1996.

Gober, Patricia. "Americans on the Move." *Population Bulletin,* vol. 48, no. 3. Washington, D.C.: Population Reference Bureau, Inc., 1993.

Goldfield, David R. *Promised Land: The South since 1945.* Arlington Heights: Harlan Davidson, 1987.

Graham, Hugh Davis. *The Civil Rights Era: Origins and Development of National Policy, 1960–1972.* New York: Oxford University Press, 1990.

Grantham, Dewey W. *The Life and Death of the Solid South: A Political History.* Lexington: University of Kentucky Press, 1988.

—— *The South in Modern America.* New York: Harper Perennial, 1995.

Green, John, ed. "The Continuing Transformation of Southern Politics." Special Issue, *The American Review of Politics* 23 (2002).

Guide to U.S. Elections. Washington, D.C.: Congressional Quarterly Inc., 1975.

Hadley, Charles D. "Blacks in Southern Politics: An Agenda for Research." *Journal of Politics* 56 (1994), 585–600.

Heard, Alexander. *A Two-Party South?* Chapel Hill: University of North Carolina Press, 1952.

Hill, Kevin A. "Does the Creation of Majority Black Districts Aid Republicans? An Analysis of the 1992 Congressional Elections in Eight Southern States." *Journal of Politics* 57 (1995), 384–401.

Hinckley, Barbara. *Congressional Elections.* Washington, D.C.: CQ Press, 1981.

Hood, M. V. III, Quentin Kidd, and Irwin L. Morris. "Of Byrd[s] and Bumpers: Using Democratic Senators to Analyze Political Change in the South, 1960–1995." *American Journal of Political Science* 43 (1999), 465–487.

Hurt, R. Douglas. *The Rural South since World War II.* Baton Rouge: Louisiana State University Press, 1998.

Jacobson, Gary C. *The Politics of Congressional Elections.* Boston: Little, Brown, 1987.

——— *The Electoral Origins of Divided Government: Competition in U.S. House Elections, 1946–1988.* Boulder: Westview Press, 1990.

Jacobson, Gary C., and Samuel Kernell. *Strategy and Choice in Congressional Elections.* New Haven: Yale University Press, 1981.

Jaffe, Natalie. "Appendix B: Attitudes Toward Public Welfare Programs and Recipients in the United States." In Lester M. Salamon, ed., *Welfare: The Elusive Consensus.* New York: Praeger, 1978.

Keech, William R. *The Impact of Negro Voting: The Role of the Vote in the Quest for Equality.* Chicago: Rand McNally, 1968.

Key, V. O., Jr. *Southern Politics in State and Nation.* New York: Alfred A. Knopf, 1949.

King, Gary, Robert O. Keohane, and Sidney Verba. *Designing Social Inquiry: Scientific Inference in Qualitative Research.* Princeton: Princeton University Press, 1994.

Klinkner, Philip A., ed. *Midterm: The Elections of 1994 in Context.* Boulder: Westview Press, 1996.

Kousser, J. Morgan. *The Shaping of Southern Politics: Suffrage Restriction and the Establishment of the One-Party South, 1880–1910.* New Haven: Yale University Press, 1974.

Krysan, Maria. "Prejudice, Politics, and Public Opinion: Understanding the Sources of Racial Policy Attitudes." *Annual Review of Sociology* 26 (2000), 136–168.

Ladd, Everett Carll, with Charles D. Hadley. *Transformations of the American Party System.* New York: W. W. Norton, 1975.

Lamis, Alexander P. *The Two-Party South.* New York: Oxford University Press, 1984.

——— ed. *Southern Politics in the 1990s.* Baton Rouge: Louisiana State University Press, 1999.

Lawson, Steven F. *Black Ballots: Voting Rights in the South, 1944–1969.* New York: Columbia University Press, 1976.

Lea, James F., ed. *Contemporary Southern Politics.* Baton Rouge: Louisiana State University Press, 1988.

Lublin, David. *The Paradox of Representation: Racial Gerrymandering and Minority Interests.* Princeton: Princeton University Press, 1997.

——— *The Republican South: Democratization and Partisan Change in the South.* Princeton: Princeton University Press, 2004.

Lublin, David, and D. Stephen Voss. "Racial Redistricting and Realignment in Southern State Legislatures." *American Journal of Political Science* 44 (2000), 792–810.

Maggiotto, Michael A., and Gary D. Wekkin. *Partisan Linkages in Southern Politics: Elites, Voters, and Identifiers.* Knoxville: University of Tennessee Press, 2000.

Matthews, Donald R., and James W. Prothro. *Negroes and the New Southern Politics.* New York: Harcourt, Brace, 1966.

Mayhew, David R. *Congress: The Electoral Connection.* New Haven: Yale University Press, 1974.

McCarty, Nolan, Keith T. Poole, and Howard Rosenthal. "Political Polarization and Income Inequality." Draft paper, January 27, 2003, 43 pp.

McKee, Seth C. "Majority Black Districts, Republican Ascendancy, and Party Competition in the South, 1988–2000." *The American Review of Politics* 23 (2002), 123–139.

McKinney, John C., and Linda Brookover Bourque. "The Changing South: National Incorporation of a Region." *American Sociological Review* 36 (1971), 399–412.

Merton, Robert K. "Patterns of Influence: Local and Cosmopolitan Influentials." Chapter 13 in Merton, *Social Theory and Social Structure,* enl. ed. New York: The Free Press, 1968.

Miller, Warren E. "One-Party Politics and the Voter." *American Political Science Review* 50 (1956), 707–725.

Nadeau, Richard, and Harold W. Stanley. "Class Polarization in Partisanship among Native Southern Whites, 1952–90." *American Journal of Political Science* 37 (1993), 900–919.

Nadeau, Richard, Richard G. Niemi, Harold W. Stanley, and Jean-Francois Godbout. "Class, Party, and South–Non-South Differences: An Update." *American Politics Research* 32 (2004), 52–67.

National Election Studies, 1952, 1956, and 1958. Ann Arbor: University of Michigan, Center for Political Studies, 1953, 1957, and 1959.

National Election Studies, 1948–2000 Cumulative Data File. Ann Arbor: University of Michigan, Center for Political Studies, 2001.

Oleszek, Walter, ed. *The 104th Congress: A Congressional Quarterly Reader.* Washington, D.C.: CQ Press, 1995.

Patterson, James T. "The Failure of Party Realignment in the South, 1937–1939." *Journal of Politics* 27 (1965), 602–617.

Petrocik, John R. "Realignment: New Party Coalitions and the Nationalization of the South." *Journal of Politics* 49 (1987), 347–375.

Petrocik, John R., and Scott W. Desposato. "The Partisan Consequences of Majority-Minority Redistricting in the South." *Journal of Politics* 60 (1998), 613–633.

Polsby, Nelson W. "A Revolution in Congress?" Inaugural Lecture, Oxford University, 1997.

Prothro, James W., Ernest Q. Campbell, and Charles M. Grigg. "Two-Party Voting in the South, Class vs. Party Identification." *American Political Science Review* 52 (1958), 131–139.

Prysby, Charles L. "The Structure of Southern Electoral Behavior." *American Politics Quarterly* 17 (1989), 163–180.

——— "Southern Congressional Elections in the 1990s: The Dynamics of Change." *American Review of Politics* 17 (1996), 23–46.

Rae, Nicol C. *Southern Democrats.* New York: Oxford University Press, 1994.

Rhodes, Terrel L. *Republicans in the South: Voting for the State House, Voting for the White House.* Westport: Praeger, 2000.

Rohde, David W. "'Something's Happening Here; What It Is Ain't Exactly Clear': Southern Democrats in the House of Representatives." In Morris P. Fiorina and David W. Rohde, eds., *Home Style and Washington Work: Studies of Congressional Politics,* 137–163. Ann Arbor: University of Michigan Press, 1991.

——— "The Inevitability and Solidity of the 'Republican Solid South.'" *American Review of Politics* 17 (1996), 23–46.

Roland, Charles P. *The Improbable Era: The South since World War II.* Lexington: University of Kentucky Press, 1975.

Scher, Richard K. *Politics in the New South.* New York: Paragon House, 1992.

Schuman, Howard, Charlotte Steeh, Lawrence Bobo, and Maria Krysan. *Racial Attitudes in America: Trends and Interpretations,* rev. ed. Cambridge, Mass.: Harvard University Press, 1997.

Scranton, Philip, ed. *The Second Wave: Southern Industrialization from the 1940s to the 1970s.* Athens: University of Georgia Press, 2001.

Seagull, Louis M. *Southern Republicanism.* New York: John Wiley, 1975.

Sears, David O., Jim Sidanius, and Lawrence Bobo, eds. *Racialized Politics: The Debate about Racism in America.* Chicago: University of Chicago Press, 2000.

Shafer, Byron E., ed. *Postwar Politics in the G-7: Orders and Eras in Comparative Perspective.* Madison: University of Wisconsin Press, 1996.

——— "We Are All Southern Democrats Now." In Shafer, ed., *Present Discontents: American Politics in the Very Late Twentieth Century.* Chatham: Chatham House, 1997.

Shafer, Byron E., and Richard G. C. Johnston. "The Transformation of Southern Politics, Revisited: The House of Representatives as a Window." *British Journal of Political Science* 31 (2001), 601–625.

——— "Economic Development, Legal Desegregation, and Partisan Change in the Postwar South." Paper presented to the annual meetings of the American Political Science Association, Boston, 2002.

Shaffer, William R. "Ideological Trends among Southern U.S. Democratic Senators: Race, Generation, and Political Climate." *American Politics Quarterly* 15 (1987), 299–324.

Shapiro, Robert Y., and John M. Young. "Public Opinion and the Welfare State: The United States in Comparative Perspective." *Political Science Quarterly* 104 (1989), 59–89.

Sitkoff, Harvard. *The Struggle for Black Equality, 1954–1980.* New York: Hill & Wang, 1981.

Sniderman, Paul M., Philip E. Tetlock, and Edward G. Carmines, eds. *Prejudice, Politics, and the American Dilemma.* Stanford: Stanford University Press, 1993.

Spengler, Joseph J. "Demographic and Economic Change in the South, 1940–1960." In Allan P. Sindler, ed., *Change in the Contemporary South.* Durham: Duke University Press, 1963.

Stanley, Harold W. *Voter Mobilization and the Politics of Race: The South and Universal Suffrage, 1952–1984.* New York: Praeger, 1987.

——— "Southern Partisan Changes: Dealignment, Realignment, or Both?" *Journal of Politics* 50 (1988), 65–88.

Statistical Abstract of the United States. Washington, D.C.: U.S. Department of Commerce, various years.

Steed, Robert P., Laurence W. Moreland, and Tod A. Baker, eds. *Southern Parties and Elections: Studies in Regional Political Change.* Tuscaloosa: University of Alabama Press, 1998.

Stonecash, Jeffrey M. *Class, Party, and American Politics.* Boulder: Westview, 2000.

Stonecash, Jeffrey M., and Mack D. Mariani. "Republican Gains in the House in the 1994 Elections: Class Polarization in American Politics." *Political Science Quarterly* 115 (2001), 93–113.

Strahan, Randall W. "Partisan Officeholders, 1946–1996." In Byron E. Shafer, ed., *Partisan Approaches to Postwar American Politics.* New York: Chatham House, 1998.

Sundquist, James L. *Dynamics of the Party System: Alignment and Realignment of Political Parties in the United States.* Washington, D.C.: Brookings Institution, 1973.

Swansborough, Robert H., and David M. Brodsky, eds. *The South's New Politics: Realignment and Dealignment.* Columbia: University of South Carolina Press, 1988.

Tindall, George Brown. *The Emergence of the New South, 1913–1945.* Baton Rouge: Louisiana State University Press, 1967.

———— *The Disruption of the Solid South.* Athens: University of Georgia Press, 1972.

Tingsten, Herbert. *Political Behavior: Studies in Election Statistics.* London: P. S. King, 1937.

Tomz, Michael, Jason Wittenberg, and Gary King. "CLARIFY: Software for Interpreting and Presenting Statistical Results," Version 2.1, 2003 (available at *http://gking.harvard.edu*).

Voss, D. Stephen. "Beyond Racial Threat: Failure of an Old Hypothesis in the New South." *Journal of Politics* 58 (1996), 1156–1170.

Voss, D. Stephen, and David Lublin. "Black Incumbents, White Districts: An Appraisal of the 1996 Congressional Elections." *American Politics Research* 29 (2001), 141–182.

Wattenberg, Martin P. "The Building of a Republican Regional Base in the South: The Elephant Crosses the Mason-Dixon Line." *Public Opinion Quarterly* 55 (1991), 424–431.

Weinstein, Bernard L. *Regional Growth and Decline in the United States,* 2nd ed. New York: Praeger, 1985.

Welch, Susan, and Lorn Foster. "Class and Conservatism in the Black Community." *American Politics Quarterly* 15 (1987), 445–470.

White, Theodore H. *The Making of the President, 1964.* New York: Atheneum, 1965.

Wilcox, Clyde. *The Latest American Revolution? The 1994 Elections and Their Implications for Governance.* New York: St. Martin's, 1995.

Wolfinger, Raymond E., and Robert B. Arseneau. "Partisan Change in the South: 1952–1976." In Louis Maisel and Joseph Cooper, eds., *Political Parties: Development and Decay.* Beverly Hills: Sage, 1978.

Woodward, C. Vann. *Origins of the New South, 1877–1913.* Baton Rouge: Louisiana State University Press, 1951.

❧ Index

Agrarian radicalism, 6
Agriculture: and economic basis of Old South, 12
Aistrup, Joseph A., 17
Arseneau, Robert B., 2

Barrett, Edith J., 202n3, 203n5
Bartley, Numan V., 13, 59
Bass, Jack, 59
Black, Earl, 2, 10–11, 63, 70, 129
Black, Merle, 2, 63, 70, 129
Black Republicanism: end of, 54
Black voters: growth in share of Southern electorate, 13, 23; enfranchisement, 51; attachment to Democratic party, 52; role in restructuring the Southern electorate, 52, 59; and demise of black Republicanism, 52, 82; racial identification, 55, 178; class differences, 55, 59, 93; as voting bloc, 55–59, 83; racial attitudes of, and vote, 58, 59; as component of Democratic and Republican electoral coalitions, 82; as unresponsive to overall Republican trend, 173
Bobo, Lawrence, 203n5
Border South. *See* Peripheral South
Bourbon Democrats, 9
Bourque, Linda Brookover, 12
"Bridging" candidates. *See* Third party candidates
Bullock, Charles S., 11
Bush, George H. W., 35–36, 180, 205n7
Butler, David, 56

Cameron, Charles, 203n4
Candidates: incumbent, 2; provision of, 2,

136–147, 163, 191–192; lack of Republican, for House, 26; and open seats in House of Representatives, 138–139; in districts with white collar majorities, 139–141; for Senate, 141; "quality" of, 147–148; local vs. cosmopolitan, 148–154, 180; decline of local, 153; "cosmopolitan" presidential, priming race, 157–159; impact of cosmopolitan vs. local, in voting for Senate, 158–159; role of, in channeling impact of social forces, 164
Carmines, Edward, 203n5
Carter, Dan T., 165
Carter, Jimmy, 16, 35–36, 156, 168, 180; as National Democrat, 154
Cash, W. J., 6
Civil Rights Act (1964), 51, 53, 54, 55; as voting issue, 68; and Lyndon Johnson, 110; and change in impact of racial context, 110
Civil rights revolution, 4, 11, 17, 51, 52, 53, 55, 61, 62, 86, 91, 110, 127, 156, 180; and Northern Democrats vs. Southern Democrats, 53–54; impact on presidential voting patterns, 110
Civil War, 3, 4, 29, 30, 41, 46, 89, 175
Claggett, William J. M., 184
CLARIFY (software), 202n1
Class. *See* Social class
Clinton, Bill, 16, 20, 35, 36, 156, 180; as National Democrat, 154
"Coattails," presidential, 136, 160–162, 180
Cobb, James C., 11, 12
Congressional districts. *See* Districts
Congressional voting: after legal desegregation, 53. *See also* House of Representatives; Senate
Connelly, William F., 137

Convergence: of social class impact across electoral arenas, 43–44, 49; social welfare policy impact across arenas, 49–50; racial policy preferences and partisan choice across arenas, 78, 85, 89; and institutional alignment, 123–128; of ideological structure of vote across arenas, 127–128; of racial context impact across arenas, 185–187; effect of economic context, 187–189; across Southern states, 187–191; of South with North, 191–199

Converse, Philip E., 15

Cook, Fay Lomax, 202n3, 203n5

"Cosmopolitan" candidates: for House, 2, 180, 181, 183; electoral strategy, 135; defined, 148–149; influence of social class and racial context on success, 150–151; for House, policy attitudes and vote for, 152–153; for President, race and, 157–159; for Senate, 158–159. *See also* "Local" candidates; Northern Democrats; Southern Democrats

94–100; in multivariate estimation, 95–98; and vote among white Southerners, 95–98, 178–179; and realignment of class relationships, 176; and "seven myths," 177

Eisenhower, Dwight, 16, 24, 30, 31, 32–33, 35–36, 44, 77, 89, 105, 136, 165, 180; and class basis of vote for in "old" Republican areas, 33; and racial conservatives, 77; vote for, and racial context, 89

Electoral College, 24; distortion of popular vote by, 195, 198

Electoral reform: effect on class composition of Southern electorate, 59, 61, 83. *See also* Civil Rights Act; Legal desegregation; Voting Rights Act

Enfranchisement (by Voting Rights Act), 52, 60–62; and class structure of white electorate, 52; direct and indirect partisan effects, 63

Epstein, David, 203n4

Eulau, Heinz, 30

Deep South: contrast with Peripheral South, 94, 129–133; defined, 129; racial and social composition, 130, 203n6; Republican success in, 131–132; share of House seats, 133; demographic decline, 133, 179

Desegregation. *See* Legal desegregation

Desposato, Scott W., 115

DeVries, Walter, 59

Dewey, Thomas, 30

Districts (House): white-collar proportion of population in, 47; as units of analysis, 67; "majority-minority," 112–113; racial composition of, and racial strategies, 113–116, 180–181; racial composition of, and candidate provision, 139–140; white-collar composition of, and candidate provision, 139–141

Dukakis, Michael, 156

Economic development, 4, 6–8, 20, 47, 86, 92, 128, 162, 180; as engine of partisan change, 2; impact on vote across electoral arenas, 41–42; as led by wartime industry, 46; considered with legal desegregation,

Fenno, Richard F., 11, 24, 136, 204n3

Forbes, H. D., 73

Fowler, Linda L., 141

Frederickson, Kari, 165

Geer, John G., 27

Gingrich, Newt, 17

Glaser, James M., 73

Gober, Patricia, 43

Goldwater, Barry, 68, 169

Graham, Hugh Davis, 12, 13, 51, 59

Great Depression, 3, 14, 15, 16, 32

Green, John, 2

Hadley, Charles D., 8

Heard, Alexander A., 15

Hill, Kevin A., 203n4

Hinckley, Barbara, 112

Hood, M. V., 142

House of Representatives: Republican proportion of seats in, before 1950, 14, 38–39; Republican proportion of seats in, after 1940, 16, 38–39; social class and voting for, 25–27, 95–98; social welfare atti-

tudes and voting for, 28–29; postwar, 43–44; welfare attitudes among partisans in voting for, 45; welfare attitudes and social class in voting for, 47–49; racial context and social class in voting for, 64–65, 98, 100–108; influence of racial attitudes and voting for, 75–77, 84–85; influence of racial feelings and voting for, 79–81, 84; impact of economic development and voting for, 95–98; joint impact of welfare and racial attitudes in voting for, 119–121; open seats and candidate provision, 138–139; power of incumbency, 142–144
Humphrey, Hubert H., 156, 166, 170

Income: change in per capita, over time, 12; as measure of social class, 23–24
Incumbents: 2, 163; and impact of racial context, 111–112; and candidate provision, 137–139; power of, 142–147; similarities between Senate and House, 144; reasons for termination of incumbency, 146–147
Independent candidates. *See* Third party candidates

Jacobson, Gary C., 141, 147
Jaffe, Natalie, 202n3
Johnson, Lyndon, 35, 68, 180; and Civil Rights Act, 110; and Voting Rights Act, 110; as "local" Southern candidate, 154; as bridge to Republican vote in 1968, 169

Keech, William R., 13
Kennedy, John F., 16, 30, 35–36, 68
Keohane, Robert, 185, 206n1
Kernell, Samuel, 141, 147
Key, V. O., 6–11, 16, 22, 26, 33, 43, 51, 64, 70, 129, 180, 185
Kidd, Quentin, 142
King, Gary, 185, 202n1, 206n1
Kousser, J. Morgan, 83
Krysan, Maria, 203n5

Ladd, Everett Carll, 8, 27
Lamis, Alexander P., 2, 15, 63, 128

Lawson, Steven F., 13, 59
Legal desegregation, 4, 6–8, 12, 20, 70, 73, 86, 92, 128, 162; and economic development, 2, 22, 94–99; and class composition of Southern electorate, 59–61; and class voting patterns, 60–63; and change in black share of total electorate, 81; and change in class composition of Southern electorate, 83–84; and impact of racial context, 96–99; and vote among white Southerners, 95–98; contrast in impact of, between electoral arenas, 176, 179; and "seven myths," 177
Literacy test, 15; effect on Southern whites, 61
"Local" candidates, 2, 180, 181, 183, 203n1; electoral strategy, 135; defined, 148–149; for House, influence of social class and racial context on success of, 150–151; for House, and priming of class, 151, 153; for House, and priming of race, 151–153; declining share, 153; for Senate, impact on vote, 158–159. *See also* "Cosmopolitan" candidates
Lublin, David, 203n4

"Majority-minority" districts: and impact of racial context, 112. *See also* Reapportionment
Mayhew, David R., 112
McGovern, George, 156
McKee, Seth C., 203n4
McKinney, John C., 12
Merton, Robert K., 148–149
Miller, Warren E., 4
Mondale, Walter, 156
Morris, Irwin L., 142

Nadeau, Richard, 12
National Election Studies, 20, 22, 23, 27, 33, 37, 54, 58, 59, 73, 75, 79
NES. *See* National Election Studies
New Deal, 3, 14, 15, 22, 26–27, 29, 45, 46, 47, 62, 72, 143
"New" Republican Areas: measure of, 33; vote for President by social class in, 34
Nixon, Richard, 35–36, 68, 166, 168, 169, 180

Northern Democrats (candidates for presidency), 180; vs. Southern Democrats, 154–155; and priming race, 155–159. See also "Local" candidates; "Cosmopolitan" candidates

O'Halloran, Sharyn, 203n4
"Old" Republican areas: measure of, 33; vote for President by social class in, 34
Oleszek, Walter, 137

Party system: alignment of, for welfare policy and racial policy, 105–107; differences in alignment among electoral arenas, 107
Patterson, James T., 4
Peripheral South: contrast with Deep South, 94, 129–133; defined, 129; racial and social context in, 130; Republican success in, 131–132; share of seats in House of Representatives, 133; and collapse of "old Democracy," 178; demographic composition of, 179, 203n6
Perot, Ross, 31, 205n7, 206n7
Petrocik, John R., 115
Pitney, John J., 137
Poll tax, 15; effect on class composition of electorate, 61
Polsby, Nelson, 24, 136
President, voting for: as site of first changes, 15; by social class, 30–34, 95–98; by social welfare attitudes, 34–36, 45; in Old Republican and New Republican areas in postwar era, 43–44; welfare attitudes and class bases, 47–49; after legal desegregation, 53; influence of racial context and social class among whites on, 64–65, 68–71, 98, 100–108, 123–125; and "racial threat" hypothesis, 65, 69–70; influence of racial attitudes on, 76–78, 84–85; influence of racial feelings on, 79–81, 84; economic development and, 95–98
Primary (election), white, 15

Racial attitudes. See Racial policy attitudes; Racial feelings
Racial context: importance of, for white voters, 57; indicators of, 57, 71; differen-

tial impact by electoral arena, 57–58, 63–71, 72, 87–91, 98, 99, 183; as surrogate for social class, 66; relationship with racial attitudes, 73, 176; influence on strategy, 86; change in impact over time, 88–91, 107–110, 184; institutional mediation, 98–108; impact with social context on voting, 100–108; interaction with social class, welfare policy, and race policy, 116–123; Deep South vs. Peripheral South, 130; "cosmopolitan" candidates and, 157–159; and convergence of impact across arenas, 185–189
Racial desegregation. See Legal desegregation
Racial feelings: indicator, 79; influence on vote, 79–81, 84; joint impact with welfare attitudes, 125–127
Racial policy attitudes, 52, 72; convergence of impact across electoral arenas, 53, 123–125; lack of impact among black voters, 58; indicator of, 58, 73–74, 125; and legal desegregation, 73; relationship with racial context, 73; impact among white voters, 75–77, 84–85, 87–91, 174, 176–177; interaction with racial context, social class, and welfare policy, 116–123; versus racial feelings, 125–127
"Racial threat": defined, 63; and voting for House, 65–66, 68, 69, 84; and voting for President, 69–70, 84; and racial policy attitudes, 78
Rae, Nicol C., 142
Reagan, Ronald, 17, 35–36, 169, 180
Reapportionment, 183; race-based, in 1990s, 110, 112–116; and racial composition of districts, 114–116; and biracial districts, 127
Reconstruction 3, 13–14
Recruitment. See Candidates
Redistricting. See Reapportionment
Rim South. See Peripheral South
Rohde, David W., 2, 24, 136, 142
Roosevelt, Franklin Delano, 27, 167
Rozell, Mark J., 11

Schuman, Howard, 203n5
Scranton, Philip, 11
Seagull, Louis M., 15

Sears, David O., 203n5
Second World War. *See* World War II
Senate: Republican seats before 1950, 14,
38–39; Republican seats after 1940, 16,
38–39, 43–44; social class and voting for,
36–41, 95–98; welfare attitudes and vote
for, 40–41; welfare attitudes among partisans in voting for, 45; joint effect of social
welfare attitudes and class basis, 47–49;
racial context and social class in voting
for, 66–68; racial attitudes and voting for,
75–77, 84–85; racial feelings and voting
for, 79–81, 84; economic development
and voting for, 95–98; racial context and
voting for, 98; social class, racial context,
and voting for, 100–108; joint impact of
welfare and racial attitudes on vote for,
121–125; provision of candidates for,
141; power of incumbency, 144–146; impact of "cosmopolitan" vs. "local" candidates, 158–159
"Seven myths," 177–185
Shapiro, Robert Y., 202n3, 203n5
Sidanius, Jim, 203n5
Sitkoff, Harvard, 12
Smith, Al, 14
Sniderman, Paul, 203n5
Social class: and vote for President, 30–34,
95–98; and vote for President in Old and
New Republican areas, 41–44; inversion
in 1950s, 46–47; impact post-1960, 47–
50; impact compared with social welfare
policy attitudes, 50; lack of impact
among black voters, 55; enfranchisement
and class composition of white electorate,
60–62; relationship with social welfare
policy attitudes, 87; impact on vote, 93,
95–98, 173–174, 184; and joint impact
with racial context, 100–108; interaction
with racial context, welfare policy attitudes, and race policy attitudes, 116–123;
local/cosmopolitan candidate success in
House, 150–151
Social class context, 52; impact on black
voters, 56–58; impact on white voters, 57,
63–66; and presidential voting, 68–69;
and racial policy attitudes, 73, 87–91; in
Deep South and Peripheral South, 130;
as primed by social backgrounds of candidates, 152–153, 157–162

Social welfare policy attitudes: indicator of,
28; and voting for House of Representatives, 28–29, 45, 117–123; and voting for
President, 34–36, 45, 117–123; and voting for Senate, 40–41, 45; change in class
basis over time, 47–49; impact on vote,
compared with social class, 50; lack of
impact among black voters, 55; and social class, 87; interaction with social
class, racial context, and race policy, 116–
123; convergence of impact across electoral arenas, 123–125; joint impact with
racial feelings, 125–127; and vote, 174,
176
Southern Democrats (candidates for Presidency), 180; differentiated from Northern Democratic candidates, 154–155;
success at repressing Republican vote in
the South, 154, 157; priming social class,
155–159. *See also* "Local" candidates;
"Cosmopolitan" candidates
Southern economy: basis of, 11; changes in
per capita income, 12
Stanley, Harold W., 12, 59
Stevenson, Adlai, 167
Stokes, Donald, 56
Sundquist, James L., 8

Tetlock, Philip, 203n5
Third party candidates, 31, 136; as
"bridges," 165, 180. *See also* Perot, Ross;
Thurmond, Strom; Wallace, George
Thurmond, Strom, 136, 205n7; as potential
"bridge" between old and new political
orders, 165–172; candidacy motivated by
racial threat, 180
Tindall, George Brown, 2
Tomz, Michael, 202n1
Tower, John, 15
Truman, Harry, 19, 27, 68, 167
"Two Souths" argument, 128–133, 165,
203n6; lack of support for, 130–133; as
causal story, 179–180. *See also* Deep
South; Peripheral South

Verba, Sidney, 185, 206n1
Voss, D. Stephen, 203n4
Voter registration, 12–13

Voting Rights Act (1965), 51, 53, 54, 55, 68; effect on Southern whites, 61; and Lyndon Johnson, 110; and change in impact of racial context, 110

Wallace, George, 31, 205n7, 206n3; as potential "bridge" between old and new political orders, 165–172; attraction of racially-based white vote, 170–171; candidacy motivated by racial threat, 180

Wattenberg, Martin P., 2
Weinstein, Bernard L., 12
Welfare. *See* Social welfare policy attitudes
Wilkie, Wendell, 30
Wittenberg, Jason, 202n1
Wolfinger, Raymond, 2
World War II, 4, 6, 12, 18, 41, 46, 51, 175

Young, John M., 202n3, 203n5